A Theology of Dao

Ecology and Justice

An Orbis Series on Integral Ecology

Advisory Board Members
Mary Evelyn Tucker
John A. Grim
Leonardo Boff
Sean McDonagh

The Orbis Series on Integral Ecology publishes books seeking to integrate an understanding of Earth's interconnected life systems with sustainable social, political, and economic systems that enhance the Earth community. Books in the series concentrate on ways to

- Reexamine human-Earth relations in light of contemporary cosmological and ecological science.
- Develop visions of common life marked by ecological integrity and social justice.
- Expand on the work of those exploring such fields as integral ecology, climate justice, Earth law, ecofeminism, and animal protection.
- Promote inclusive participatory strategies that enhance the struggle of Earth's poor and oppressed for ecological justice.
- Deepen appreciation for dialogue within and among religious traditions on issues of ecology and justice.
- Encourage spiritual discipline, social engagement, and the transformation of religion and society toward these ends.

Viewing the present moment as a time for fresh creativity and inspired by the encyclical *Laudato Si'*, the series seeks authors who speak to ecojustice concerns and who bring into this dialogue perspectives from the Christian communities, from the world's religions, from secular and scientific circles, or from new paradigms of thought and action.

A Theology of Dao

by

Heup Young Kim

ORBIS BOOKS

Maryknoll, New York 10545

ORBIS BOOKS
Maryknoll, New York 10545

Fathers and Brothers
MARYKNOLL™
TOGETHER IN GOD'S MISSION OF MERCY

Founded in 1970, Orbis Books endeavors to publish works that enlighten the mind, nourish the spirit, and challenge the conscience. The publishing arm of the Maryknoll Fathers and Brothers, Orbis seeks to explore the global dimensions of the Christian faith and mission, to invite dialogue with diverse cultures and religious traditions, and to serve the cause of reconciliation and peace. The books published reflect the views of their authors and do not represent the official position of the Maryknoll Society. To learn more about Maryknoll and Orbis Books, please visit our website at www.maryknollsociety.org.

Library of Congress Cataloging-in-Publication Data

Names: Kim, Heup-Young, 1949- author.
Title: A theology of Dao / Heup Young Kim.
Description: Maryknoll : Orbis Books, 2017. | Series: Ecology and justice series | Includes bibliographical references and index.
Identifiers: LCCN 2016048020 (print) | LCCN 2017007374 (ebook) | ISBN 9781626982192 (pbk.) | ISBN 9781608336845 (e-book)
Subjects: LCSH: Christianity and other religions—East Asian. | Christianity—East Asia. | Tao. | Philosophical theology. | Taoism. | Confucianism.
Classification: LCC BR127 .K49 2017 (print) | LCC BR127 (ebook) | DDC 261.2/9514—dc23
LC record available at https://lccn.loc.gov/2016048020

Contents

CHAPTER EIGHT
**Multiple Religious Belonging as Hospitality:
A Korean Confucian-Christian Perspective**

PART III
Theodao in Action: An Ecological and Scientific Age

CHAPTER NINE
**Trialogue: Christian Theologies, Asian Religions, and
Natural Sciences**

Preface

This book is a humble presentation of an example of doing theology from a Korean or East Asian Christian perspective to locate Christianity more thoughtfully within the global community. Works of East Asian theologians published in English are relatively rare. There are two main reasons for this scarcity. The first reason is the language barrier. Unlike theologians in South Asia, those in East Asia (Korea, Japan, Taiwan, and China) have been less exposed to English, with no strong history of Western colonialism. Second, East Asians have a radically different religious worldview and way of thinking from both Western and other Asian people. Western Christianity and other Asian religions tend to be theistic (including Buddhism as an antithesis to theism). East Asian religions, however, are not so much theistic as sapiential, as is saliently expressed in Confucianism and Daoism. The late Bede Griffiths made an insightful and prophetic comment about the value of East Asian religions for this age, referring to *Dàodéjīng*, one of their foundational scriptures:

> This may sound very paradoxical and unreal, but for centuries now the western world has been following the path of *Yang*—of the masculine, active, aggressive, rational, scientific mind—and has brought the world near destruction. It is time now to recover the path of *Yin*, of the feminine, passive, patient, intuitive and poetic mind. This is the path which the *Tao Te Ching* sets before us.[1]

---

1. Bede Griffiths, *Universal Wisdom: A Journey through the Sacred Wisdom of the World* (San Francisco: HarperSanFrancisco, 1994), 27-28.

The thesis of this book is that East Asian theological perspectives, as an antidote to Western modes of thinking, present an alternative paradigm that can effectively address the problems of Christian theologies due to the enduring legacy of Greek dualism (e.g., theory and praxis) and substantialism in Western thought. Contemporary theologies (including Asian theologies), heavily influenced by this dualism, are divided by two macro-paradigms, namely, theo-logos (classical theology) and theo-praxis (liberationist theology). To overcome this dualism, I propose a third way, the *dao* [*tao*] paradigm of theology, namely, a *theo-dao*. This theo-dao, I argue, is contextually appropriate for East Asian Christians (doing theology in our own metaphors). In the Bible, furthermore, Jesus never identified himself as the logos, nor as the praxis, but the *hodos* ("way"; John 14:6), and the *hodos* of Jesus was the original name for Christianity in the Bible (Acts 9:2; 19:9; 22:4; 24:14, 22). Since *dao* is a homologous East Asian term to *hodos*, dao would be even biblically a more relevant root-metaphor for Christ than logos and praxis.

As a product of my theological contemplation for the last three decades, this book reflects my theological journey in three stages: (1) dialogue and crossing the boundaries between the two great hermeneutical worlds of Christianity and Neo-Confucianism; (2) engaging a construction of theodao, an East Asian theology, by the employment of dao as the root-metaphor; and (3) further exploring theodao in an eco-scientific age, through trialogue among theology, East Asian religions, and natural sciences. Thus, the journey is composed of three main parts, titled "Theodao in Construction," "Theodao in Bridge-building," and "Theodao in Action."

Part 1 consists of four chapters that present some basic methodological and doctrinal insights to construct theodao as a new paradigm of Christian theology. In chapter 1, I share my experience that, even though I have diligently studied and practiced Western theology and spirituality, I do not sufficiently feel that I belong there as a person from a family with the long tradition of Confucianism. In chapter 2, as a way to overcome those inadequacies in the prevailing paradigms of both theologos and theopraxis, I propose a macro-paradigm shift to a theology of dao (*theo-dao*), introducing a radically different hermeneutical world of the dao such as an intriguing notion of *ki* (*qi*). In chapter 3, from this vantage point, I elaborate some christological insights (*Christo-dao*), conceiving of Jesus Christ as the Dao, the Great Ultimate (*T'aegŭk* [*Tài jí*]), and the Being-in-Non-Being. In chapter 4, I formulate a new *East Asian* interpretation of the Trinity, suggesting that Confucian and Daoist insights can effectively address long-standing trinitarian dilemmas within the parameters of Western theologies.

Part 2 begins with two Confucian–Christian dialogues I developed in the beginning of my theological career. Chapter 5 introduces the first Confucian–Christian dialogue between Wang Yang-ming (1472–1529), a seminal Neo-Confucian thinker, and Karl Barth (1886–1968), an enormously important Christian theologian of the twentieth century. In this comparison of Confucian sincerity (*chèng*) versus Christian love (*agapē*), I discovered thick resemblances between these two radically different traditions and realized that the dao (the wisdom of life) is a concrete meeting point between the two traditions. Chapter 6 summarizes the second Confucian–Christian dialogue between Yi T'oegye (1502–1571), the most important scholar in Korean Confucianism, and John Calvin (1509–1564), as Presbyterianism is the largest branch of Christianity in Korea. This comparative study between the two seminal thinkers shows even more striking similarities that, I argue, are a root (or theological) reason for the great success of the Presbyterian mission in Korea. Chapter 7 introduces intriguing christodaoist insights of Ryu Yŏng-mo (1890–1981), a most innovative Christian thinker in Korea. Ryu provided a unique interpretation of Christian (biblical) faith in and through intrareligious dialogue and cross-canonical study with East Asian religious scriptures of Confucianism, Daoism, and Buddhism. In chapter 8, evaluating today's hot topic of multireligious belonging in the West, from a Korean Confucian-Christian perspective, I propose trinitarian hospitality as its theological basis.

Part 3 discusses challenging issues from the planetary ecological crisis and explosive developments of natural sciences and technologies. In chapter 9, I advocate for a trialogue of Christian theology, East Asian religions, and natural sciences, integrating interreligious dialogue with interdisciplinary study between religion and science. In this scientific age, on the one hand, interreligious dialogue should take seriously discoveries of science and advances of technologies. In this multireligiously global age, on the other hand, the dialogue between religion and science must include dimensions of interreligious dialogue beyond the domination of Western theologies. In chapter 10, I formulate a new (theodaoist) way of doing eco-theology (namely, *eco-dao*). In chapter 11, I introduce an East Asian Christian (theodaoist) reflection on life science and biotechnology (*bio-dao*), focusing on the debates on human embryonic stem-cell research. This also introduces the issue of transhumanism, the radical transformation of humanity in the future by the maximum use of scientific and technological advances. In the last chapter, I discuss this complicated issue, a most challenging theological and anthropological subject in this century (*techno-dao*).

For some key conceptual terms originating in Chinese characters, I use mainly the Chinese romanization system of Pinyin except where there are available citations and book titles already published in the Wade-Giles system. I also use the Korean romanization system of McCune-Reischauer for the terms relevant to the historical discourse of Korean Neo-Confucianism, for example, the Great Ultimate (*T'aegŭk*), Non-Ultimate (*Mugŭk*), principle (*li*), energy (*ki*), and reverence (*kyŏng*). The Glossary of Terms at the end of the book summarizes these technical terms with their conversion table of romanizations.

PART I

Theodao in Construction: An East Asian Theology of Dao

CHAPTER ONE

Owning Up to Our Own Metaphors: A Christian Journey in the Confucian Stronghold

1. A Journey in the Confucian Stronghold

In the summer of 1998, I stayed for a month in an art colony in the district of Andong, an ancient city in a southeastern part of Korea. Famous for the preservation of our cultural heritages, particularly the Neo-Confucian tradition, this area is recognized as the last stronghold of Korean culture.[1] Hidden deep in the mountains, it is free from the noise, disturbances, pollution, and other by-products of the rapid industrialization of this so-called tiger nation in the Far East. It is rare to find such a place today that preserves the beauty and solitude of the old Confucian Korea, a country previously recognized as "the hermit kingdom" or "the country of the morning calm" (as the great Indian poet Tagore once described it).

Adapted from Heup Young Kim, "Owning up to Our Own Metaphors: A Christian Journey in the Neo-Confucian Wilderness," originally published in *Third Millennium* 4, no. 1 (2001): 31-40. It was reprinted in *Visioning New Life Together among Asian Religions: The Third Congress of Asian Theologians (CATS III)*, ed. Daniel S. Thiagarajah and A. Wati Longchar (Hong Kong: Christian Conference of Asia, 2002), 243-53; and in Heup Young Kim, *Christ & the Tao* (Hong Kong: Christian Conference of Asia, 2003), 123-34.

1. This area is perhaps that of Neo-Confucianism in the world as well. Tu Wei-ming claimed that Korea, not China, is the most Confucianized country in the world. See Tu Wei-ming, *Confucianism in a Historical Perspective* (Singapore: Institute of East Asian Philosophies, 1989), 35.

The main mansion in the colony, a typical home of Confucian literati in the seventeenth century, is composed of three compartments—an inner chamber, an outer chamber, and a shrine hall. This architecture epitomizes the way of living in traditional Korean society. Women in the inner chamber were engaged in the procreation of descendants, rearing children, and housekeeping. Men in the outer chamber dealt with everyday matters in relation to the outside world. And occasionally all of the family members assembled in the shrine to perform ancestor rites.

This arrangement, first of all, signifies a lucid division of labor among the members of the traditional household. Its more profound implication, however, lies in their comprehension of community, which is closely related to the notion of time. The inner chamber, as the womb of the house, is assigned to the preparation for the future of the family (descendants), the outer chamber to the present affairs (the living), and the shrine to their communal memory of the past (ancestors). Here, community does not imply merely a temporal gathering of family members presently living together but includes both those in the past and those yet to come. Almost every family in Korea preserves a genealogy, a comprehensively written record of the lives of their ancestors from the beginning to the present. People in this society live their everyday lives in intimate association with their collective past and future. Community here has a transhistorical nature.

The transhistorical nature of community reaches its peak in the ancestor rite, a memorial service for those who have passed away. Both the family of the house and the relatives living near and far gather together to participate in the ritual. The participants remember that they share the common collective past, the common memory of the same ancestors. They experience a transhistorical moment, transcending their separations in space and time, to be united again as one community, one collective identity. In addition, sharing food constitutes an important part in this ritual. After dedicating food to their ancestors, the participants set the table to eat together with guests and their children. There is a certain parallelism between ancestor rites and Christian communion. In communion, participants also realize their collective identity as Christian, sharing bread and wine with the common memory of Jesus Christ. Hence, the ancestor rite plays a significant role as a cultural sacrament for this family-centered society.

Spiritually, furthermore, I felt at home in the colony. With a keen interest in Christian spirituality, I had surveyed various Christian retreat centers, ranging from a Pentecostal prayer house to a Benedictine monastery. Although overwhelmed by their fervent prayers and rich traditions, I was not completely sure that I belonged there. In the solitude and carelessness of the Neo-Confucian wilderness, I felt genuine spiritual freedom. Returning to the spiritual realm that Daoists describe as Nature in nonaction action,[2] I could experience deep relaxation and charming delight in being one with God.

Frankly, this experience surprised me. Elsewhere, I have made a confession about my existential struggle as a Christian who was raised in a Korean family steeped in a thousand-year history in Confucianism:

> The more I study Christian theology, the more I become convinced how deeply Confucianism is embedded in my soul and body, my spirituality. Subtly but powerfully, Confucianism still works inside me, as my native religious language. If theology involves the response of one's total being to God, it entails a critical wrestling with this embedded Confucian tradition. Doing East Asian theology necessarily involves the study of Confucianism as a theological task.[3]

Although I declared this theologically and spiritually, I had been hesitant to adopt those methods and principles that I learned from our own spiritual traditions such as Confucian quiet sitting, Buddhist Zen meditation, and Daoist breathing technique. As the first Christian convert in a family who acquired a full theological education in the West (America), I was still not free from the educated taboo against non-Christian spiritual practices. The experiences

---

2. Bede Griffiths, *Universal Wisdom: A Journey through the Sacred Wisdom of the World* (San Francisco: HarperSanFrancisco, 1994), 27-28.

3. Heup Young Kim, *Wang Yang-ming and Karl Barth: A Confucian–Christian Dialogue* (Lanham, MD: University Press of America, 1996), 1.

in the colony, however, liberated me from the taboo. More deeply than I had realized, our own religions are rooted in my spirituality, constituting an essential part of my spiritual identity (something like a religio-cultural DNA), yet the Western Christianity I was taught superficially hangs on. Spiritually and religiously, Confucianism and Daoism (Neo-Confucianism) still function as my native languages, while Western Christianity remains a foreign language like English.

In this context, the Western form of Christianity is not enough, not appropriate, and not viable. I need a new form of Christianity. To be fully Christian, I should be able to utter my faith and experiences of God in my own native religious languages, as fully—without restraint and shame—as possible. I do need to *own up* to my own religions. In this regard, I completely agree with the statements that Dr. Anto Karokaran, the chief editor of the *Third Millennium*, made in his letter to me:

> In this context, it is absolute necessary that church should be able to *own up* [to] the genius, religions, experience, yearnings and the spiritual heritage of people. That alone will give the churches in Asia in-depth identity with the people. If we in Asia really seek an identity of our own church, this can be attained only through an owning up of the religions and traditions of our people. Surely an integration of these with the God-experience in Christ is to be effected.

"Owning up to the religions of one's own country as part of one's identity." Yes, but not so much in a pejorative sense (a confession of guilt) as in a constructive sense (a full acknowledgment). Generally, "to own up to" means "to admit or confess frankly and fully" (*Webster's Third International Dictionary*). We should be frank and honest about the spiritual, religious, and cultural traditions of our own country to fully confess that they are important parts of our own identity, functioning as native religious languages or spiritual DNA. Any Christian identity disconnected from our own people, community, and collective identity is not only inappropriate but also false. To articulate our Christian identity in the fullest way, I argue that we need to move one step forward. That is to say, we should critically appreciate the symbols and metaphors of

our religions and cultures and apply them to our theological thinking, which is the most important meaning of owning up. This does
not entail merely a translation of Western Christianity into our religious languages, or a speculative syncretism of multiple religious
traditions, but a confession of the integrated Christian selfhood in
the network of our own community.

The colony, the last stronghold of Korean culture and spirituality, presented me with profound symbolic implications. There I
could find the heart of our Korean spiritual and cultural identity.
I cannot complete my mission in doing Korean theology unless I
respond properly to those symbols, metaphors, and messages crying
out from the depth of our collective soul. I regard them as a barom-
eter or a vantage point to examine the appropriateness of Korean
theology. Hence, owning up to our own religions and culture as
part of our own identity entails two tasks: (1) critically examin-
ing theology from this Korean vantage point, and (2) theologically
owning up to our own metaphors and symbols. In the remaining
discourse, I deal with these two subjects.

In the next section, I criticize three prevailing doctrines in
Korean theologies, namely, soteriology, original sin, and religious
pluralism. In the final section, I suggest a new paradigm of Asian
theology by owning up to the Dao (the Way), a religio-cultural
root-metaphor[4] for East Asian people, namely, theo-dao (theology
as the way of life).

2. Theology from the Korean Vantage Point

Soteriology

The salvation of Jesus Christ is not temporal and partial but transhistorical and complete. It empowers us to transcend our existential limitation in space and time to be united with the Ultimate
Being. If one justifies the sacrifice of others in one's community for
the sake of one's salvation, it is not only a violation of the gospel of

---

4. Root-metaphors denote the central metaphors such as logos and praxis
that have shaped and governed narrative structures, cultural-linguistic matrices, or paradigms of theology and Christology in wider definitions.

Jesus Christ, who taught us sacrificial love on the cross but also a distortion of Christian soteriology with an ideology of individualism. In order for the gospel to be truly good news for Asian people, the Christian doctrine of salvation should surmount a soteriological individualism and incorporate the transhistorical nature of the community noted above. Christian salvation is by no means limited to the present and the future, but it importantly includes the past. The division of linear time in terms of the past, the present, and the future is not real but artificial and speculative. The genius of Augustine's great book *Confessions* lies in his enlightenment that there is no true salvation without the salvific dealing with one's past (memories), though his individualistic interpretation unfortunately gave rise to theological individualism. Overcoming this theological individualism, Asian theology must own up to and make honest confessions of our own collective memories of the past.

A reason why Confucianism is so attractive to the people in this postmodern period is that it does not conceive of a person as an isolated ego (essentialism) but as a center of relatedness in the network of communal relationships (relational view). From the Asian relational viewpoint, one's salvation in separation from one's own community does not make sense at all. Furthermore, Christianity is no longer a minority religion in Korea, but the most powerful one in the society with membership of more than a quarter of the total population. No more should the Korean Church praise the dissociation from one's own community and traditions as a victory of Christian faith for salvation or a heroic act of Christian evangelism. Such schizophrenic soteriology of amnesia and individualistic evangelism hinders a proper contextualization of Christianity in Korea. The remarkable membership growth of the Korean Church within the short period of two centuries is often cited as a miracle of modern Christian mission. Yet Christianity has not been rooted firmly in Korean soil. Christianity is still recognized as a Western religion in Korea, both in society and in academia. There is Christianity in Korea but no Korean Christianity! There are Christians in Korea but no Korean Christians! Therefore, it is an urgent task for us to search our new Christian identities to know what it means to be a Korean Christian in the global context of today. We should be honest with our religio-cultural traditions and make confessions of those collective memories. In order to cultivate Korean Christianity, furthermore, we should be humble enough to admit Christianity as a Korean religion, one among multiple Korean religions.

Original Sin

The individualistic soteriology and missiology of amnesia disconnect people from their own past and communities to impede the Koreanization of Christian faith. Moreover, the Protestant doctrine of original sin is often used venomously to demolish the values and ethics of traditional Confucian society. Augustine's doctrine of original sin was primarily intended to solve the problem of theodicy, but it was rhetorically exaggerated to dispute Pelagius and the Manicheans. Protestantism inflated this doctrine to defend their Reformation principle of *sola fide* (faith alone) against medieval Catholicism. To make the situation even worse, Protestant missionaries, fearing syncretism, implanted this doctrine deliberately to exclude indigenous religions and cultures. Religious plurality, however, is an everyday reality for the people in Korea and Asia. For example, one might see a family where the father is a stern Confucian, the mother a pious Buddhist, the grandmother a customary Shamanist, the son a carefree Daoist, the daughter-in-law a gentle Catholic, the daughter an evangelical Protestant, and the son-in-law a careless atheist. All religions except Christianity have existed in this country for more than a millennium. (Thus, multiple religious identities among family members are no extraordinary thing in Asian societies!) Yet we see many cases where the excessive doctrine of original sin plays an ill-fated role in breaking up a previously peaceful familial community. Being self-righteous as a born-again Christian, a newly converted Christian daughter indiscriminately accuses others in her own family—parents, siblings, and spouse—of being "non-Christian" sinners and aggressively teaches them with the "right" doctrines.

The central principle of Korean society before the advent of Christianity was the Confucian notion of human morality and fiduciary community, based on a Mencian belief in the original goodness of humanity. Taking for granted that these relationships are made in accordance with the heavenly decree, we believed the eternal bond among family and the faithfulness of our friends. In this society, we could fully trust our own family and neighbors, and we regarded it as a cardinal virtue to make sacrifices to rectify the name of our family and to keep faithfulness with our friends. The Christian doctrine of original sin shattered this foundational principle of Confucian society. Family and friends are no longer "we" but "they." Since they are also merely sinners, we cannot fully trust them. The doctrine of original sin plays a certain role in bringing about the destruction of Confucian society based on mutual trust. Korean Christianity, however, seems not to have been successful in establishing an alternative societal principle in the moral vacuum that was created after the withdrawal of Confucianism. Instead, extreme forms of materialism and individualism are rampant. The Confucian belief in fiduciary community and human faithfulness at least enabled us to keep confidence and hope in our own people and society. Unfortunately, however, the Christian doctrine of original sin has helped to foster severe distrust among the people in contemporary Korean society.

Religious Pluralism

Religious Pluralism is a Western concept that originated from an epistemological shock that Western theologians and scholars from religiously homogeneous Christian backgrounds experienced when they encountered and realized the profundities of other religions. Hence, advocates of religious pluralism generally have no real experience in a multireligious situation such as is common among Asian people, an example of which we saw in the Korean family. Religious pluralism legitimately corrects the abuses of ecclesiocentric soteriology, which reserves to the church exclusive hegemony over salvation and revelation, but pluralism still conceals an epistemological outlook that views everything from a Western perspective.

Therefore, it is inadequate and odd for us to engage in the Western debates of religious pluralism. For more than a millennium before Christianity came to this land, there already had existed plural religions such as Daoism, Confucianism, Buddhism, and Shamanism. These living traditions have shaped our religious and cultural identities, something like our religious genome or cultural

DNA. Those religions are ontologically given to our existences. They are not others but our own. We do not have an epistemological distance to put them in the subject/object dichotomy. An urgent task of Korean theology is not in a speculative discussion of religious pluralism but in an articulation of our Christian identity in this context of religious plurality. Korean religions for us are not so much a subject of religious epistemology as an immediate matter of theological hermeneutics. In proper reverence to our own Korean religions and by owning up to them as part of our own identity, Christian theology should help Christianity take part in the religious plurality of our country.

3. *Owning Up to Our Own Metaphors: Toward a Theology of Dao (Theodao)*[5]

Theologies have developed through continuous paradigm shifts in relation to their surrounding religions and cultures, sometimes by owning up to their root-metaphors.[6] Generally, theologies can be divided in two paradigms, the logos paradigm and the praxis paradigm. The logos paradigm was developed by owning up to a key concept of Greek philosophy, logos, as the root-metaphor of theology (theo-logos). This paradigm flourished for almost two millennia. In addition to its metaphysical and dogmatic propensities, however, Enlightenment rationalism reduced the logos to a system of technical knowledge. Then, liberation theologies uncovered the sociological plots hidden in the metaphysics of orthodoxy. Instead, they adopted an alternate root-metaphor, praxis, to develop the praxis paradigm (theo-praxis). Although its emancipatory emphasis is historically a necessary corrective, theo-praxis cannot present a comprehensive program without its dialectical counterpart, theo-logy.

Asian theologies seem to inherit this dualism. On the one hand, Asian theologies of the conservative camps uncritically import the Western logos theologies with the blind belief in the myth of orthodoxy. On the other hand, creative Asian theologies, while being

---

5. For more discussion, see chap. 2.

6. See Hans Küng, *Christianity: Essence, History, and Culture*, trans. John Bowden (New York: Continuum, 1995).

reactionary to the logos theology, are not much beyond the corrective manifesto of liberation theology for orthopraxis. The socioeconomic situations of Asia do call on Asian theology to adopt the emancipatory tenet of theopraxis. The praxis paradigm, however, consists in the modern myth of history, an unqualified belief in teleological progress.[7] Unlike their dualistic, exclusivistic, and mechanistic Western counterparts, Asian religious visions are more holistic, inclusive, and ecological. Asian theology, as an integrated articulation of the Asian Christian community of faith about God, humanity, and life in the world, should be not only emancipatory but also open-ended, dialogical, ecological, and inclusive. We should construct a new paradigm of Asian theology that can break down the vicious cycle of the socioeconomic injustice that prevails in Asia and at the same time can own up to Asian religions and cultures as part of our identities.

God cannot be reduced to logos or praxis, but God transcends Greek dualism such as form and matter, body and soul, or theory and practice. I argue that the dao (way), a cardinal religio-cultural metaphor of East Asian people, is the root-metaphor—that is more appropriate and biblical—for Christian theology in the third millennium than the logos and the praxis. The dao is the ultimate way of life, as Jesus said, "I am the way [*hodos*], and the truth, and the life" (John 14:6a). Jesus did not identify himself either as truly God (*verus Deus*) and truly human (*verus homo*) or as the incarnate logos, but he simply said that he is the Way (dao) toward God (John 14:6b). He is Christ in such a way that he was a fully embodied Dao of God. Also remember that the Greek word *hodos* (way) was the original name for Christianity (Acts 9:2; 19:9; 22:4; 24:14, 22). I call this dao paradigm *theo-dao* vis-à-vis theo-logy and theo-praxis. Theodao calls forth a theological paradigm shift, from a mechanistic and materialistic paradigm to an organismic and life-generating one. The dao means both the source of cosmic being (logos) and the way of historical becoming (praxis). That is to say, the being in becoming, or the logos in transformative praxis.

---

7. See Raimon Panikkar, *The Cosmotheandric Experience: Emerging Religious Consciousness* (Maryknoll, NY: Orbis Books, 1993).

The dao is not an option of either-or but embraces the whole of both-and. The dao as the ultimate way embodies the transformative praxis of the cosmic trajectory of life in the unity of knowing and acting and with a preferential option toward the sociocosmic biography of the exploited life.

If the primary concern of traditional theology is the epistemology of faith, and if that of modern theopraxis is the eschatology of hope, the cardinal theme of Asian theodao is the pneumatology of love. Theology is classically defined as the *faith-seeking-understanding (fides quaerens intellectum)* and theopraxis as the *hope-seeking-practice;* theodao can be defined as the *love-seeking-way.* Theology (God-talk) focuses on the right understanding of Christian doctrines (orthodoxy) and theopraxis (God-walk) on the right practice of Christian ideologies (orthopraxis); theodao (God-live) searches for the wisdom of Christian life (orthodao). What Jesus taught us was not so much an orthodox doctrine, a philosophical theology, a manual of orthopraxis, or an ideology of social revolution but rather the way of life toward God. Jesus Christ cannot be divided between the historical Jesus (theopraxis) and the kerygmatic Christ (theology). Rather, theodao conceives of Jesus Christ as the crossroad of the Heavenly Dao and the human dao. It comprehends Jesus as the crucified Dao that reveals the way of salvation, with his own sociocosmic biography of the exploited life. It receives Christ as the Dao of resurrection, the way of sociocosmic reconciliation and sanctification. Jesus Christ teaches us the dao of how we, cosmic sojourners, can live fully human in solidarity with other cosmic co-sojourners. Theodao as a dao of Asian people invites us to participate in the common quest for our true subjectivity, in solidarity with the exploited life including minjung, women, and polluted nature, through the pneumatology of outpouring and harmonizing *ki* (氣 vital energy; *qì [ch'i]*).[8]

---

8. *Ki* is a Korean romanization of 氣 (vital energy; Pinyin: *qì*; Wade-Giles: *ch'i*]). *Ki* is a key East Asian term, very similar to *pneuma*, with various translations such as energy, vital force, material force, and breath. For more discussion of this term, see chapter 2.

CHAPTER TWO

God as the Dao: Toward a Theology of Dao (Theodao)

1. A Call for a Macro-Paradigm Shift in Theology

There is no *the theology*, objective, universal, and relevant to every context. There are *theologies*, open-ended, always on the way, and in dialogue with surrounding cultures and religions. (Theology is inevitably contextual!) Historically, theologies have been developing through continuous paradigm shifts with changes in their relating cultures.[1] Even today, however, I argue that Western theologies are still divided basically into two macro-paradigms—the logos paradigm (theo-logy) and the praxis paradigm (theo-praxis)— both holding leftovers of Greek dualism (form and matter, soul and body, theory and practice, etc.).

The Logos Paradigm

Traditional Western theologies developed in dialogue with Greek philosophy and flourished for almost two millennia with the

---

Adapted from Heup Young Kim, "A Tao of Asian Theology in the Twenty First Century," originally published in *Asia Journal of Theology* 13, no. 2 (1999): 276-93. It was reprinted in Heup Young Kim, *Christ & the Tao* (Hong Kong: Christian Conference of Asia, 2003), 135-54.

1. Hans Küng classified six macro-paradigms in the development of Christianity: early Christian apocalyptic, early church Hellenistic, medieval Roman Catholic, Reformation Protestant, Enlightenment modern, and contemporary ecumenical (postmodern) paradigms. See Hans Küng, *Christianity: Essence, History, and Culture*, trans. John Bowden (New York: Continuum, 1995).

employment of the key concept of that philosophy, logos, as the root-metaphor of theology (*theos* + *logos*). In the early Christian church, *theologia* had wider meanings, interrelated with *sophia* (wisdom) and other ideas.[2] However, the narrower definitions of later Christian theologians, for instance, of logos as logical and technical knowledge, and the excessive focus of Protestant theologians on the Word of God made this paradigm more and more metaphysical, dogmatic, and phonocentric. The goal of theology, primarily as God-talk, is to transmit universal orthodoxy. Most contemporary theologians, however, claim that this logosphonocentric paradigm is anachronistic and is no longer viable, not to mention criticisms from deconstructionists such as J. Derrida.

The Praxis Paradigm

Ever since Latin American liberation theologies uncovered the sociological plots in the metaphysics of orthodoxy, the logos paradigm has been under fire. Various liberationist theologies and first world political theologies argue for the employment of a somewhat neglected root-metaphor, praxis. In the praxis paradigm, theology (precisely, theopraxis) is defined rather as God-walk, and orthopraxis becomes the primary issue instead of orthodoxy. The emancipatory emphasis of Christian practice is the necessary and legitimate corrective to traditional theology. Yet the praxis paradigm can hardly present an independent and comprehensive program, because it is incomplete without the logos and still remains within the boundary of the Western dualism between theory and practice.

Both the logos and praxis paradigms hold to this hierarchical Western dualism and, hence, are basically heteronomous, whatever distinctions they make between superstructure and infrastructure or between heteronomy and autonomy. A subtler problem in the praxis paradigm is its uncritical belief in the dialectical progress of history. The strength of theopraxis is its expression of the emanci-

---

2. See Jean Pepin, "Logos," in *The Encyclopedia of Religion*, ed. Mircia Eliade (New York: Macmillan, 1987), 9:9–15; also Edward Farley, *Theologia: The Fragmentation and Unity of Theological Education* (Philadelphia: Fortress, 1983), 31-44, 162, 165-69.

patory dimension, but it is weak in facilitating the ecological and dialogical dimensions, highly demanded in our broken, polluted, postmodern world.

Yet most Asian theologies seem to remain within the boundaries of these dualistic macro-paradigms. On the one hand, Asian theologies of the conservative camps uncritically import the Western logos theologies with a blind belief in the myth of orthodoxy. On the other hand, creative Asian theologies, while being reactionary to the logos theology, are not much beyond the corrective manifesto of liberation theology for orthopraxis. The socioeconomic situations of Asia do call Asian theology to adapt the emancipatory tenet of theopraxis. Asian theology, however, needs to admit that the hidden presupposition of the praxis paradigm consists in the modern myth of history, a belief in teleological progress, whose validity is now questionable.[3]

Furthermore, nonlinear Asian religious visions challenge Asian theologians to demythologize this myth of history, the modern modification of salvation history inherited from Judeo-Christianity. Unlike its dualistic and mechanistic Western counterparts, Asian religious visions are characteristically more holistic, inclusive, and ecological, namely, "anthropocosmic" (humanity and cosmos being interrelated) or even "theanthropocosmic" (God, humanity, and cosmos being interrelated).[4] Eventually, these visions will provide rich resources for Asian theology. Asian theology in the twenty-first century, as an integrated articulation of the Asian Christian community of faith about God, humanity, and life in the world at a given time, should be not only emancipatory but also open-ended,

---

3. See Raimon Panikkar's analysis in his *The Cosmotheandric Experience: Emerging Religious Consciousness* (Maryknoll, NY: Orbis Books, 1993).

4. For the anthropocosmic vision, see Tu Wei-ming, *Centrality and Commonality: An Essay on Confucian Religiousness*, rev. ed., SUNY Series in Chinese Philosophy and Culture (Albany: State University of New York Press, 1989), 102-7. For the theanthropocosmic vision, see Panikkar, *Cosmotheandric Experience*. For a comparative study of these, see Heup Young Kim, *Wang Yang-ming and Karl Barth: A Confucian–Christian Dialogue* (Lanham, MD: University of Press of America, 1996), 175-77, 185-88.

dialogical, ecological, inclusive, and holistic. However, Asian theology of religions, active in inter- and intrareligious dialogue, has been too politically naïve and too retrospectively romantic. A most important issue for Asian theologians today is how to construct an Asian revolutionary theology to break the vicious cycle of the socioeconomic injustice prevailing in Asia without falling into Western dualism and historicism.[5]

The Dao Paradigm

Constructing such a viable Asian theology for the twenty-first century solicits a macro-paradigm shift beyond the two paradigms of the traditional logos-oriented theo-logy and the modern praxis-oriented theo-praxis. The days for these two Western root-metaphors for theology, logos and praxis, have passed. Asian theology in the day of new wine needs a new wineskin. I argue that the East Asian root-metaphor of dao is the new wineskin (it is as old as logos and praxis in the history of East Asian thought, though, perhaps, new for Christianity).[6]

Then what is Dao (道; Way [Tao])? First and foremost, just as God is, dao is inexplicable. You would be idolatrous if you defined it with any intention. Compare "The Dao that can be told of is

---

5. Among Asian theologians of the first generation, this dichotomy appeared saliently between Raimon Panikkar and M. M. Thomas; see Panikkar, *The Unknown Christ of Hinduism*, rev. ed. (Maryknoll, NY: Orbis Books, 1964); and Thomas, *The Acknowledged Christ of the Indian Renaissance* (London: SCM, 1969). According to Paul Knitter, Aloysius Pieris formulated this issue in a slightly different way as "a nondualistic understanding/ experience of the liberative activity of God and the liberative activity of the poor as 'one indivisible Saving Reality'" ("Foreword," in Pieris, *An Asian Theology of Liberation* [Maryknoll, NY: Orbis Books, 1988], xiv).

6. As the widely used root-metaphor of all classical East Asian religions, including Confucianism, Daoism, and Buddhism, dao is a very inclusive term with various meanings. Tentatively, I use the Confucian definition formulated by Herbert Fingarette: "Tao is a Way, a path, a road, and by common metaphorical extension it becomes in ancient China the right Way of life, the Way of governing, the ideal Way of human existence, the Way of the Cosmos, the generative-normative Way (Pattern, path, course) of existence as such" (*Confucius—The Secular as Sacred* [New York: Harper & Row, 1972], 19).

not the eternal Dao" (*Dàodéjīng* [*Tao-te Ching*]: 1) and "You shall not make yourself an idol, whether in the form of anything that is in heaven above, on the beneath, or in the water under the earth" (Exod. 20:4). In light of the biblical expression of Jesus, we might say provisionally that Dao is the ultimate way of life, as Jesus said, "I am the way, and the truth, and the life" (John 14:6a). In fact, Jesus did not identify himself as either true God (*verus Deus*) and true human (*verus homo*) or the incarnate logos, but he simply said that he is the way (*hodos, dao*) toward God (John 14:6b). He is Christ in such a way that he was a fully embodied *dao* of God. In that sense, Jesus was *the* way to God (John 14:6b), without reference to any so-called exclusivism.

2. The Ugŭmch'i Phenomenon

What does the dao paradigm look like? Kim Chi Ha, a well-known Korean poet, once told an intriguing story in his essay "The Ugŭmch'i Phenomenon." This story suggests an example of the dao paradigm. It introduces some valuable insights that help us to envision a theology in the East Asian way of life and to solve the problematic of Asian theology, an inner conflict between the Christian liberation imperative and Asian anthropocosmic vision. I will begin with this story to search out a new dao paradigm of Christian theology.

The Ugŭmch'i Phenomenon (우금치 현상)[7]

> In front of my house in Haenam,[8] there is a little stream. This stream originates at Kumgang-bo, the largest reservoir in the neighborhood of Haenam. In the past, the water was so clean and fresh that people could swim and catch fish in the stream. Now, however, it has become a smelly ditch, darkly

---

7. In Kim Chi Ha, *Saengmyŏng* [Life] (Seoul: Sol, 1992), 188-92. Since this theologically profound essay is a good parable by which to awaken to the vista of dao, I translate the whole essay here with the permission of the author.

8. Translator: A city located in Chŭllanamdo, the Southwestern state of Korea.

rotten with wastewater, synthetic detergents, briquette ashes, garbage, Coke bottles, cans, etc. Nevertheless, the stream changes entirely when it rains. At midnight, it makes a sound as big as what we can hear from refreshing rapids in Mt. Sŏlak or Mt. Odae. And it sweeps wastes downward so that it becomes as clean again as it used to be. When I [Kim Chi Ha] sat down by the stream and noticed it had much better fish jumping, I was greatly astonished. There are about ten big cement stepping-stones across the stream, and rapid currents flow down between them like a waterfall. This scene forms a little spectacle. There are many fishes jumping from below to cross over the stepping-stones in order to return upward! It is a great scene with scores of fish in various sizes, from little daces to hand-sized crucians continuously jumping up and straining.

I sat down by the stream and thought over and over.

How on earth can those fish move upward against such strong downward currents? Is it only what evolution theory calls a groping in the dark which leads to endless failure? To see that some among them go upward very smoothly, it seems not to be a failure or a groping in the dark. What on earth is the mystery that enables them to do so? Unless those fish are fools, there is no reason why they so persistently put forth every ounce of their energies in vain. It must be obvious to them that they swim upward in the opposition to the currents pouring down upon them. But I do not know more. Perhaps, the fishes are returning to the reservoir to find the ecological conditions most appropriate to them in terms of water temperature, water pressure, water habitus, plankton, etc. However, how can they swim upward along the water currents flooding downward so rapidly and forcefully? It might be enough to explain that it is a mysterious creation of the Creator. But this still does not solve the mystery. It is easy and simple to say that it is an adaptation to the environment according to evolutionary theory. But that does not explain everything, either.

In the night, I sat in the lotus position and looked at the face of my wife, straight at the pupils of her eyes. At that time, a strange thought occurred to me. Through her eye-pupils, I could feel what she was thinking in her mind, and, through my pupils, my wife likewise felt that I could feel the same. It happened for an instant. It was like the movement of *sin-ki* [神氣; vital or divine energy; *shén qì* (*shen-ch'i*)].[9] I realized then that it is the movement of *sin-ki* insofar as one movement of *sin-ki* enables to know the other movement of *sin-ki* and vice versa.

Aha, now I know.

The mystery of how a feeble fish can swim upward along the turbulent down flow to return to its destined birthplace.

That is to say, such a thing occurs in the moment when the *sin-ki* of a fish is united with the *sin-ki* of the water flow. Nature is another good word for this. In other words, it happens in the moment when the nature of a fish is united with the nature of water.

The *ki* (*qì*)[10] of water moves in both directions of *yin* and *yang*.[11] While the *yang* of water runs the downward movement, the *yin* of water runs the upward movement. While water flows downward, water flows upward at the same time. In the river, counter-currents must occur in the majestic movement of big waters! This is a phenomenon that occurs simultaneously in the movement of *il-ki* of water.[12] This phe-

---

9. Translator: *Sin* (神; in Chinese, *shén* [shen]) has various meanings such as ghost, spirit, soul, vitality, sacred, etc. Although this word is translated as vitality in this chapter, it also connotes divinity. Translating *shén qì* as vital spiritual energy, this chapter uses primarily its Korean romanization, *sin-ki*, because of author's special emphasis.

10. Translator: *Ki* (氣; in Chinese, *qì* [ch'i]) is a term very similar to *pneuma* and translated variously such as energy, vital force, material force, and breath. This chapter uses primarily its Korean romanization, *ki*, translating as energy.

11. Translator: *Ki* is interpreted to have two forms of movement, the *yin* (negative or female) and the *yang* (positive or male) that forms a unity of complementary opposites such as the Great Ultimate (太極 *T'aegŭk*; in Chinese, *Tài jí* [*T'ai-chi*]).

12. Translator: *Il-ki* (一氣; in Chinese, *yī qì* [*i-ch'i*]) means the one or primordial *qì* or the primordial vigor.

nomenon arises exactly when the nature of a fish's *sin-ki* becomes united with the nature of this *ki*. Does history progress forward only? No. While history progresses forward, it goes backward at the same time. Although it is described in terms of quality and quantity, this is a matter that arises simultaneously. Certainly, it is not right to say this in terms of either front and back or progression and retrogression. Rather, it would be better to say this in terms of a simultaneously converging-diverging movement of "in and out" and "quality and quantity." And all the movements after all return to their origin. They return, not in vain but creatively. This is the *yin-yang* movement of *il-ki*, i.e., the primordial vigor of the cosmos. Humans can do this with self-consciousness.

Aha, I also know now.

From the palpitation of the persistent and dynamic *sin-ki* of the fish in returning home, [I now understand] the mystery of the Ugŭmch'i War[13] where the exalted *sin-ki* had the minjung[14] of several hundred thousands jumping soaked with blood and going persistently upstream.

We should not understand it simply as a battle or a struggle in terms of victory or failure between this and that. By that understanding, we fail to see or, after all, misconceive the mystery of that tremendous collective life energy discharged by the minjung in the Tonghak Revolution in 1894. It may end with such misconceptions as a literary expression like the explosion of continuously accumulated *han*[15] or as a superfi-

---

13. Translator: The last and fiercest battle during the second uprising of Tonghak minjung, which broke out on a hill of Kongju, named Ugŭm, in December of 1894. Tonghak (東學), literary meaning Eastern Learning, was a religious movement founded by Ch'oe Che-u [1824–1864] in reaction to the so-called Western Learning (西學), i.e., Catholicism.

14. Translator: Minjung literally means the multitude of people, but in minjung theology, this term is closely related to the oppressed, exploited, and marginalized groups.

15. Translator: This term became well known by the use of Korean minjung theologians. According to Suh Nam-dong (1918–1984), a founder of minjung theology, *han* is "the suppressed, amassed and condensed experience

cial socio-economic observation like an upward uprising or a poverty uprising.

But it is not.

Although it looks like that, it is not.

Han, poverty, or the demand for class liberation, without the knowledge of the movement of minjung's collective *sin-ki* that acts in everything, cannot uncover the mystery of Ugǔmch'i. Nor can *han*, poverty, or the demand for class liberation receive a legitimate evaluation on the basis of historical meaning.

What kind of force on the earth made the minjung of several hundred thousands, who were almost bare-handed, armed only with firelocks and bamboo spears, attempt to climb the hill through the scorching fires of the demonic cannons of Japan and the Yi Dynasty?[16] What was the origin of the power that empowered them to advance for freedom, forming a mountain of corpses and a sea of blood, experiencing failure after failure and death after death?

Where is the clue to understand the mystery of Tonghak, that had constituted the roots of the main forces in the righteous armies of 1895, in the second and the third great righteous armies, and in the Minhoe Movement during the Russo-Japanese War, again in the March First Movement, in the Ch'ǔngudang Movement[17] of the Ch'ǔndogyo, in many

---

of oppression caused by mischief or misfortune so that it forms a kind of 'lump' in one's spirit" (Kim Yong Bock, ed., *Minjung Theology: People as the Subjects of History* [Singapore: Commission on Theological Concern, Christian Conference of Asia, 1981], 65). In fact, Suh's theology of *han* was heavily influenced by Kim Chi Ha's thought. However, afterwards Kim changed his mind on this issue and went beyond it, as appears in this essay.

16. Translator: Yi Dynasty is the last dynasty in Korea (1392–1910).

17. Ch'ǔngudang was a national movement organization of Ch'ǔndogyo organized in North Korea with the institute of religious affairs of Ch'ǔndogyo in North Chosǔn after the independence of August 15, 1945. It attempted a revival movement of the March First Movement in 1948 to develop a general election for the unification of the South and the North. However, the plan was revealed beforehand, many people were arrested, and the movement was systematically suppressed since then.

tenancy disputes in the peasant history of Chosŭn,[18] in strike movements in the labor history of Chosŭn, in the movements of numberless liberation armies in Kando, Siberia, Tumen River, and in the region of Yalu River, and in the movements of the underground organizations to support them, and going further even in the change of the forms of ideologies and organizations?

In short, it is in the great self-awakening of minjung on the collective *sin-ki* through Tonghak. Minjung became aware of and became the embodiment of vitalization and spiritualization and the vital energy *ki* that endlessly and immensely evolves, socializes, self-sanctifies, and self-divinizes.

The collective *sin-ki* of the self-conscious minjung is a great cosmic movement to be united with the primordial *sin-ki* of history, i.e., the *yin-yang* movement of *ki*, against the demonic currents of the history that poured down against them. I will call this the ugŭmch'i phenomenon.

Ah, Ah. The *sin-ki* of our minjung, the vitalization and spiritualization, with the climax of 1894, has been displaced, alienated, rooted out, oppressed, disgraced, divided, imprisoned, neglected, destroyed, and enslaved—therefore, has been slaughtered until now—by the wrong foreign ideas of the West or Japan. Even now, the flags of death are waving in the street. Only few people are searching around for the true subjectivity of minjung.

This is the time when we look into the ugŭmch'i phenomenon in order to find our genuine subjectivity.

Yes. For, even against the demonic currents of the history, we have not failed completely and descended out, but have ascended this much!

3. The Phenomenology of Sin-ki (Shén qì)

This provocative story of the ugŭmch'i phenomenon puzzles the dualistically oriented Western mind in general and the analyti-

---

18. Translator: Chosŭn is the original name of the Korea.

cally trained modern mind in particular (including the westernized Asian mind). However, it is a very original East Asian way of grasping reality, and it has profound theological implications. Furthermore, it introduces some passwords that may open the vision of a new East Asian paradigm in theology. Although it requires further thematization, it would be worthwhile mentioning five points at this juncture.

1. Neither the logos paradigm (traditional Western theology) nor the praxis paradigm (liberationist theology) fits simply with this phenomenology of *sin-ki* and falls short of the analogical imaginations it presents. If the polluted flood metaphorically refers to the force of destruction, the feeble fish represent the force of life. Deconstuctionists have unveiled that the logos-centric paradigm has had more affinity to the force of destruction than to the force of life. It rather has helped the demonic movement of the historical flood, by its involvement with sociological plots such as androcentrism and ethnocentrism, and by endangering life by its dualistic fragmentation.

Although the praxis paradigm aggressively resists the force of destruction, it remains within the limit of narrowly defined historico-socioeconomic concerns that do not proceed completely beyond the logic constituted by the force of destruction. It does not propound a self-sufficient description for the force of life but ends with a reactionary articulation against the force of destruction. Nor does it retain a profound understanding of the complex relations among God, humanity, and the cosmos such as those expressed in the Asian theanthropocosmic vision and the phenomenology of *sin-ki*.

2. The ugŭmch'i phenomenon lures Asian theology one step forward. For example, Korean minjung theologies have made some valuable contributions to contemporary theology with the prophetic calling to the Christian movement for justice and freedom in solidarity with minjung. Yet this call seems to be too narrow, romantic, or Western from the perspective of Kim Chi Ha's ugŭmch'i phenomenon.

Kim Yong-bock argued that the social biography (the underside history) of minjung is a more authentic historical point of reference for theological reflection than the doctrinal discourses (the official history) superimposed by the church and in the orientation of Western rationality.[19] It was an important and creative proposal for Asian theology to be situated on a concrete ground so as to evoke the self-awakening of minjung as the subjects of history. To employ the sociobiography of minjung as a main theological agenda serves as a legitimate correction to traditional theology, primarily based on autobiographical (psychological) or church (official) narratives. Nevertheless, this more or less exclusive focus on the political economy of God looks too historical to be liberated fully from the myth of history in Western modernism and to locate Asian religious dimensions properly.

Chung Hyun Kyung's provocative proposal of *"hanpuri"* (a participatory event to release *han*-riddenness) was an authentic appeal from the perspective of Korean women.[20] Asian theology should take seriously the reality of *han*, the accumulated psychosomatic experiences (and dangerous memories) of collective suffering. The *hanpuri* does have psychologically and socially therapeutic and salvific dimensions. Nevertheless, with such a simple hermeneutics of *han*, we cannot reach the depth of Asian spiritual complexity, as Kim Chi Ha claimed in the ugŭmch'i phenomenon. To thematize Christian confessional agendas more comprehensively in the profundity of Asian spiritual complexity, Asian theology needs to move forward beyond the proposals of these minjung theologies so as to overcome this potential reductionism (or "misconceptions," according to Kim Chi Ha).

3. *The Hermeneutics of* Ki [Qì]. Kim Chi Ha's phenomenology of *sin-ki*, though based on his creative interpretation of the original Tonghak, offers some fascinating clues for the re-visioning of Asian theology for the twenty-first century beyond the (Western) logos

---

19. See Kim Yong-bock, "Theology and the Social Biography of Minjung," *CTC Bulletin* 5, no. 3–6, no. 1 (1984–85): 66-78.

20. See Chung Hyun Kyung, "'Han-puri': Doing Theology from Korean Women's Perspective," *Ecumenical Review* 40, no. 1 (January 1988): 27-36.

paradigm and the (Asian) praxis paradigm. It illuminates that *ki*, a term very comparable to *pneuma*, provides a significant hermeneutical key and rich theological resource for Asian theologies in the future. He argues lucidly that *ki* (more correctly, *sin-ki*) is the key to unveil the reason for the mystery of how the feeble fishes in the turbulent flood and the multitude of minjung in the Ugŭmch'i War can manifest such a tremendously life-empowering force. *Ki* is a very East Asian term, and, like *pneuma*, it is not dualistic and analytic but holistic and embracing; it is both the source (primordial energy) and the medium of primordial empowerment. Hence, with this new hermeneutics of *sin-ki*, we can develop an appropriate answer to our starting question—how to construct a revolutionary theology to fight against the vicious structure of socioeconomic injustice without falling into dualism and historicism. An answer would be a revolutionary theology of *sin-ki* with the hermeneutics of *ki*.

4. *The Pneumato-anthropocosmic (Ki-anthropocosmic) Vision.* The phenomenology of *sin-ki* expands the East Asian anthropocosmic vision to a new horizon in the unity of Heaven (God), the human, and Earth (cosmos) through the spirit (*ki*). Neo-Confucianism developed a vision of "cosmic togetherness" in an organismic unity with Heaven, Earth, and the myriad things, as is well expressed in Zhang Zai's *Western Inscription*:

> Heaven is my father and Earth is my mother, and even such a small creature as I find an intimate place in their midst. Therefore that which fills the universe I regard as my body and that which directs the universe I consider as my nature. All people are my brothers and sisters, and all things are my companions.[21]

---

21. Chan Wing-tsit, trans., *A Source Book in Chinese Philosophy* (Princeton, NJ: Princeton University Press, 1963), 497-98. Wang Yang-ming further developed the doctrine of the Oneness of All Things, as expressed in the following. For more discussion, see Kim, *Wang and Barth*, 42-46:

The great man regards Heaven, Earth, and the myriad things as one body. He regards the world as one family and the country as one per-

Kim Chi Ha enhanced this East Asian anthropocosmic vision dramatically by the phenomenology of *sin-ki.* Since it implies a spiritual communion between humanity and the universe through the interpenetration of *ki,* I call it pneumato- or ki-anthropocosmic vision. In East Asian thought, this vision is heavily embedded in the *yin-yang* correlation, the sophisticated cosmology of Changes (易), and the Neo-Confucian metaphysics of the Great Ultimate (太極). The anthropocosmic vision expressed in various Asian religions should be a reservoir of great potential to heal, vitalize, and even save today's fragile and fragmented Christian theologies from the swamp of postmodern crises, as many Asian and Western scholars suggest.

Nevertheless, this potentiality does not necessarily endorse a ret-

---

son. As to those who make a cleavage between objects and distinguish between the self and others, they are small men. That the great man can regard Heaven, Earth, and the myriad things as one body is not because he deliberately wants to do so, but because it is natural humane nature of his mind that he does so. Forming one body with Heaven, Earth, and the myriad things is not only true of the great man. Even the mind of the small man is no different. Only he himself makes it small. Therefore, when he sees a child about to fall into a well, he cannot help a feeling of alarm and commiseration. This shows that his humanity [*rén*] forms one body with the child. It may be objected that the child belongs to the same species. Again, when he observes the pitiful cries and frightened appearance of birds and animals about to be slaughtered, he cannot help feeling an "inability to bear" their suffering. This shows that his humanity forms one body with birds and animals. It may be objected that birds and animals are sentient beings as he is. But when he sees plants broken and destroyed, he cannot help a feeling of pity. This shows that his humanity forms one body with plants. It may be said that plants are living things as he is. Yet, even when he sees tiles and stones shattered and crushed, he cannot help a feeling of regret. This shows that his humanity forms one body with tiles and stones. This means that even the mind of the small man necessarily has the humanity that forms one body with all. Such a mind is rooted in his Heaven-endowed nature, and is naturally intelligent, clear, and not beclouded. (Chan Wing-tsit, trans., *Instructions for Practical Living and Other Neo-Confucian Writings* [New York: Columbia University Press, 1963], 272).

rospective and uncritical romanticization of Asian religions and cultures. On the contrary, it should be emphasized that Asian religious visions are not totally innocent of distortion and exploitation. Historically, they also committed much evil against minjung and women. For example, Cheng Chung-ying succinctly characterized the East Asian mode of orientation in terms of "natural naturalization" (nature and naturality in Chinese philosophy: *Yìjīng /Dàodéjīng*) and "human immanentization" (Confucianism and Neo-Confucianism), which contrasts with the Western mode in terms of "rational rationalization" (reason and rationality in Greek philosophy: Socrates/Plato/Aristotle) and "divine transcendentalization" (Judeo-Christianity).[22] Although this is a lucid distinction, we must question whether such a beautiful mode of natural naturalization and human immanentization does not contain the dimension for a paradise indwelling, the myth that has been broken. (A big question is why those who inherit those beautiful ecological traditions now live in the most polluted regions in the world?)[23] The human reality people experience today is rather in a post-paradise situation. Christianity is at least correct in that observation. After the lost battle vis-à-vis Western modernization, we Asians can no longer be "innocent dreamers" (Paul Tillich). We need to employ modern critical thinking and a hermeneutics of suspicion. At the same time, we must admit with the postmodern consciousness that the modern mode of thinking has reached its limits and that there might be hope in our own resources, though they must be reinterpreted in new ways.

From this vantage point, the revolutionary theology of *sin-ki* should take very seriously Asian hermeneutics of suspicion including minjung, feminism, neo- and post-colonialism, and orientalism. Asian theology in the future solicits an entirely new paradigm that

---

22. Cheng Chung-ying, *New Dimensions of Confucian and Neo-Confucian Philosophy,* SUNY Series in Philosophy (Albany, NY: State University of New York Press, 1991), 4-22.

23. See Heup Young Kim, "Response to Peter K. H. Lee," in *Christianity and Ecology: Seeking the Well-Being of Earth and Humans,* ed. Dieter T. Hessel and Rosemary Radford Reuther(Cambridge, MA: Harvard University Press, 2000), 357-61.

can utilize fully the profundity of the Asian pneumatoanthropocosmic vision, while remaining faithful to these Asian hermeneutics of suspicion.

5. *The Sociocosmic Narrative of the Exploited Life:* By reinforcing Kim Yong-bock's proposal with the ki-anthropocosmic vision, we can commence the thematization of an Asian revolutionary theology of *sin-ki.* In addition to the sociobiography of minjung, Asian theology should embrace also the cosmic biography of the exploited life (metaphorically, the feeble fishes in the turbulent currents). Asian theology should liberate the underside of history of the exploited life, including animals and nature, from the captivity of modern imperialism and scientific fundamentalism that could bring us the doomsday of massive ecological destruction. As hinted in the ugŭmch'i phenomenon, the Asian ki-anthropocosmic vision cultivates a symbiosis of the life network through the communication of *ki.* This vision fosters the human race's relationship with other lives more holistically and profoundly than *societas* (by contract), *communitas* (by fellowship [*koinōnia*]). While being enhanced by a holistic vision, Asian theology should demythologize the dimensions of innocent dreaming and individualistic mysticism in the Asian anthropocosmic visions. To do it, Asian theology needs to thematize what I call the *sociocosmic narrative of the exploited life,* creatively pushing beyond both the sociobiography of minjung and the anthropocosmic vision. Asian theologians are impelled to tell the story of the sociocosmic network of the exploited life constituted by the spiritual communion of *ki,* whose primordial energy is salvific, both emancipatory and reconcilatory. The ugŭmch'i phenomenon is an example of such a sociocosmic narrative of the exploited life, metaphorically telling the story of the two exploited lives, the feeble fishes in the turbulent stream and the multitude of minjung in the Ugŭmch'i War.

4. A Dao of Asian Theology in the Twenty-First Century

God can be reduced neither to logos nor to praxis. God cannot be fully grasped with these two dualistic root-metaphors. God transcends Greek dualisms such as form and matter, body and soul, divinity and humanity, logos and praxis. I have argued that the dao is a root-metaphor to articulate God more appropriately than these two metaphors. I call this theological paradigm to be constructed with the root-metaphor of dao theo-dao (*theos* + *dao*) vis-à-vis theo-logy (*theos* + *logos*) and theo-praxis (*theos* + *praxis*).

In the light of the ugŭmch'i phenomenon, theodao, as a proper Asian theology in the twenty-first century, envisions the Dao of God operative in the ki-anthropocosmic trajectory. Theodao introduces an Asian pneumatological hermeneutics of *ki* that embodies the vital spiritual energy in exploited lives in order for them to swim dynamically upward against the demonic down-flood of history, for example, the manipulative global market controlled by technocratic dictatorship and centralized cyber space in our days. To do that, theodao calls forth Asian theology to make a macro-paradigm shift from mechanistic cosmology to that of life, from the materialistic paradigm to that of *ki*, and from the ontological paradigm to that of life-generation.

As its Chinese word consists of two ideographs, meaning "head" (首, *shŏu*, being) and "vehicle" (辶, becoming), dao means both the source of being (logos) and the way of cosmic becoming (praxis). Accordingly, dao can be reduced neither to being nor to becoming; rather, it is the being in becoming or the logos in transformative praxis. Thus, dao is not an option of either-or but embraces the whole of both-and. It does not force one to stay at the crossroad of logos (being) and praxis (becoming) but actualizes one to participate in a dynamic movement to be united with the cosmic track.[24] The dao as the ultimate way and reality embodies the transforma-

---

24. Tu Wei-ming said: "Since the Way is not known as a norm that establishes a fixed pattern of behavior, a person cannot measure the success or the failure of his conduct in terms of the degree of approximation to an external ideal. The Way is always near at hand, and the journey must be constantly renewed here and now. . . . It is like the art of archery. . . . The Way, then, does not provide an ideal norm or a set of directives to be complied with. It functions as a governing perspective and a point of orientation" (Tu, *Humanity and Self-Cultivation: Essays in Confucian Thought* [Berkeley: Asian Humanities Press, 1979], 36-37).

tive praxis of the sociocosmic trajectory of life in the unity of knowing and acting. Hence, while theology is the perspective from above and while theopraxis is that from below, theodao is the perspective from an entirely different dimension, theanthropocosmic intersubjectivity, or, in the light of the ugŭmch'i phenomenon, pneumatoanthropocosmic communion (through the network of *ki*). Furthermore, as already mentioned, theodao particularly focuses on the sociocosmic biography of the exploited life.

Theodao argues that Asian theology can be neither logos-centric (knowledge) nor praxis-centric (acting), but dao-centric (cf. *sophia* in action). Asian theology as a theodao can be reduced neither to an ortho-doxy (a right doctrine of the church) nor to an ortho-praxis (a right practice in history), but should embrace holistically the right way of life (ortho-dao), the transformative wisdom of living in a pneumatoanthropocosmic trajectory. The issue is neither only an orthodoxy nor only an orthopraxis, but an orthodao—that is, whether we are in the right way of God revealed in Jesus Christ and live wisely under the direction of the Holy Spirit. Remember that the Greek word *hodos* ("way," also meaning path, road, route, journey, march, etc.) was the original name for Christianity (Acts 9:2; 19:9; 22:4; 24:14, 22). Hence, the key issue is whether we are in proper communication with the Spirit to participate fully in the loving process of theanthropocosmic reconciliation and sanctification. See the end of 1 Corinthians 13! If orthodoxy emphasizes faith and orthopraxis hope, the orthodao focuses on love. Whereas the primary theme of the traditional logos theology was the epistemology of faith and whereas that of the modern praxis theology was the eschatology of hope, the cardinal theme of Asian dao theology is the pneumatology of love (that is the goal of the hermeneutics of *ki*). A comparison between the following two Christian and Daoist statements illuminates the gravity of this pneumatology of love:

> Love never ends. But as for prophecies [theopraxis], they will
> come to an end; as for tongues, they will cease; as for knowledge [theology], it will come to end. For we know only in part,
> and we prophesy only in part; but when the complete comes,
> the partial will come to an end. When I was a child, I spoke

like a child, I thought like a child, I reasoned like a child; when I became an adult, I put an end to childish ways. For now we see in a mirror dimly, but then we will see face to face. Now I know only in part; then I will know fully; even as I have been fully known. And now faith, hope, and love abide, these three; and the greatest of these is love. (1 Cor. 13:8-13 NRSV)

The fish trap exists because of the fish; once you've gotten the fish, you can forget the trap. The rabbit snare exists because of the rabbit; once you've gotten the rabbit, you can forget the snare. Words exist because of meaning; once you've gotten the meaning, you can forget the words. Where can I find a man who has forgotten words so that I can have a word with him? (*Zhuāngzǐ*) [25]

Asian theology as a theodao takes the definition of the *love-seeking-dao* rather than the classical definition of theology, the *faith-seeking-understanding (fides quaerens intellectum* [theology]), or the *hope-seeking-practice* (theopraxis). Whereas theology (God-talk) focuses on the right understanding of the Christian doctrines, and theopraxis (God-walk) on the right practice of the Christian ideologies, theodao (God-live) searches for the way and wisdom of Christian life. In fact, Jesus taught neither an orthodox doctrine, a philosophical theology, a manual of orthopraxis, nor an ideology of social revolution but the dao of life and living. Jesus Christ cannot be divided between the historical Jesus (theopraxis) and the kerygmatic Christ (theology). Hence, with the first Korean Catholic theologian Yi Pyŏk (1754–1786),[26] theodao conceives of Jesus as the crossroad of the Heavenly Dao and the human dao; that is to say, the theanthropocosmic Dao. Further, theodao comprehends Jesus as the crucified Dao that reveals the way of salvation, with

---

25. Translation from Burton Watson, trans., *The Complete Works of Chuang Tzu* (New York: Columbia University Press, 1968), 302.

26. See Jean Sangbae Ri, *Confucius et Jésus Christ: La première théologie chrétienne en Corée d'après L'oeuvre de Yi Piek lettré Confucéen, 1754–1786* (Paris: Beauchesne, 1979).

his own sociocosmic biography of the exploited life. Theodao sees Jesus as the Dao of resurrection, the way of cosmic reconciliation and sanctification that teaches us in such a way that we, cosmic sojourners, can live fully human in solidarity with other cosmic co-sojourners, particularly with the fullness of other exploited lives.

Finally, the dao of Asian theology in the twenty-first century is to invite us to participate in the common quest for the true subjectivity of the exploited life, including minjung, women, and polluted nature through the hermeneutics of *ki*. In light of the ugŭmch'i phenomenon, the dao of Asian theology revitalizes us by the outpouring power of the *sin-ki* (*ki*) through self-awakening. That has been manifested in the sociocosmic narratives of the exploited lives in Asia, but "has been displaced, alienated, rooted out, oppressed, disgraced, divided, imprisoned, neglected, destroyed, and enslaved—therefore, has been slaughtered until now—by the wrong foreign ideas."[27] To re-vision us with the correction of those wrong foreign ideas and re-embody us in the outpouring power of *ki* through self-awakening is an important task of theodao, as a new paradigm of Asian theology in the twenty-first century.

---

27. See Kim Chi Ha, *Saengmyŏng* [Life], 192.

CHAPTER THREE

Christodao:
Jesus Christ as the Dao

1. A Koan: *Christological Impasse*

The contemporary christological crisis consists of two basic problems: modern historicism and the dualism in Western thought between logos and praxis. The most salient example of modern historicism in the biblical field is the quest for the historical Jesus that began in the nineteenth century and continues today through the so-called second and third quests.[1] Demanding historical proofs, these scholars have challenged Christian faith and created a strange dichotomy between the historical Jesus and the kerygmatic Christ, between the earthly Jesus and the risen Christ, or between the pre-Easter Jesus and the post-Easter Christ. They reflect a historical

---

Adapted from Heup Young Kim, "Toward a Christotao: Christ as the Theanthropocosmic Tao," first published in *Studies in Interreligious Dialogue* 10, no. 1 (2000): 5-29. It was reprinted in *The Chinese Face of Jesus Christ*, vol. 3, ed. Roman Malek, Monumenta Serica Monograph Series 50 (Sankt Augustin, Germany: Institut Monumenta Serica and China-Zentrum, 2007), 1457-79; and in Heup Young Kim, *Christ & the Tao* (Hong Kong: Christian Conference of Asia, 2003), 155-82.

1. See Albert Schweitzer, *The Quest of the Historical Jesus: A Critical Study of Its Progress from Reimarus to Wrede* (1910; repr., New York: Macmillan, 1968); Rudoph Bultmann, *The History of the Synoptic Tradition*, rev. ed. (New York: Harper & Row, 1976); Günther Bornkamm, *Jesus of Nazareth*, rev. ed. (Minneapolis: Fortress, 1995); John Dominic Crossan, *The Historical Jesus: The Life of a Mediterranean Jewish Peasant* (San Francisco: HaperCollins, 1994); and Marcus J. Borg, *Jesus in Contemporary Scholarship* (Valley Forge, PA: Trinity Press International, 1994).

positivism or absolutism, an uncritical attitude toward or a blind faith in the modern myth of history.[2]

The dualism between logos and praxis, two root-metaphors of theology, has deepened with the emergence of liberation theology.[3] Many liberation theologies have radically questioned the relevance of church doctrines to historical situations (especially in the problem of radical evil). They argue that the primary task of theology has to do with right practice (orthopraxis) to transform unjust socioeconomic conditions, and they reject traditional logos theology (orthodoxy) as oppressively dogmatic, metaphysically abstract, and naively ahistorical. This powerful challenge divides contemporary systematic theology into two major camps, theo-logy and theo-praxis. This division is further sharpened in Christology, namely, between Christo-logy (Christ as [the incarnate] logos) and Christo-praxis (Jesus as the praxis [of the reign of God]).[4]

---

2. For an analysis of the myth of history, see Raimon Panikkar, *The Cosmotheandric Experience: Emerging Religious Consciousness* (Maryknoll, NY: Orbis Books, 1993), 79-134.

3. Root-metaphors denote the central metaphors such as logos and praxis that have shaped and governed narrative structures, cultural-linguistic matrices, or paradigms of theology and Christology in wider definitions. The terms theology (*theos* + *logos*) and Christology (*christ* + *logos*) were formulated in the process when the ancient Christian church borrowed the logos from Greek philosophy and adopted it as the root-metaphor in its understanding of God and Christ.

4. This dualism is comparable to the distinction between a Christology "from above" and a Christology "from below"; see Wolfhart Pannenberg, *Jesus, God and Man,* trans. Lewis L. Wilkins and Duane A. Priebe (Philadelphia: Westminster, 1974), 33-37. For Christopraxis of Latin American liberation theology, see Leonard Boff, *Jesus Christ Liberator: A Critical Christology for Our Time,* trans. Patrick Hughes (1978; repr., Maryknoll, NY: Orbis Books, 1991); Jon Sobrino, *Jesus the Liberator: A Historical-Theological Reading of Jesus of Nazareth,* trans. Paul Burns and Francis McDonagh (Maryknoll, NY: Orbis Books, 1993). For Occidental Christopraxis, see Tom F. Driver, *Christ in a Changing World: Toward an Ethical Christology* (New York: Crossroad, 1981); Jens Glebe-Møller, *Jesus and Theology: Critique of a Tradition,* trans. Thor Hall (Minneapolis: Fortress, 1989); and Edmund Arens, *Christopraxis: A Theology of Action,* trans. John F. Hoffmeyer (Minneapolis: Fortress, 1995).

Despite their holistic religious contexts, Asian theologies are also divided into two poles between Asian liberation theologies (liberationists) and Asian theologies of religions (inculturationists). Focusing on the historical situations of Asia, the liberationists call for an emancipatory struggle for socioeconomic justice; the inculturationists emphasize the contextual and hermeneutical imperative of Asian "anthropocosmic" (humanity and the cosmos being interrelated) religious visions.[5] A classic example of this dualism appears in the Christologies of two great Indian theologians, M. M. Thomas and Raimon Panikkar.[6] On the one hand, Thomas'a *a posteriori* Christology sees the functional Christ in the historical and inner transformation (reformation through modernization) of Asia and Asian religions (*The Acknowledged Christ of the Indian Renaissance*). On the other hand, Panikkar's *a priori* Christology finds the suprahistorical presence of a homologous Christ in Asian religions (*The Unknown Christ of Hinduism*). In Korean Christologies also, there appears a sharp distinction between the two opposite camps of minjung theology (Jesus as the oppressed people) and contextual theology of religions (Christ as the Sage or Bodhisattva).[7]

---

5. Neo-Confucianism had developed this vision of the "cosmic togetherness" in an organismic unity with Heaven, Earth, and the myriad things, as is well expressed in the following passage of Zhang Zai's *Western Inscription*: "Heaven is my father and Earth is my mother, and even such a small creature as I find an intimate place in their midst. Therefore that which fills the universe I regard as my body and that which directs the universe I consider as my nature. All people are my brothers and sisters, and all things are my companions." (Chan Wing-tsit, trans., *A Source Book in Chinese Philosophy* [Princeton, NJ: Princeton University Press, 1963], 497-98). Also see Tu Wei-ming, *Centrality and Commonality: An Essay on Confucian Religiousness*, rev. ed. (Albany: State University of New York Press, 1989), 102-7.

6. M. M. Thomas, *The Acknowledged Christ of the Indian Renaissance* (London: SCM, 1969); also R. Panikkar, *The Unknown Christ of Hinduism*, rev. ed. (Maryknoll, NY: Orbis Books, 1981).

7. For a version of minjung Christology, see C. S. Song, *Jesus, The Crucified People* (New York: Crossroad, 1990). For a (Confucian) sage Christology, see Heup Young Kim, *Wang Yang-ming and Karl Barth: A Confucian–Christian Dialogue* (Lanham, MD: University Press of America, 1996), 180-88; also M. Thomas Thangaraj, *The Crucified Guru: An Experiment in Cross-*

Hence, dualism is a dilemma prevalent in contemporary Christology. It is an unavoidable consequence as long as a Christology holds logos as the root-metaphor, because logos, based on dualistic Greek thinking, is vulnerable to an unfortunate split between theory (logos) and practice (praxis), between form and content, or between thought and feeling. Furthermore, blind faith in the modern myth of scientific history forces Western Christologies to reach an impasse, as is soberly illustrated by the recent North American debates among scholars surrounding the Jesus Seminar.[8]

How can we escape this dualism between logos and praxis and the myth of history? This is the *koan* (an evocative question) of this paper. That is to say, in our context how can we construct an East Asian Christology that neither neglects historical situations nor falls into Western dualism and historicism? In other words, how we can thematize an emancipatory Christology embodied in the soteriological nucleus of Asian anthropocosmic religions?

This christological enterprise may call for an entirely new hermeneutical paradigm with a new root-metaphor. I will argue that dao is such an alternative root-metaphor for Jesus Christ.[9] And I

Cultural Christology (Nashville: Abingdon, 1994). For a (Buddhist) bodhisattva Christology, see Keel Hee-sung, "Jesus the Bodhisattva: Christology from a Buddhist Perspective," *Buddhist-Christian Studies* 16 (1996): 169-85; John P. Keenan, *The Meaning of Christ: A Mahāyāna Theology* (Maryknoll, NY: Orbis Books, 1993); also Donald S. Lopez Jr. and Steven C. Rockfeller, eds., *The Christ and the Bodhisattva*, SUNY Series in Buddhist Studies (Albany: State University of New York Press, 1987).

8. The Jesus Seminar seems to be a scholarly movement initiated by those who, epistemologically shocked by the destruction of their innocent image of the ethnocentric Christ through historical-critical study, have substituted a faith in scientific history for that ethnocentrically controlled Christian faith. See Luke Timothy Johnson, *The Real Jesus: The Misguided Quest for the Historical Jesus and the Truth of the Traditional Gospels* (San Francisco: HarperSanFrancisco, 1996); also N. T. Wright, *Jesus and the Victory of God, Christian Origins and the Question of God 2* (Minneapolis: Fortress, 1996).

9. As the widely used root-metaphor of all classical East Asian religions, including Confucianism, Daoism, and Buddhism, *dao* [*tao*] (道) is a very inclusive term with various meanings. For example, a Confucian definition: "Tao is a Way, a path, a road, and by common metaphorical extension it becomes

will propose a *Christodao* that may overcome the dualism between Christology and Christopraxis. The comparison among the three theological and christological paradigms based on the three root-metaphors can be illustrated as follows:

Root-metaphor	Theology	Christology	Metaphor	Character	Objective
logos	theo-logy	Christo-logy	faith	under-standing (doctrine)	orthodoxy
praxis	theo-praxis	Christo-praxis	hope	action (ideology)	orthopraxis
dao	theo-dao	Christo-dao	love	living (the way of life)	orthodao

Vindications for this adoption are already apparent from several sources. First of all, from the confessional point of view, the adoption of dao for the formation of East Asian Christology is as legitimate as that of logos was for the fourth-century Christian church in developing the Nicene-Chalcedonian Christology. Further, remember that the original title for both Jesus and Christianity was the "way" (*hodos*) (John 14:6; Acts 16:17; 18:25; 18:26).[10] Furthermore, contemporary theologies and biblical scholarship illuminate, more and more transparently, the viability and cogency of the adoption of dao as an alternative postmodern title and metaphor for Jesus.

Ironically, the third quest for the historical Jesus seems to have arrived at a conclusion close to my thesis; that is, Jesus is more like

---

in ancient China the right Way of life, the Way of governing, the ideal Way of human existence, the Way of the Cosmos, the generative-normative Way (Pattern, path, course) of existence as such" (Herbert Fingarette, *Confucius—The Secular as Sacred* [New York: Harper & Row, 1972], 19). Dao also can be interpreted as "the logos in praxis" or "a being in becoming," as its Chinese character consists of two graphs meaning a head (首) and a movement ("to run"); see Wing-tsit Chan, *The Way of Lao Tzu: Tao-te ching* (Indianapolis: Bobbs-Merrill, 1963), 6-10.

10. The term "logos" does not appear in the *Gospel of Thomas*; see Stevan L. Davies, *The Gospel of Thomas and Christian Wisdom* (New York: Seabury, 1983), 81.

a sapiential teacher of the Way (dao), a sage, than either a founder of orthodox religion (logos) or an eschatological revolutionary (praxis).[11] German theologian Jürgen Moltmann rejected the classical logos Christology and explicitly employed the metaphor of the way in his christological formulation. He claimed, "I am trying to think of Christ no longer statically, as one person in two natures or as a historical personality. I am trying to grasp him dynamically, in the forward movement of God's history with the world." Moreover, Moltmann submits three reasons for the adoption of the way-symbol; it "embodies the aspect of process," "makes us aware that every human christology is historically conditioned and limited," and "invites" the unity of Christology and Christopraxis.[12]

Asian theologian Aloysius Pieris also made a helpful suggestion. He attempted to overcome the division among Asian theologies between liberationists and inculturationists by formulating an Asian liberation theology of religions through a genuine intrareligious dialogue between Asian religions (*Love Meets Wisdom*).[13] In a subsequent book, he divided Christian theology into three patterns—the logos model ("philosophical or scholastic theology"), the *dabhar* model ("liberation theology"), and the *hodos* model ("theology as search for wholeness"), and searched for a holistic model that "weaves together all three aspects of Christian discourse: Jesus as the

---

11. See Borg, *Jesus in Contemporary Scholarship*, esp. "Portraits of Jesus in Contemporary North American Scholarship," 18-43; also see Ben Witherington III, *Jesus the Sage: The Pilgrimage of Wisdom* (Minneapolis: Fortress, 1994). In addition, Bernard Lee analyzed the metaphors used for Jesus in the New Testament and proposed "a new development of a *Ruach/Dabhar* christology" to prevent ethnic violation (against the Jewishness of Jesus) and free from the metaphysical captivity of the logos Christology; see his *Jesus and The Metaphors of God: The Christs of the New Testament,* Studies in Judaism and Christianity 2 (New York: Paulist, 1993), 189.

12. Jürgen Moltmann, *The Way of Jesus Christ: Christology in Messianic Dimensions,* trans. Margaret Kohl (San Francisco: HarperSanFrancisco, 1990), xv, xiv.

13. See Aloysius Pieris, *Love Meets Wisdom: A Christian Experience of Buddhism,* Faith Meets Faith (Maryknoll, NY: Orbis Books, 1988); also *An Asian Theology of Liberation,* Faith Meets Faith (Maryknoll, NY: Orbis Books, 1988).

word that interprets reality, the *medium* that transforms history, and the *way* that leads to the cessation of all discourse."[14]

These are some examples of clear signs anticipating the coming of Christodao, the dao paradigm of Christology. However, the holistic but fundamentally apophatic and elusive universe of dao is strange and foreign to modern people (including modernized Asians). We may need an enlightenment to leap into this new hermeneutical vista from the contemporary linear, scientific worldview. This enlightenment requires an experience more profound than that of "rhythmic pulses" and "cosmic dance of energy" that Fritjof Capra described.[15] For an innocent dance of the cosmos is a romantic interpretation of dao. An adequate interpretation must be more complex, because *dao* is a fully loaded term as old as *logos*. And dao has often been used in ideologies of the powerful to oppress the powerless in the political history of East Asia. Dao also should be regarded as a broken symbol in a fragmented form. Thus, its interpretation must be not only creative and imaginative but also critical. An imaginative hermeneutics of retrieval should be combined with a proper hermeneutics of suspicion.

2. Dao: A New Root-Metaphor for Jesus Christ

As Jaroslav Pelikan has pointed out, the "momentous" adoption of logos as the title for Jesus (Christo-logy) by the fourth-century Christian church was accompanied by another kind of monumental adaptation of Jesus as the cosmic Christ (the Savior of the cosmos).[16] Although it brought unfortunate consequences in the modern

---

14. Aloysius Pieris, *Fire and Water: Basic Issues in Asian Buddhism and Christianity*, Faith Meets Faith (Maryknoll, NY: Orbis Books, 1996), esp. 146; also see 138-46.

15. See Fritjof Capra, *The Tao of Physics: An Exploration of the Parallels between Modern Physics and Eastern Mysticism*, 3rd ed. (Boston: Shambhala, 1991), 11.

16. Jaroslav Pelikan, *Jesus through the Centuries: His Place in the History of Culture* (New York: Harper & Row, 1985), 58. For the cosmic Christ in the Bible and Christian traditions, also see Matthew Fox, *The Coming of the Cosmic Christ: The Healing of Mother Earth and the Birth of a Global Consciousness* (San Francisco: Harper & Row, 1988), esp. 75-128.

period, the adoption of logos was to articulate not only the cosmic but also the cosmogonic natures of Christ in the Greek philosophical language. The Nicene Creed explicitly states, "[We believe] in one Lord Jesus Christ, the Son of God . . . by whom all things were made." This faith in the *cosmogonic Christ* was not new but had been already articulated by John and Paul: "All things have been created through him and for him. He himself is before all things, and in him all things hold together" (Col. 1:16-17 NRSV; cf. John 1:3).

Dao is a metaphor more congenial to the cosmogonic nature of Christ than logos: "Tao is Great in all things, complete in all, universal in all, whole in all. These three aspects are distinct, but the reality is one" (*Zhuāngzǐ*: 22).[17] Dao refers to the ultimate reality beyond the realm of naming with any cultural-linguistic metaphor, symbol, and form; it is radically apophatic: "The Tao that can be told of is not the eternal Tao; The name that can be named is not the eternal name. The Nameless is the origin of Heaven and Earth; The Named is the mother of all things" (*Dàodéjīng*: 1).[18] Hence, the naming of dao is only heuristic: "I do not know its name; I call it Tao, for the lack of

---

17. [Wade-Giles: *Chuang-tzu*] Translation from Thomas Merton, *Thoughts on the East* (New York: New Directions, 1995), 25-26. For a general introduction to the dao, see Max Kaltenmark, *Lao Tzu and Taoism*, trans. Roger Greaves (Stanford: Stanford University Press, 1969); also A. C. Graham, *Disputers of the Tao: Philosophical Argument in Ancient China* (La Salle, IL: Open Court, 1989). For Zhuāngzǐ's understanding of the dao, see Chad Hansen, "A Tao of Tao in Chuang-tzu," in *Experimental Essays on Chuang-tzu*, ed. Victor H. Mair (Honolulu: University of Hawaii Press, 1983), 24-55; Philip J. Ivanhoe, "Zhuangzi on Skepticism, Skill, and the Ineffable Dao," *Journal of American Academy of Religion* 91, no. 4 (1993): 639-53. For comparative studies between dao and logos, see Zhang Longxi, *The Tao and the Logos: Literary Hermeneutics, East and West*, Post-contemporary Interventions (Durham, NC: Duke University Press, 1992); Mark Berkson, "Language: The Guest of Reality—Zhuangzi and Derrida on Language, Reality, and Skillfulness," *Essays on Skepticism, Relativism, and Ethics in the Zhuangzi*, ed. Paul Kjellberg and Philip J. Ivanhoe, SUNY Series in Chinese Philosophy and Culture (Albany: State University of New York Press, 1996), 97-126; and James W. Stines, "I Am the Way: Michael Polanyi's Taoism," *Zygon* 20, no. 1 (1995): 59-77.

18. [Wade-Giles: *Tao-te ching*] Translation from Chan, *Source Book*, 139.

the better word" (*Dàodéjīng*: 25). Remember again that Jesus and primitive Christianity originally had a similar heuristic name, *hodos*.

Dàodéjīng describes dao with basically feminine metaphors: "mother of all things," "the root," "the ground" (of Being), or "the uncarved block" (the original nature). Dao is called "the mystical female": "The spirit of the valley never dies. It is called the mystical female. The gateway of the mystical female is called the root of Heaven and Earth" (6). "Can you play the role of the female in the opening and closing the gates of the Heaven?" (10).[19] This feminine vision is based on Lǎozǐ's principle of "reversal." A. C. Graham explicated that Lǎozǐ (老子) always put the preferential option for the strategy of *yin* rather than that of *yang* in the following chain of oppositions:[20]

Yang	Yin	Yang	Yin
Something	Nothing	Before	Behind
Doing Something	Doing Nothing	Moving	Still
Knowledge	Ignorance	Big	Small
Male	Female	Strong	Weak
Full	Empty	Hard	Soft
Above	Below	Straight	Bent

This principle of reversal is closely connected with the principle of return. In fact, this is the hidden source for the vitality depicted metaphorically by the return of fish in the ugǔmch'i phenomenon (see chapter 2). "Attain complete vacuity, maintain steadfast quietude. All things come into being, and I see thereby their return. All things flourish, but each one returns to its destiny. To return to destiny is called the eternal (Dao). To know the eternal is called enlightenment" (*Dàodéjīng*: 16).[21] The paradoxical power of weakness and emptiness is further developed in the principle of *wú wéi* (nonaction action). Bede Griffiths (1907–1993), a Benedictine mystic who lived many years in Indian ashrams, made helpful remarks on the implications of *Dàodéjīng* for Western religion:

---

19. Ibid., 144.
20. Graham, *Disputers of the Tao*, 223.
21. Chan, *Source Book*, 147.

The most typical concept in the *Tao Te Ching* is that of *wu wei*, that is "actionless activity." It is a state of passivity, of "non-action," but a passivity that is totally active, in the sense of receptivity. This is the essence of the feminine. The woman is made to be passive in relation to the man, to receive the seed which makes her fertile. But this passivity is an active passivity, a receptivity which is dynamic and creative, from which all life and fruitfulness, all love and communion grow. The world today needs to recover this sense of feminine power, which is complementary to the masculine and without which man becomes dominating, sterile and destructive. But this means that western religion must come to recognize the feminine aspect of God. This leads to *the paradox of the value of emptiness*. "We make pots of clay," it is said, "but it is the empty space in them which makes them useful. We make a wheel with many spokes joined in a hub, but it is the empty space in the hub which makes the wheel go round. We make houses of brick and wood, but it is the empty spaces in the doors and windows that make them habitable." This again is the value of "non-action," what Gandhi called *ahimsa*.[22]

3. Korean Quests for Christodao: Jesus as the Theanthropocosmic Dao[23]

How can we conceive of Jesus Christ with this new root-metaphor? In fact, Korean Christians in this hermeneutical universe have com-

---

22. Bede Griffiths, *Universal Wisdom: A Journey through the Sacred Wisdom of the World* (San Francisco: HarperSanFrancisco, 1994), 27.

23. As a composite adjective of *theos* (God), *anthrōpos* (humanity), and *cosmos* (universe), literally, theanthropocosmic refers to the interrelation of God, humanity, and the cosmos. It is comparable to the cosmotheandrism of Raimon Panikkar; see his *Cosmotheandric Experience*; also *The Trinity and the Religious Experience of Man: Icon–Person–Mystery* (Maryknoll, NY: Orbis Books, 1973). But my position comes from my experiences of the concrete context where the fusion of horizons has been in progress between the two great traditions, namely, the anthropocosmic paradigm of Neo-Confucianism and the theohistorical paradigm of Christianity. For this, see Kim, *Wang Yang-ming and Karl Barth*, esp. 175-88.

prehended Christ from this vantage point of dao since the beginning. For Korean Christians, the adoption of dao as the root-metaphor in understanding Christ is no less legitimate but more congenial than that of logos was for the fourth-century Greco-Roman Christians. The following are three examples of Christodao formulated by Korean Christian thinkers, Yi Pyŏk (1754–1785), Ryu Yŏng-mo (1890–1981), and Lee Jung Young (1935–1996).

Jesus as the Crossroads of the Heavenly Dao and the Human Dao

Lǎozǐ [Lao-tzu] claimed that the ultimate Dao (the Way) is apophatic and ineffable beyond human reason and language. At the same time, however, he said even more about sapiential daos (ways) of life (dé). Dao refers to the heuristic metaphor not only for the ineffable ultimate but also for practical ways people can participate in the transformative praxis of the anthropocosmic trajectory. In the history of East Asian thought, this distinction is normally recognized by the complementary opposites of Daoism and Confucianism.[24] Daoist tradition takes more seriously the apophatic dimension of the Ultimate (the Heavenly Way); Confucian tradition focuses on the kataphatic side of human living (the human way). Hence, Yi Pyŏk, a brightest Neo-Confucian scholar of his time, the first Christian theologian in Korea, and the spiritual founder of the Korean Catholic Church, found the unity of these two daos in Jesus Christ.[25] Yi conceived of Christ as the Sage par excellence, the crossroads of the Heavenly Way and the human way, in whom divinity and humanity become united.[26]

---

24. For a general introduction to Daoism, see Liu Xiaogan, "Taoism," in Our Religions, ed. Arvind Sharma (San Francisco: HarperSanFrancisco, 1993), 229-89; for Confucianism, see Tu Wei-ming, "Confucianism," in ibid., 139-227.

25. Jean Sangbae Ri, Confucius et Jésus Christ: La première théologie chrétienne en Corée d'après L'oeuvre de Yi Piek lettré Confucéen, 1754–1786 (Paris: Beauchesne, 1979).

26. Etymologically, dao also denotes a beginning at the crossroads.

Jesus as Being-in-Non-Being

Ryu Yŏng-mo, a Korean Christian-Daoist ascetic, heavily influenced by Confucianism and Buddhism, thematized the cosmogonic Christ from the deepest heart of the East Asian hermeneutical universe of dao. The statement on the Non-Ultimate and the Great Ultimate in the Zhou Dunyi's diagram denotes the ultimate complementary and paradoxical opposites of the ineffable Vacuity and the Cosmogony. From the vantage point of this supreme cosmogonic paradox of Dao, Ryu "understood the cross as both the Non-Ultimate and the Great Ultimate. . . . Jesus is the one who manifested the ultimate in Asian cosmology. Through the sacrifice of himself, he achieved genuine humanity (*rén*). That is to say, by offering himself as a sacrifice, he saved the human race and opened the kingdom of God for humanity."[27]

In Christ, the Non-Ultimate and the Great Ultimate become one. In the historical scene, this is revealed as the affectionate and filial relation between father and son, as Jesus uttered, "I [the Son] am in the Father and the Father is in me" (John 14:11). Ryu described the cross as "the blood of the flower" (*kkot-pi*)[28] through which the Son reveals the glory of the Father and the Father the glory of the Son. Seeing the blossom of this flower of Jesus (at the cross), Ryu envisioned the glorious blossom of the cosmos (cosmogony). For Ryu, "the cross is a rush into the cosmic trajectory, resurrection is a participation in the revolution of the cosmic trajectory, and lighting up the world is the judgment sitting in the right-hand side of God."[29]

From the perspective of the supreme paradox of non-being and being, Ryu formulated furthermore a unique Korean pneumato-apophatic Christodao. He called Jesus "the Primordial Breathing"

---

27. Kim Heung-ho, "Ryu Yŏng-mo's View of Christianity from the Asian perspective," in *Dasŏk Ryu Yŏng-mo*, ed. Park Young-ho (Seoul: Sungchun Institution, 1994), 299.

28. By this Korean word, Ryu expressed two metaphorical meanings of the cross simultaneously. On the cross, Jesus spilled blood like the blood of the flower, which is also like the blossoming of the flower (of life).

29. Kim Heung-ho, "Ryu Yŏng-mo's View," 301.

(*sumnim*). Jesus is the One who "Is" in spite of "Is-Not," that is to say, "Being-in-Non-Being" (*Ŏpshi-gyeshin nim*). Whereas we are those of non-being-in-being, he is the One of Being-in-Non-Being. Whereas we are the "forms" that are "none other than emptiness" (*Heart Sutra*), he is the "emptiness" that is "none other than form."[30]

Jesus as the Perfect Realization of Change

Lee Jung Young, a Korean constructive theologian, formulated an East Asian Christology in a systematic fashion with the metaphysics of change. Advocating for change as an appropriate mode of future theology, Lee argued consistently for a paradigm shift in the theological mode of thinking from the substantial mode (being), through the process (becoming), to that of change (being and becoming).[31] As the discoveries of modern physics such as Einstein's relativity theory and quantum theory have revealed, the ultimate reality is neither so much being (substance) in Greek metaphysical terms (Aristotelian logic, Euclidean geometry, and Newtonian physics), nor becoming in (Whiteheadian) process metaphysics, as being and becoming in change (or the Great Ultimate in the complementary opposites of *yin* and *yang*). "Change is, then, the matrix of all that was, is, and shall be. It is the ground of all being and becoming."[32] Thus, he advocated the theology of change, which views the ultimate as both being and becoming.

The "either-or" logic is so deeply rooted in the intellectual life of the West that it is hard for Western theology (including process theology) to transcend it. The either-or logic, however, is false as Wilfred Cantwell Smith also said: "In all ultimate matters, truth lies not in an either-or, but in a both-and."[33] Lee argued that the "both-

---

30. Kim Heung-ho, *Jesori* [The Genuine Voice: The Words of Ryu Yŏng-mo] (Seoul: Pungman, 1985), 68. For more on Ryu Yŏng-mo's Christo-dao, see chapter 7 below.

31. Lee Jung Young, *The Theology of Change: A Christian Concept of God in an Eastern Perspective* (Maryknoll, NY: Orbis Books, 1979), 11–28.

32. Ibid., 20.

33. Wilfred Cantwell Smith, *The Faith of Other Men* (New York: New American Library, 1963), 72.

and" logic of change is the right metaphysics of theology (God as the Change). "Change in the *I-Ching* [*Yìjīng*] is certainly beyond categorization. It is simultaneously personal and impersonal, male and female, immanent and transcendent."[34] This total affirmation (both-and), however, is complementary to total negation (neither-nor). In the supreme paradox, the Great Ultimate signifies the total affirmation; the Non-Ultimate, the total negation. Hence, God as the great Dao is simultaneously personal and impersonal, male and female, immanent and transcendent. At the same time, however, it is neither personal nor impersonal, neither male nor female, neither immanent nor transcendent.

Furthermore, Jesus Christ can be conceived of as the perfect realization of change:

> In Jesus as the Christ man and God are in perfect harmony. Jesus' identity does not preclude his humanity but presupposes it, just as *yang* presupposes the existence of *yin*. Furthermore, perfect humanity presupposes perfect divinity. In his perfect complementarity of divinity and humanity, or of the change and the changing, he is both perfect man and perfect God. Being the symbol of perfect harmony between the change and the changing, Jesus Christ is the ultimate reality of change and transformation.[35]

Christ, as the perfect realization of change, is also both personal and impersonal, male and female, and individual and communal.[36]

Lee's proposal, though it has many brilliant points, has not received as much attention as it deserves. His proposal is, perhaps, metaphysically positivistic and excessively rhetorical, as if making a universal claim for change as an alternative metaphysics for a new theology. His hermeneutics of retrieval is excellent, but innocent and romantic, without a proper hermeneutics of suspicion with regard to his own tradition. His theology is a good model for Asian spec-

---

34. Lee, *Theology of Change*, 22.
35. Ibid., 99.
36. See Lee Jung Young, *The Trinity in Asian Perspective* (Nashville: Abingdon, 1996), 78-82.

ulative theology of religions, but not for Asian liberation theology, another pole of Asian theology, without a sufficient consideration of historical situations. In a passionate polemic against the Western metaphysics of contradiction, Lee, contrary to his intention, also fell into the metaphysical assumption that dao can be named objectively. By definition, however, dao cannot be described objectively but only heuristically. Dao as constant change has no fixed face; it has many faces constantly changing from context to context and from people to people. Hence, in the dynamic hermeneutics of dao, the context and the role of an interpreter are mutually important. The dao hermeneutics requires a creative and holistic engagement consisting of an interpreter (a community of interpretation), the context, and the trajectory of dao. At the same time, it itself is a dao (skill) for an interpreter to discern how she or he can participate appropriately in the cosmic movement of dao at any given time.

4. *Jesus Christ as the New* T'aegŭk (*Great Ultimate;* 太極 [Tài jí]*)*

A more profound dimension of dao thinking lies in the possibility of christological utterance with respect to the ultimate in such a way that the ineffable dao can be somehow articulated while transcending fallacies of metaphysical positivism, namely, by the both-and and the neither-nor modes of thinking. In fact, the genius of the Nicene-Chalcedonian formulas lies in its articulation of the ultimate and cosmogonic nature of Christ beyond the Greek dualistic framework. Christian faith empowered the fourth-century Christians to transcend the either-or logic of Greek philosophy. The Nicene Creed (325 CE) used the both-and mode to articulate Christ as both *vere deus* and *vere homo*. Furthermore, the Chalcedonian formula (451 CE) employed the neither-nor mode to express that the two natures in the Christ are neither confused, changed, divided, nor separated. To say it more sharply in East Asian terms, the fourth-century Christians intuitively had perceived the cosmogonic nature of Christ as the supreme paradox of the Great Ultimate (total affirmation of the both-and) and the Non-Ultimate (total negation of the neither-nor).

In fact, this dao mode of paradoxical thought appears not only in the Gnostic Gospels but also in creative early Christian theologians such as Gregory of Nyssa (ca. 395) and Dionysius the Areopagite (fl. 500), in Christian mystics such as Francis of Assisi (1182–1226), Meister Eckhart (d. 1327), and Julian of Norwich (b. 1343), and most explicitly in the principle of *coincidentia oppositorum* formulated by Nicholas of Cusa (1401–1464).[37] Remember that St. Paul already proclaimed, "There is no longer Jew or Greek, there is no longer slave or free, there is no longer male and female . . . in Christ" (Gal. 3:28).

With Ryu's profound pneumato-apophatic insights, Christodao can be further thematized. Jesus is the Dao, the supreme paradox of the Great Ultimate and the Non-Ultimate (*T'aegŭk* and *Mugŭk* [*Wú jí* 無極]), the Primordial Breathing, the Being-in-Non-Being, and the complete emptiness (*kenōsis* or *sunyata*) that is none other than the complete form. The cross refers to the rush to the cosmic path, and resurrection signifies the christological transformation of the theanthropocosmic trajectory. The crucifixion of Jesus was a cosmogonic crucifixion, which changed the cosmic path. Furthermore, it signifies a radical opening of the vicious circle of the old metaphysical world of Dao (*T'aegŭk* and Yì 易).[38] This is the great openness of the Ultimate. The cosmogony of the old *T'aegŭk* was

---

37. For a comparative study with dao, see Holmes Welch, *The Parting the Way: Lao Tzu and the Taoist Movement* (Boston: Beacon, 1957), esp. 50-82. For Christian mystical traditions, including Hildegard of Bingen (1098–1179), Bonaventura (1221–1274), and Dante Alighieri (1265–1321), see Ewert H. Cousins, *Christ of the 21st Century* (Rockport, MA: Element, 1992); also Fox, *Cosmic Christ*, 109-26. For an introduction to Nicholas of Cusa, see Karl Jaspers, *The Great Philosophers: The Original Thinkers*, trans. Ralph Manheim (New York: Harcourt, Brace & World, 1966), 116-272. For Julian of Norwich, see Brant Pelphrey, *Christ Our Mother: Julian of Norwich*, Way of the Christian Mystics 7 (Wilmington, DE: Michael Glaizer, 1989).

38. The understanding of logos has been modified and developed notably since Western Christologies adopted it as their root-metaphor. The similar fusion of hermeneutical horizons will evolve in the process of making a Christodao. Likewise, dao would also need to adapt and change partly when East Asian Christians articulate their faith in Jesus Christ. A formulation here demonstrates an example of the modification.

crucified into the *Muguk* and resurrected as the New *T'aeguk*, that is to say, a great eschatological movement of the supreme paradox. It is neither just a dogmatic revolution (logos) nor only a messianically inspired social revolution (praxis), but it is a cosmogonic revolution (dao). The Christodao of the crucified and risen *T'aeguk* entails the cosmogonic revolution of the Christ. Christ rushed into the old anthropocosmic cycle of *T'aeguk* through the crucifixion, changed it to the new "serendipitous" theanthropocosmic trajectory (Dao), and opened the new aeon of *T'aeguk*.

Christ as the Serendipitous[39] Pneumatosociocosmic Trajectory

This new serendipitous theanthropocosmic trajectory is real but hidden. It is not yet fully waxed but eschatological.[40] The ugumch'i phenomenon renders *ki* (氣; *pneuma*) as a significant hermeneutical key, which introduces a pneumatoanthropocosmic vision. *Ki*, a holistic and embracing term, signifies both the spiritual power and its material manifestation, and both the source of primordial *ki* and the medium of its empowerment. The pneumatoanthropocosmic vision can cultivate a symbiosis of the life network through the communication of *ki* which fosters the human race's relationship with other lives more holistically and profoundly.

Furthermore, this vision invites us to thematize the *sociocosmic biography of the exploited life*, creatively pushing beyond the dialectical sociobiography of minjung and the innocent anthropocosmic vision.[41] Theodao tells the story of the sociocosmic network

---

39. I borrowed this expression from Gordon D. Kaufman, though I do not fully agree with his vision of the cosmic evolutionary-historical trajectory, which still is more or less linear, pragmatist, and historicist. See his *In Face of Mystery: A Constructive Theology* (Cambridge, MA: Harvard University Press, 1993), 264-80.

40. In this *T'aeguk* Christology, eschatology is conceived of as the other side of history; for example, if history refers to the visible part of the moon, eschatology signifies its invisible part.

41. Kim Yong-bock argued that the social biography of minjung is a more authentic historical point of reference for theological reflection than the

of the exploited life constituted by the spiritual communion of *ki* whose primordial *ki* is salvific, both emancipatory and reconcilatory. The ugŭmch'i phenomenon is an example of the sociocosmic biography of the exploited life, metaphorically telling the story of the two exploited lives, the feeble fishes in the turbulent stream and the multitude of minjung in the Ugŭmch'i War. In addition, *ki* as both spirit and matter can be a clue to solving the problem of incarnation. The birth story of Jesus depicts the pneumatoanthropocosmic vision par excellence, and the passion narratives of Christ tell the sociocosmic biography of the exploited life par excellence. Therefore, Jesus Christ as the theanthropocosmic Dao entails the *serendipitous pneumatosociocosmic trajectory* in the life-giving spirit of the primordial *ki*.

Since the pneumatic hermeneutics of *ki* and the sociocosmic biography of the exploited life are its constitutive parts, Christodao (Christ as the serendipitous pneumatosociocosmic trajectory, the Dao) is a spiritual and emancipatory Christology. Hence, Christodao (Christ as the New *T'aegŭk*) is a paradigm of emancipatory Christology embodied in the soteriological nucleus of Asian spirituality. That is to say, Christodao (Jesus as the theanthropocosmic Dao) is an appropriate solution to the *koan* of this paper, overcoming modern historicism and Western dualism, the two basic problems of the contemporary christological impasse.

5. The Coming of Yin Christ

Christ as the New *T'aegŭk* (both *yang* and *yin*) is both divine and human, male and female, personal and impersonal, individual and communal. Nonetheless, this description is erroneous if it falls again into an objective and abstract description of Christ as the old *T'aegŭk*. But Christodao must involve a prophetic hermeneutics of the Dao of Jesus Christ as the New *T'aegŭk*—that is to say, a responsibility to expose the new manifestation of *pneumatocos-*

---

doctrinal discourses superimposed by the church and in the orientation of Western rationality; see his "Theology and the Social Biography of Minjung," *CTC Bulletin* 5, no.3–6, no. 1 (1984–85): 66-78.

mogonic transformation, that is, the great reversal of the Dao. Whereas the time of yang Christ is waning, the period of yin Christ is waxing! Griffiths affirmed:

> This may sound very paradoxical and unreal, but for centuries now the western world has been following the path of Yang—of the masculine, active, aggressive, rational, scientific mind—and has brought the world near destruction. It is time now to recover the path of Yin, of the feminine, passive, patient, intuitive and poetic mind. This is the path which the Tao Te Ching sets before us.[42]

Indeed, we are now witnessing a kairological moment of the great christological turning point. Yijing describes: "After a time of decay comes the turning point. The powerful light that was banished returns. There is movement, but it is not brought about by force. . . . thus the movement is natural, arising spontaneously. . . . The old is discarded and the new is introduced."[43] There are already plenty of these natural and spontaneous signs for the coming of Yin Christ; for example, ecofeminist (sister), sophia, Christo Mater, Christa, female, black and Asian womanist, liminal-marginal, and the second axial cosmic Christologies.[44] The contemporary christologi-

---

42. Griffiths, Universal Wisdom, 27-28.

43. Richard Wilhelm, trans., The I Ching or Book of Changes, 3rd ed. (Princeton, NJ: Princeton University Press, 1967), 97.

44. For example, Rosemary Radford Ruether, Sexism and God-Talk: Toward a Feminist Theology (Boston: Beacon, 1983), 116-38; Elisabeth Schüssler Fiorenza, Jesus, Miriam's Child, Sophia's Prophet: Critical Issues in Feminist Christology (New York: Continuum, 1995); Mark Kline Taylor, Remembering Esperanza: A Cultural-Political Theology for North American Praxis (Maryknoll, NY: Orbis Books, 1990), 194-245; Julie M. Hopkins, Towards A Feminist Christology: Jesus of Nazareth, European Women, and the Christological Crisis (Grand Rapids: Eerdmans, 1995), 81-97; Rita Nakashima Brock, Journeys by Heart: A Christology of Erotic Power (New York: Crossroad, 1983); Rose Horman Arthur, The Wisdom Goddess: Feminine Motifs in Eight Nag Hammadi Documents (Lanham, MD: University Press of America, 1984); Jacquelyn Grant, White Women's Christ and Black Women's Jesus, American Academy of Religion Academy Series 64 (Atlanta: Scholars Press, 1985); Chung Hyun Kyung, "Who Is Jesus for Asian Women?"

cal impasse is de facto an impasse of the white androcentric logos Christologies, namely, the impasse of *yang Christ*. Those Christologies are false and based on an ethnocentric myth whose demythologization provokes some emotional and awkward scholarship, the clear signs that these Christologies have reached their points of reversal. Remember that *T'aegŭk* has the subtle principle of reversal: when *yang* reaches its maximum intensity, it will revert to *yin*. Hence, in fact, this is a most creative moment for the interpretation of Jesus Christ. Whereas those "masculine, expansive, demanding, aggressive, competitive, rational, analytic" *yang* ("old") Christologies are "discarded," "feminine, contractive, conservative, responsive, cooperative, intuitive, synthesizing" *yin* ("new") Christodaos are "introduced."[45] The contrast between the *yang* Christology and the *yin* Christodao can be characterized as follows:[46]

---

in *Asian Faces of Jesus*, ed. R. S. Sugirtharajah, *Faith and Cultures* (Maryknoll, NY: Orbis Books, 1993), 223-46; Majella Franzmann, *Jesus in the Nag Hammadi Writings* (Edinburgh: T&T Clark, 1996); Lee Jung Young, *Marginality: The Key to Multicultural Theology* (Minneapolis: Fortress, 1995); Cousins, *Christ of the 21st Century*; and Fox, *Cosmic Christ*.

45. Fritjof Capra, *The Turning Point: Science, Society, and the Rising Culture* (Toronto: Bantam Books, 1982), 37-38. For the need of the transformation of Western culture, see ibid., 21-49.

46. These characterizations connote not an essentialism (related to an Aristotelian theory of sexuality) but a "dynamic balance," as Capra clarified well (see ibid., 35-37). Thus, I reject both the patriarchal and the feminist biases in the association of *yin*. Christodao is thematized in the context of the Great Ultimate (the Change), which transcends both substantialism (being) and processism (becoming), identifying the reality as the constant change. It is related no longer to a mutually exclusive choice of sexuality between female and male (the Western logic of either-or) but to the mutually inclusive relationship not only between male and female but also between personal and impersonal (the Asian mode of both-and). In this paradigm of the complementary opposites, "nothing is only *yin* or only *yang*." Simply, they refer to a responsible hermeneutics for the dynamic balance of the serendipitous pneumatosociocosmic trajectory at a given time (as *Yìjīng* reads a hexagram pertinent to a historical context).

As Richard Wilhelm clarified, these characterizations do not refer to objective representations of entities as such but to their functional tendencies in movement (see Wilhelm, *I-ching*, 1). As Karl Jüng observed, this hermeneu-

Yin	⟵	*Yang*		*Yin*	⟵	*Yang*
dao		logos/praxis		feminine		masculine
Christodao		Christology/		uterine (womb)		phallo
		Christopraxis				
intuitive		analytic		holistic		dualistic
(contemplative)		(rational)				
apophatic		kataphatic		mutuality		domination
(kenotic)		(phonocentric)				
circular		linear		receptivity		violence
(cyclical)		(historical)				

wú wéi (non-action action)   *yu-wei* (action action)

Christ as Mystical-Prophetic Female

In the coming ages, Jesus as the Dao will be the mystical female, the cosmic womb. Christ as the New *T'aegŭk* will be the prophetic cosmogonic energy, and Jesus Christ will be the "Mystical-Prophetic" Female who embraces and heals the sociocosmic trajectory of the exploited life in her great bosom.[47] Christ, the Dao and the New *T'aegŭk*, will overcome cosmic violence with her mysterious power of *wú wéi* (non-action action), with her paradoxical power of weakness and emptiness (according to Graham, "the preferential option to the strategy of *yin*"), and with her revolutionary power of the return.[48] *Dàodéjīng* states, "In Tao the only motion is returning;

---

tics is related not to the chain process of causality (the prime logic of Western science and philosophy) but to what he calls "synchronicity," which "takes the coincidence of events in space and time as meaning something more than mere chance, namely, a peculiar interdependence of objective events among themselves as well as with the subjective states of the observer or observers" (ibid., xxiv).

47. I borrowed this composite adjective from David Tracy; see his *Dialogue with the Other: The Inter-religious Dialogue*, Louvain Theological and Pastoral Monographs 1 (Louvain: Peeters, 1990), 7.

48. Jesus used the principle of reversal masterfully, as he said, "Whoever wants to be first must be last of all" (Mark 9:35), or "For those who want to save their life will lose it, and those who lose their life for my sake will find it" (Matt. 16:25). Furthermore, he stated in the Sermon on the Plain:

Blessed are you who are poor, for yours is the kingdom of God. Blessed are you who are hungry now, for you will be filled. Blessed are you who

the only useful quality, weakness. For though Heaven and Earth and the Ten thousand Creatures were produced by Being, Being was produced by Non-being" (40). The ugŭmch'i phenomenon is a metaphorical example of these mysterious, paradoxical, revolutionary, and radical powers of return. The return of fish introduces a simple sign for the Great Return of the Mystical-Prophetic Female (the Dao) with the cosmogonic breathing of the Primordial *Ki*.

The millennial crusade of the patriarchal, hegemonic (kataphatic), phallo-onto-Christology with the Western face of the *yang* (masculine) Viking-Rambo Jesus is now waning; a millennial march of the matrilineal, kenotic (apophatic), uterine-sapiential-Christodao in the Asian heart of the *yin* (feminine) Sage Christ is rising. Through great non-action action in her uterine tranquillity and sociocosmic serenity, Christ as the Mystical-Prophetic Female will heal this fragmented, divided world torn down by the aggressive lynching of incarnated macho images and will recover the harmonious wholeness through a radical return to the pneumato-sociocosmic trajectory. The revolutionary non-action action is the dynamic spiritual upward movement of life against the apocalyptically disastrous downstream of history. Christ will dance not just an innocent cosmic dance but a revolutionary pneumatosociocosmic dance of life reverting upward against and transforming the vicious downstream of gloomy history together with (*perichoresis*) the feeble fishes in the polluted river (the exploited nature) and the minjung in Ugŭmch'i (the marginalized people).

Then the task of Christian theology in the coming age will be the telling of the Dao of Jesus Christ, that is, the sociocosmic narrative of her and his pneumatic dancing with the exploited lives to transform the theanthropocosmic trajectory to the right path (so to speak, orthodao). Jesus Christ is the New *T'aegŭk* who has com-

---

weep now, for you will laugh. Blessed are you when people hate you.
. . . Rejoice in that day. . . . But woe to you who are rich, for you have received your consolation. Woe to you who are full now, for you will be hungry. Woe to you who are laughing now, for you will mourn and weep. . . . do good to those who hate you, bless those who curse you, pray those who abuse you." (Luke 6:20-28 NRSV)

pleted and generates the cosmogonic paradigm shift through crucifixion and resurrection. Christ as the theanthropocosmic Dao is
also the outpouring primordial *ki*, the life-generating Energy-Spirit
who empowers the exploited lives to return to the serendipitous
pneumatosociocosmic trajectory.

Zhuāngzǐ had Confucius saying: "*Ki* [Qi] is empty and waits for
the external things. Only the Tao gathers in emptiness. The cause
of emptiness is the fasting of the mind-and-heart" (4). After all,
Christ the Dao directs us to "return" to the Dao, like the fish of the
ugŭmch'i phenomenon, in the radical power of emptiness (*kenōsis*)
and reversal (the Sermon on the Plain), through the fasting of the
mind-and-heart (*metanoia*), under the direction of the Spirit (*sin-
ki*). And Jesus said to Simon and Andrew: "Follow me and I will
make you fish for people" (Mark 1:17).[49]

---

49. The pictogram of *T'aegŭk* (as in the national flag of South Korea) por-
trays the dancing of two fishes.

CHAPTER FOUR

The Dao and the Trinity

1. The "Easternization" of the Trinity

Since its renaissance initiated by Karl Barth and Karl Rahner, the doctrine of the Trinity has regained its status as the center of Christian theology. In this chapter, I will not pursue the fascinating story of the rediscovery of the Trinity in contemporary theology; however, one observation may be in order. As an East Asian theologian, I am intrigued by the fact that in this impressive retrieval of the trinitarian doctrine there has been a rediscovery of the East and a turn of Christian theology to the East.

In this restoration of the trinitarian center, the pendulum of Christian theology seems to have swung toward the East. At first, Western trinitarian theology appears to have reached a climax with "Rahner's Rule" and "Pannenberg's Principle."[1] The former identifies the immanent Trinity with the economic Trinity and vice versa, while the latter underscores the history of divine rule over the world. Then, at its the next stage, trinitarian theology turned to the East. Moving to the Near East, it rediscovered the significance of Eastern

---

Adapted from Heup Young Kim, "The Tao in Confucianism and Taoism: The Trinity in East Asian Perspective," originally published in *The Cambridge Companion to the Trinity*, ed. Peter C. Phan (Cambridge: Cambridge University Press, 2011), 293-308. Reprinted with permission.

1. See Stanley J. Grentz, *Rediscovering the Triune God: The Trinity in Contemporary Theology* (Minneapolis: Fortress, 2004), 96. See also Karl Rahner, *The Trinity*, trans. Joseph Donceel (New York: Crossroad, 1997), 22; and Wolfhart Pannenberg, *Theology and the Kingdom of God* (Philadelphia: Westminster, 1969), 55-56.

Orthodox trinitarian theology, embodied in "Zizioulas's dictum," according to which the divine being is the communion of the three trinitarian persons.[2] This encounter brought about the recovery and reconstruction of ontology in the doctrine of the Trinity, especially that of relationship, personhood, or "personal relatedness." This discovery also shows how essentialism and the reduction of the person to self-consciousness constitute the root cause of the modern impasse in trinitarian theology. Moving to South Asia, especially India, trinitarian theology encountered religious plurality and gave rise to the "Panikkar project."[3] Since the Trinity constitutes an archetypical structure for world religions, Panikkar argues, the Trinity is an ideal locus for inter-/intrareligious dialogue.

This trajectory of the development of contemporary trinitarian theology already reveals an Easternizing movement. It should not stop at India, however, but should move farther to East Asia. My contribution is an East Asian Christian interpretation of the Trinity in light of Confucianism and Daoism. Specifically, I will discuss how the Trinity can be understood in the religio-cultural matrix of East Asia, which is heavily influenced by Confucianism and Daoism. My goal is not to replace Western interpretations of the Trinity with this East Asian approach, which may at first appear strange to some. Rather, my hope is that an East Asian interpretation of the Trinity will enrich the contemporary theology of Trinity and situate it in the global context. Furthermore, such Easternization of trinitarian doctrine in light of Confucian/Daoist insights may offer valuable clues to resolve some of the long-standing problems in trinitarian theology.

2. Confucian and Daoist Insights

Confucianism/Daoism (Neo-Confucianism): The Third Great Religious River System

Hans Küng makes an important correction to the geography of world religions. Instead of the generally accepted dipolar view of

---

2. See Grentz, *Rediscovering the Triune God*, 134-35, 141-43, 134.

3. Raymundo Panikkar, *The Trinity and the Religious Experience of Man: Icon–Person–Mystery* (Maryknoll, NY: Orbis Books, 1973).

Middle Eastern and Indian religions, he argues for a tripolar view that includes East Asian religions such as Confucianism and Daoism. He claims that Confucianism and Daoism are "a third independent religious river system" of sapiential character, comparable to the other two great river systems, the first being of Semitic origin and prophetic character (Judaism, Christianity, and Islam), and the second of Indian origin and mystical character (Hinduism, Buddhism, and so on).[4]

Although often neglected by the dominant bipolar view of world religions, Confucianism and Daoism represent a most distinctive feature of the East Asian religio-cultural matrix. More precisely, Neo-Confucianism, a reformed Confucianism in synthesis with Daoism, is recognized as "the common background of the peoples of East Asia" and "the most plausible rationale" in attempting to understand the attitude of "the inward-looking civilization of East Asia" (Korea, China, Japan, Taiwan, Vietnam, and Singapore).[5] Tu Wei-ming states, "East Asians may profess themselves to be Shintoists, Taoists, Buddhists, Muslims, or Christians, but by announcing their religious affiliations seldom do they cease to be Confucians."[6] Consequently, "doing East Asian theology necessarily involves the study of Confucianism as a theological task."[7] Confucianism and Daoism are broad and complex religio-cultural traditions with a history longer than Christianity. In the following I will present only some basic concepts relevant to the theology of the Trinity.

Anthropocosmic Vision and Inclusive Humanism

One axiomatic pillar of Confucianism is what has been termed the "anthropocosmic vision" inherent in the Confucian belief in the

---

4. Hans Küng and Julia Ching, *Christianity and Chinese Religions*, trans. Peter Beyer (New York: Doubleday, 1989), xi–xv

5. Wm. Theodore de Bary, *East Asian Civilizations: A Dialogue in Five Stages,* Edwin O. Reischauer Lectures 1986 (Cambridge, MA: Harvard University Press, 1989), 44.

6. Tu Wei-ming, *Confucianism in an Historical Perspective* (Singapore: Institute of East Asian Philosophies, 1989), 3.

7. Heup Young Kim, *Wang Yang-ming and Karl Barth: A Confucian–Christian Dialogue* (Lanham, MD: University Press of America, 1996), 1.

"mutual dependence and organic unity" of Heaven and humanity.[8] *The Doctrine of the Mean*, one of the Confucian Four Books, begins, "What Heaven imparts to man is called human nature. To follow our nature is called the Way (Dao). Cultivating the Way is called education."[9] In this anthropocosmic vision, humanity (anthropology) is not only inseparable from Heaven (cosmology) but is also conceived of as its microcosm. This East Asian cosmocentric approach to anthropology is different from the anthropocentric approach to cosmology prevalent in the West.[10]

Cheng Chung-ying called this view "inclusive humanism," in contrast to the "exclusive humanism" dominant in the West since Descartes' dualistic rationalism. Whereas exclusive humanism "exalts the human species, placing it in a position of mastery of and domination over the universe," inclusive humanism "stresses the coordinating powers of humanity as the very reason for its existence." He points out that "humanism in the modern West is nothing more than a secular will for power or a striving for domination, with rationalistic science at its disposal." He continues, "Humanism in this exclusive sense is a disguise for the individualistic entrepreneurship of modern man armed with science and technology as tools of conquest and devastation." In contrast, the inclusive humanism that is rooted in Confucianism "focuses on the human person as an agency of both self-transformation and transformation of reality at large. As the self-transformation of a person is rooted in reality and the transformation of reality is rooted in the person, there is no dichotomy or bifurcation between the human and reality"[11]

---

8. Tu Wei-ming, *Centrality and Commonality: An Essay on Confucian Religiousness,* SUNY Series in Chinese Philosophy and Culture (Albany: State University of New York Press, 1989), 107.

9. Wing-tsit Chan, trans., *A Source Book in Chinese Philosophy* (Princeton, NJ: Princeton University Press, 1963), 98.

10. See Jung Young Lee, *The Trinity in Asian Perspective* (Nashville: Abingdon, 1996), 18.

11. Cheng Chung-ying, "The Trinity of Cosmology, Ecology, and Ethics in the Confucian Personhood," in *Confucianism and Ecology: The Interrelation of Heaven, Earth, and Humans,* ed. Mary Evelyn Tucker and John

This point, albeit controversial, is important not only to demonstrate the relevance of Confucianism for our age of ecological crisis but also to clarify the confusion in the modern concept of person as applied to the Trinity. In retrieving the Eastern Orthodox tradition, contemporary Western theologies of the Trinity to some extent rehabilitate the ontology of personhood beyond Barthian modalism (*Seinweise*, modes of being). However, they still seem not to have been liberated completely from the modern notion of person as an isolated self-conscious ego and are still prone to exclusive humanism, which Barth vehemently resisted.

This exclusive anthropology perpetuates the long-standing trinitarian dilemma between modalism and tritheism. Inclusive humanism may help solve this problem by showing how exclusive humanism, which underwrites individualism and essentialism, is the root cause of many problems in the modern theology of the Trinity. Over against the essentialist and exclusivist view of human person, inclusive humanism stresses the "between-ness" or "among-ness" of the person. (The Chinese character for the human being 人間 connotes in-between-ness). In inclusive humanism, a person is not so much a static substance as a network of relationships in constant change (*Yì* 易).[12] This relational vision of being in continual change is called "ontocosmology."[13]

Confucian/Daoist Ontocosmology:
The Great Ultimate (太極, *T'aegŭk* [*Tài jí*])[14]

The Confucian/Daoist ontocosmology originates from the notion of *T'aegŭk* (which incidentally is the main symbol on the Korean

---

Berthrong, Religions of the World and Ecology (Cambridge, MA: Harvard University Press, 1998), 213-15.

12. This key Confucian/Daoist notion is presented in *Y jing*, one of the Five Confucian Classics. See Richard Wilhelm, trans., *The I Ching or Book of Changes*, 3rd ed., Bollingen Series 19 (Princeton, NJ: Princeton University Press, 1967).

13. Cheng, "Trinity of Cosmology," 216.

14. Romanization of 太極 (the Great Ultimate): *T'aegŭk* (Korean); *Tài jí* (Pinyin), *T'ai-chi* (Wade-Giles).

national flag). In *An Explanation of the Diagram of the Great Ulti-mate*, Zhou Dunyi (1017–1073) states:

> The Ultimate of Non-being and also the Great Ultimate! The Great Ultimate through movement generates *yang*. When its activity reaches its limit, it becomes tranquil. Through tranquility the Great Ultimate generates *yin*. When tranquility reaches its limit, activity begins again. So movement and tranquility alternate and become the root of each other, giving rise to the distinction of *yin* and *yang*, and the two modes are thus established.[15]

T'aegŭk, symbolized by a circle enclosing *yin* and *yang*, denotes the complementarity of opposites. The circle signifies "an inex-haustible source of creativity, which is one and undifferentiated," and the dynamic process of *yin-yang* interaction is "always ready to be differentiated into concrete and individual things." It is "the constant fountainhead amidst all things and provides the integra-tive and purposive unity of any type or any individual token while, at the same time, it also serves as the impetus for the diversity of things as types of tokens."[16] *T'aegŭk* so conceived entails precisely unity in multiplicity or diversity in unity, which is a crucial prin-ciple for trinitarian theology.

The ontocosmology of *T'aegŭk* is pertinent not only to Confu-cianism but also to Daoism. Lǎozǐ states:

> Tao [the Way] produced the One.
> The One produced the two.
> The two produced the three.
> And the three produced the ten thousand things.
> The ten thousand things carry the yin and embrace the yang, and through the blending of the material force (*ki* [*qì*]) they achieve harmony.[17]

---

15. Chan, *Source Book*, 463.
16. Cheng, "Trinity of Cosmology," 219.
17. *Dàodéjīng*: 42. Chan, *Source Book*, 160-61. Romanization of 氣 (material force or vital energy): *ki* (Korean); *qì* (Pinyin); *ch'i* (Wade-Giles).

This statement refers to the dynamic creative process of *T'aegŭk* or Dao, which produces the One, which produces the Two (*yin-yang*), which produces the Three (offspring of *yin-yang*), all of which, as will be shown, has profound implications for understanding the Trinity. "The whole is both absolute and relative, it is both one (singularity) and two (plurality) at the same time."[18] The creativity of Dao is the creative process of *T'aegŭk* through the dynamic *yin-yang* interaction and always in the process of change. It stipulates the dialogical paradigm of harmony or equilibrium in East Asian thought, in contrast to the dialectical paradigm of strife or conflict in Western thought. *T'aegŭk* "signifies both a process and world *qua* the totality of things in which there is a profound equilibrium from the beginning and a pervasive accord or harmony among all things at any time."[19]

Confucian Ontology of Relation:
The Yin-Yang *Complementary Opposites*

The *yin-yang* relation is a key to understanding the Dao in East Asian thought. In the *yin-yang* relationship, the two opposites are not in conflict but complement each other in order to attain harmony and equilibrium. In the Western model of strife (conflicting dualism), we must choose one of the two alternatives and eliminate the other (an either-or paradigm). In the East Asian model of harmony (complementary dualism), the two opposites are complementary and belong to each other (a both-and paradigm). It is analogous to the relationship between a male and a female who, though opposite in gender, become one couple through marriage (and bring forth the child, which is the third).

The East Asian holistic way of *yin-yang* thinking is more allied with the both-and paradigm, whereas the modern critical method is more allied with the either-or paradigm. Wilfred Cantwell Smith states, "We in the West presume that an intelligent man must choose *either* this *or* that. . . . [But] in all ultimate matters, truth lies not in

---

18. Lee, *Trinity in Asian Perspective*, 30.
19. Cheng, "Trinity of Cosmology," 291.

an either-or, but in a both-and."[20] Since the doctrine of the Trinity pertains to the ultimate reality of the whole, it is to be envisaged with the both-and paradigm rather than with the either-or mode of thinking, which is more pertinent to penultimate matters.

The Ontology of Change

Furthermore, the yin-yang mode of thinking entails the ontology of change in contrast to the ontology of substance that is dominant in the West. The yin and yang relationship is characterized by continuous change; change is primary and prior to ontic being or substance. In this ontocosmology of T'aegŭk, change is not a function of being, as Western ontology generally assumes. On the contrary, change is the ultimate itself, whereas being or substance is a penultimate manifestation of change. The ontology of change where only change is changeless calls for a paradigm shift in the philosophy of being.

Confucian Trinity: Heaven, Earth, and Humanity

Inclusive humanism rooted in Neo-Confucian ontocosmology is luminously expressed in the Western Inscription of Zhang Zai (1022–1077), as the Confucian Trinity of Heaven, Earth, and Humanity:

> Heaven is my father and Earth is my mother, and even such a small creature as I finds an intimate place in their midst. Therefore, that which fills the universe I regard as my body and that which directs the universe I consider as my nature. All people are my brothers and sisters, and all things are my companions.[21]

The universe is visualized as a cosmic triune family, and a human being as a cosmic person, a member of the cosmic Trinity. From this vantage point, a Confucian-Christian idea of the Trinity

---

20. Wilfred Cantwell Smith, *The Faith of Other Men* (New York: New American Library, 1963), 72.

21. Chan, *Source Book*, 497.

has been suggested: "We might see God the Son as the ideal human, God the Father would be heaven (the creative spirit), and God the Holy Spirit the earth (the receptive co-spirit), or agent of the world which testifies to the accomplishment of the divinity."[22]

3. A Confucian/Daoist Interpretation of the Trinity

Jung Young Lee is a pioneer in developing an East Asian Christian theology of the Trinity, particularly through the *yin-yang* paradigm. Although his project is not yet widely known, his challenging insights deserve careful consideration in articulating a contemporary trinitarian theology.

One and Three

Because of the dominant either-or paradigm of substance metaphysics, the trinitarian paradox of one nature (*una substantia*) and three persons (*tres hypostaseis*) has been a vexing problem to Western theology. In light of the *yin-yang* way of complementary opposites, however, this one-and-three paradox is no longer a problem but can be reconciled within the both-and paradigm of relational thinking. The "one and two" and the "one and three" principles are the foundation of the ontocosmology of Dao (*Dàodéjīng*: 42). The ontocosmology of *T'aegŭk* replaces the essentialist ontology of being with the relational ontology of change. Pursuing this line of thought, Lee proposes a Trinity of change, namely, God the Father as "change itself," God the Holy Spirit as "the power of change," and God the Son as "the perfect manifestation of change."[23]

Perichoresis

In the diagram of *T'aegŭk*, there is an eye (a small circle of *yang*) inside *yin*, and another eye (a small circle *yin*) inside *yang*. They symbolize the "in-ness" (inclusion) of *yang* "in" *yin* and of *yin* "in" *yang*, or the existence of "the inner connecting principle" between *yin* and *yang* (when *yin* reaches its limit, it becomes *yang*, and vice

---

22. Cheng, "Trinity of Cosmology," 225.
23. Lee, *Trinity in Asian Perspective*, 66.

versa). This insight of in-ness or the inner connecting principle in *yin* and *yang* illuminates the meaning of *perichoresis* (coinherence) in Jesus's saying, "Believe me that I am *in* the Father and the Father is *in* me" (John 14:11).

Furthermore, from this vantage point of in-ness, Rahner's Rule that the immanent Trinity *is* the economic Trinity and vice versa can be made more precise by maintaining their distinction. Thus writes Lee, "Just as *yin* and *yang* always coexist without losing their distinctive identity, the economic Trinity and the immanent Trinity always coexist, but they are different." Hence, Lee revises Rahner's Rule: "In this inclusive rather than identical relationship, we can revise Rahner's rule: The immanent Trinity is *in* the economic Trinity and the economic Trinity is *in* the immanent Trinity. This rule will help us retain their distinctiveness as well as their unity."[24]

Cosmic Family Analogy

This ontocosmology always in the process of change is also conceived of as "a procreative process" (*Dàodéjīng*: 42). As we have seen in the *Western Inscription*, this trinitarian process culminates in the expression of a cosmic family of Trinity (Heaven, Earth, and Humanity). Lee further develops a family analogy of the Trinity, identifying the Father as the "heavenly Father," the Holy Spirit as the "sustainer" of the earth in the feminine symbol of "mother," and the Son as the "child" of the father and the mother. From the vantage point of a cosmic vestige of the trinitarian family, the Holy Spirit is conceived of as feminine, as mother, just as "spirit" is feminine in Hebrew (*ruaḥ*). Lee claims that "the gender balance between mother and father is possible."[25] Furthermore, in the both-and paradigm of the Cosmic Trinity, God is not only both male (*yang*) and female (*yin*) but also both personal and non-personal and ultimately transcends all of these categories as the ineffable Dao.

---

24. Ibid., 58, 67-68.
25. Ibid., 63- 65.

God the Son: The Connecting Principle (Dao Christology)

In developing his theology of the Trinity, Lee starts from the Son rather than from the Father. Lee argues that it is through the Son that we know the Father and that the idea of two (i.e., divinity and humanity in Christ) is a prerequisite for understanding the three. Furthermore, in light of East Asian cosmo-anthropology, the incarnation can be understood in a closer connection with creation. The Son (anthropology) is "a fulfillment of Trinitarian process in creation" (cosmology), and Christ (the prototype of cosmo-anthropology) is "the perfect manifestation of change in the world."[26] Lee formulates a trinitarian interpretation of creation: the Son as the act of creation, the Father as the source of creation, and the Spirit as the power of creation.

Just as the Christ is identified as the Logos (Word) in the first-century Greco-Roman milieu (John 1), he can be understood as the Dao (Way) in the East Asian context. Christ as the Word as well as the Way is not so much "a form of structure" as "the act of creativity."[27] The ineffable Dao that transcends verbal limitations is the Ultimate Reality and the power of all creativities. As *Dàodéjīng* says about the "supraessential" Dao:

> The Tao that can be told is not the eternal Tao.
> The Nameless is the origin of Heaven and Earth.
> The Named is the mother of all things.[28]

The Daoist complementary paradox of fullness (*yang*) and emptiness (*yin*) is comparable to the Letter to the Philippians' christological paradox of *kenōsis* (self-emptying) and exaltation (Phil. 2:5-9). "The Word as the Tao, which is also known as *I* or change, is a ceaseless act of emptying and fulfilling process." From the cosmo-anthropological perspective, "death is inseparable from life, just as life cannot exist independently from death."[29] When *yin* reaches

---

26. Ibid., 71.
27. Ibid., 72. The Hebrew word *dābār* (Word) can mean the creative act.
28. Chan, *Source Book*, 144.
29. Lee, *Trinity in Asian Perspective*, 73, 83.

its maximum, *yang* begins to arise (like the wax and wane of the moon), and vice versa. Likewise, if the death of Jesus refers to the maximum expansion or the perfection of *yin*, then the resurrection of Christ is regarded as the *yang* that begins to expand toward perfection.

The obedience of the Son to the Father until the death on the cross can be well understood in the context of filial piety, a cardinal virtue serving as the gate to attain the supreme Confucian goal of human relatedness, *rén* (仁, benevolence or co-humanity). The Son's filial piety becomes a clue to understanding salvation as the restoration of the harmonious relationship in creation. Thus, "it was not the divine substance of the Son but his filial piety that saved us."[30] Hence, salvation is not so much substantial as relational, and sin is a disruption of this harmonious relationship not only among creatures but also between humans and the divine Trinity.

God the Holy Spirit:
Mother and the Material Principle

In light of the East Asian Trinity of cosmic family, the Spirit can be understood as the feminine member of the Trinity, "she," the Mother (*Yin*), who complements the Father (*Yang*). Furthermore, this vision embraces the intriguing East Asian notion of *ki*, "the vital energy," the material principle. The concept of *ki* [*qì*] (氣) is very similar to the biblical notion of spirit, *ruaḥ* in Hebrew and *pneuma* in Greek, both of which have the double meaning of wind and breath. "While wind brings nature to life, breath makes the living alive," as God's breathing is a life-giving power (Gen. 2:7).[31]

In the diagram of *T'aegŭk*, *ki* is the embodiment and materialization of the Great Ultimate through the complementary actualization of tranquillity and activity (*yin* and *yang*). While the Father is transcendent as the heavenly principle (理 *li* [*lǐ*]), the Spirit, the Mother, is immanent as the material principle (*ki*). And the Son is both transcendent and immanent in the unity of Heaven (*li*) and

---

30. Ibid., 89.
31. Ibid., 96, 97.

Earth (*ki*). In this context of Trinity as cosmic family, the doctrine of *filioque* is unacceptable, in Lee's view: "In this respect, it is not the Spirit which proceeds from the Father and the Son, but the Son which proceeds from the Spirit and the Father." The *Dàodéjīng* describes the Dao basically with feminine metaphors such as the female spirit or the womb of the "mystical mother," which is the root or the ground of being, Heaven and Earth:

> The spirit of valley never dies.
> This is called the mysterious female [or mother].
> The gateway [or womb] of the mysterious female [mother]
> Is called the root of Heaven and Earth.
> Dimly visible, it seems as if it were there,
> Yet use will never drain it.[32]

God the Father: The Unifying Principle

Li (*Lǐ*), generally translated as "principle," is the key concepts in Neo-Confucianism. It is usually discussed in association with *ki*, usually translated as "material force." If the *T'ai-chi* refers to *li* as the ontological principle, *yin* and *yang* signifies the movement of *ki* (the material embodiment). The relationship between *li* and *ki*, particularly as to which of them is prior to the other, was hotly debated in the history of Korean Neo-Confucianism. Lee introduces this discussion into the trinitarian discourse, identifying the Father with *li* and the Holy Spirit with *ki*, respectively. In light of the *li-ki* relationship, Lee understands the trinitarian relationships as follows: "God as the Father is analogous to a universal principle (*li*), while the Spirit as the Mother is analogous to a material principle (*ki*). In the Son both *li* and *ki* are united, for the Son serves as a connecting principle in the relationship between the Father and the Mother."[33]

Romanticism toward the patriarchal family in the context of East Asian ontocosmology is certainly a defect in Lee's otherwise

---

32. *Dàodéjīng*: 6. Lao Tzu, *Tao te ching*, trans. D. C. Lau (Harmondsworth: Penguin, 1963), 62.

33. Lee, *Trinity in Asian Perspective*, 112.

splendid theology of the Trinity. Siding with Chu Hsi's orthodoxy, he insists on justifying the priority of the Father, which is highly controversial in this age of post-feminist revolution. "It belongs to the Tao of *li*, 'above-shaped,' while all others belong to *ki*, 'within-shaped.' Even though the 'above-shaped' and 'within-shaped' are inseparable, the former seems to take priority." In this interpretation, the Father—the masculine (*yang*) member of the Trinity—represents "the transcendent moral and spiritual Principle of Heaven," whereas the Spirit—the feminine (*yin*) member—represents "the immanent Principle of the Earth."

Burdened with memories of his father, however, Lee seems to have forgotten that the Dao is primarily feminine, and he focuses exclusively on the paradoxical reversal of weakness (in his term, the margin). As he states, "Here we notice that the center becomes the margin, and the margin becomes the center, in the process of creativity and change. In trinitarian thinking, the centrality of the Father is marginalized by the Spirit, and the marginality of the Spirit is recentered in the Son."[34]

4. Review and Conclusion

These East Asian interpretations of the Trinity, especially those of Jung Young Lee, may sound odd to readers accustomed to the analytical thinking associated with substantialism, individualism, and exclusive humanism. They require a radical rethinking of the fundamental worldview, ontology, anthropology, and pneumatology that incorporate the anthropocosmic vision, the notion of change, inclusive humanism, and *ki*. Of course, all these concepts should be subject to a rigorous scrutiny before their adoption to the Christian doctrine of the Trinity. In conclusion, I will highlight four issues that seem to be significant for a future trinitarian theology.

Decentering Western Theology

East Asian interpretations of the Trinity welcome the direction of contemporary trinitarian theology, which I have called "Eastern-

---

34. Ibid.,150.

ization." The East Asian notion of inclusive humanism enriches the concept of person in trinitarian theology and shows that the root cause of the impasse in contemporary trinitarian theology lies in the Western anthropology of exclusive humanism. Furthermore, the *yin-yang* paradigm promotes the "triumph of relationship" in contemporary theology of the Trinity, replacing the ontology of substance with the ontology of relations.[35] The ontocosmology of *T'aegŭk* endorses the Cappadocian Fathers' privileging of relation over substance and the "Zizioulas's Rule" of "Being as Communion."[36]

Lee and John D. Zizioulas converge at this point in saying, "God is not first one and then three, but *simultaneously* One and Three," based on the East Asian onto-*cosmology* of change (*Yi*) and the Eastern onto-*personality* of communion (*koinōnia*), respectively.[37] Lee's explication of "in-ness" in the *T'aegŭk* (*yang* in *yin* and *yin* in *yang*) is in line with Leonardo Boff's affirmation of *perichoresis* as "the structural axis" of an "open" trinitarian theology,[38] thus modifying "Rahner's Rule" to the effect that "the immanent Trinity is *in* the economic Trinity and the economic Trinity is *in* the immanent Trinity." In this movement of Trinity from the West toward the Middle East and the Far East, the process of decentering Western theology is carried out further.

Relation with Feminist Theology

Lee's patriarchal bias undermines the efficacy of his project. In contrast to Lee's interpretation, the Confucian and Daoist understanding of the Trinity has a lot in common with feminist theology. In

---

35. Grentz, *Rediscovering the Triune God*, 5.

36. See John D. Zizioulas, *Being as Communion: Studies in Personhood and the Church*, Contemporary Greek Theologians 4 (Crestwood, NY: St. Vladimir's Seminary Press, 1985).

37. John D. Zizioulas, "Communion and Otherness," *St. Vladimir's Theological Quarterly* 38, no. 4 (1994): 353 (italics are mine); cf. Lee, *Trinity in Asian Perspective*, 63.

38. Leonard Boff, *Trinity and Society*, trans. Paul Burns, Theology and Liberation (Maryknoll, NY: Orbis Books, 1988), 119-20.

the both-and paradigm of *yin-yang*, God is not only both female and male but also both personal and non-personal and ultimately transcends those categories. The cosmic Trinity rooted in the onto-cosmology of *T'aegŭk* definitely includes a feminine personhood and encourages the view of the Holy Spirit as God-Mother. Like Sophia, the Dao refers to Wisdom primarily in feminine metaphors. The *Dàodéjīng* notes how the seemingly weak feminine (*yin*) exerts power over the apparently strong masculine (*yang*). Primordially, the ultimate reality (the Dao) lies in the *yin* rather than in the *yang*. The Dao is the Mysterious Female or Mother who is the root of Heaven and Earth.

Although Lee criticizes the christocentric focus of Western theology, he himself unfortunately falls into the same pitfall by making Christology the starting point for trinitarian discourse. Since the notion of *ki* offers great pneumatological possibilities and since Lǎozǐ gives more power to *yin* and "the feminine spirit" ("the Spirit of Valley"), East Asian theology of the Trinity can endorse the feminist "methodological shift to the Spirit" (Elizabeth Johnson) as the point of departure for trinitarian theology.[39]

From an East Asian perspective, however, feminist theologies in general have not yet been fully freed from exclusive humanism, even though they radically oppose essentialism or substantialism. This is due perhaps to the lack of an alternative ontology in the West. In this regard, the Confucian and Daoist ontology of change or nothingness can offer a viable alternative.

The Ontology of Nothingness

The *Dàodéjīng* is the book for the empowerment (*dé* 德) of the ineffable Dao. The foundation of the ontocosmology of *T'aegŭk* (太極; the Great Ultimate) is *Mugŭk* [*Wú jí*] (無極; the Non-Ultimate).[40] Together, *Mugŭk* (Non-Being) and *T'aegŭk* (Being) constitute the Ultimate Complementary Paradox of Opposites. In this ultimate

---

39. Grentz, *Rediscovering the Triune God*, 173.

40. Romanization of the Non-Ultimate (無極): *Mugŭk* (Korean); Chinese, *Wú jí* (Pinyin), *Wu chi* (Wade-Giles).

paradox, Nothing-ness (Non-Being) is primordial and prior to Thing-ness (Being). "All things are born of being. Being is born of non-being. . . . The Tao is nowhere to be found. Yet it nourishes and completes all things" (*Dàodéjīng*: 40, 41).

The notion of the ineffable Dao as the Non-Being is akin to that of "supraessential Trinity." Here, again, the East Asian Daoist ontology of nothingness converges with the Eastern apophatic theology. Reminiscent of the opening lines of the *Dàodéjīng*, John of Damascus states, "The Deity being incomprehensible is also assuredly nameless. Therefore since we know not His essence, let us not seek for a name for his essence."[41] The supraessential ontology of nothingness and emptiness is a subject requiring further discussion in contemporary theology of the Trinity. Eastern apophatic theology and East Asian theology of the Dao (which I call "theodao," in contrast to traditional theology's "theologos" and liberation theology's "theopraxis") have a lot in common and deserve further discussion.[42]

The Power of Kenotic Return

Lǎozǐ enthusiastically speaks of the Dao's "super-*kenōsis*."[43] The ontocosmology of *T'aegŭk* and the superkenotic Dao endorse a "perichoresic kenotic trinitarian ontology."[44] However, they do not imply an abstract, powerless metaphysics of the Trinity. On the contrary, they reveal the concrete trajectory of the revolutionary and subversive life force (the *ki* of great *yin*). Like the divine breath, this cosmogonic energy makes all things alive.

A clue to understanding the mystery of the hidden but unquench-

---

41. John of Damascus, *On the Orthodox Faith*, 1,12, cited from Thomas Hopko, "Apophatic Theology and the Naming of God in Eastern Orthodox Tradition," in *Speaking the Christian God: The Holy Trinity and the Challenge of Feminism*, ed. Alvin Kimel Jr. (Grand Rapids: Eerdmans, 1992), 157.

42. See chapter 2 above.

43. Grentz, *Rediscovering the Triune God*, 221.

44. Robert Kess, "Unity in Diversity and Diversity in Unity: Toward an Ecumenical Perichoresic Kenotic Trinitarian Ontology," *Dialogue & Alliance* 4, no. 3 (1990): 66-70.

able power of the Dao is the principle of "reversal" and the power of radical return. Jesus occasionally speaks of the principle of reversal: "Blessed are you that are hungry now, for you will be filled. . . . Woe to you who are full now, for you will be hungry" (Luke 6:21, 25). St. Paul also says, "Whenever I am weak, then I am strong" (2 Cor. 12:10).

A vivid symbol of the Dao's power of radical return is a feeble fish's jumping up against the mighty downstream to return to its origin.[45] With its preferential option for the *yin*, the non-being, the powerless (minjung), and the margin, East Asian trinitarian theology of the Dao is not just a romantic hankering after past things East Asian. Rather, it is a serious reinterpretation of the Christian mystery of the crucifixion as non-being and the resurrection as being, the ultimate paradox of apophatic reversal and superkenotic return. A Korean theologian Ryu Yŏng-mo offers an intriguing insight that Christ is "the Being-in-Non-Being," that is to say, the great cosmogonic Trinity (*T'aegŭk in Mugŭk*).[46] Jesus Christ is therefore also a or the supreme Dao of the East Asian Trinity. These insights on the supraessential Dao of superkenotic Return provide rich resources for developing a global trinitarian theology in the third millennium. Lǎozǐ presents a tantalizing hint:

> Attain complete vacuity [emptiness],
> Maintain steadfast quietude.
> All things come into being,
> And I see thereby their return.
> All things flourish,
> But each one returns to its root.
> This return to its root means tranquility.
> It is called returning to its destiny.
> To return to destiny is called the eternal (Dao).
> To know the eternal is called enlightenment.[47]

---

45. For this subversive power of return, see the parable of ugŭmch'i phenomenon in chapter 2 above.

46. See chapter 7 below.

47. Chan, *Source Book*, 147.

PART II

Theodao in Bridge-building: Christianity and East Asian Religions

CHAPTER FIVE

Chéng *and* Agapē: *Wang Yang-ming Meets Karl Barth*

1. Introduction to Confucian–Christian Dialogue

Since Confucianism is an embedded cultural-linguistic matrix for East Asian people, doing East Asian theology entails a critical wrestling with this living tradition. East Asian Christians are compelled to thematize a Christian theology of Confucianism that calls forth Confucian–Christian dialogue. To facilitate the dialogue between two different religious persuasions, I start with three presuppositions: (1) Confucianism as an expression of a faith, (2) confuciology as a heuristic device for a Confucian–Christian dialogue, and (3) the orthopraxis of radical humanization (self-cultivation and sanctification) as a point of contact between Confucianism and Christianity.

1. Whether Confucianism is an articulation of a *faith* is a controversial issue. The term *faith* in this context has a much broader definition than the Christian one, that is, the informed trust in the salvific person. Rather, faith is conceived of as "genetically human" (W. C. Smith) and "a constitutive dimension" of human being that involves primarily orthopraxis (R. Panikkar).[1] If faith is defined as

---

* Adapted from Heup Young Kim, "*Jen* and *Agape*: Toward a Confucian Christology," originally published in *Asia Journal of Theology* 8, no. 2 (October 1994): 335-64. For more comprehensive discussion, see Heup Young Kim, *Wang Yang-ming and Karl Barth: A Confucian–Christian Dialogue* (Lanham, MD: University Press of America, 1996).
1. See Wilfred Cantwell Smith, *Faith and Belief* (Princeton, NJ: Princeton

an integrated human attitude toward transcendence, Confucianism is a faith. Although Confucianism is no institutional and dogmatic religion, it has a dimension of "being religious" (W. C. Smith).[2] Being religious in the Confucian context means to be engaged in "ultimate self-transformation as a communal act and a faithful response to the transcendent."[3] Tu Wei-ming defined Confucianism as "a faith in the living person's authentic possibility for self-transcendence." Tu further postulated a Confucian soteriology as "the full realization of the anthropocosmic reality inherent in our human nature."[4]

Furthermore, the point of departure for the Confucian enterprise is the establishment of the will (立志; *lì zhì* [*li-chih*]), as Confucius said in the *Analects* (2:4), "At fifteen, I set my heart on learning." *Lì zhì*, a crucial notion of Wang Yang-ming (王陽明, 1472–1529), refers to an ethico-religious commitment to a fully integrated humanity that involves a fundamental determination and radical turn of the will, similar to the Christian notion of *metanoia* (repentance).[5] Although partially analogous to the Kierkegaardian notion of qualitative change,[6] *lì zhì* signifies not an "either-or" leap

University Press, 1979), 129-42; and Raymond Panikkar, "Faith—A Constitutive Dimension of Man," trans. Pheme Perkins, *Journal of Ecumenical Studies* 8 (1971): 223-54.

2. W. C. Smith established a distinction between "religion" and "being religious." See Smith, *The Meaning and End of Religion* (1963; repr., Minneapolis: Fortress, 1991), 19-74. While religion signifies an institution distinguished by a set of dogmas, being religious means "a spiritual self-identification of the living members of a community of faith" (Tu Wei-ming, *Confucian Thought: Selfhood as Creative Transformation*, SUNY Series in Philosophy [Albany: State University of New York Press, 1985], 132).

3. Tu Wei-ming, *Centrality and Commonality: An Essay on Confucian Religiousness*, rev. ed., SUNY Series in Chinese Philosophy and Culture (Albany: State University of New York Press, 1989), 94.

4. Tu, *Confucian Thought*, 55. In addition, Keum Jang Tae regards Confucianism as a faith and advocates for its systematic formulation; see his *Problems of Confucian Thought* (Seoul: Ryugang, 1990).

5. See Tu Wei-ming, *Neo-Confucianism in Action: Wang Yang-ming's Youth* (1472–1509) (Berkeley: University of California Press, 1976), 142.

6. For the comparison of *lì zhì* and qualitative change, see Tu, *Humanity*

in response to the revelation of the divine ("the wholly other") but a "both-and" return to human subjectivity in immanent-transcendence.[7] This conception is not totally different from the Christian notion of faith. For example, the mature Barth also understood that faith is not merely an either-or leap related to the passive justification but, rather, a spontaneous human self-determination for subjectivity that entails the process of sanctification, continuous repentance and regeneration, corresponding to gracious divine election.[8] The point of departure for both Confucianism and Christianity is not so much a logically construed metaphysics or a philosophy of religion as a full ethico-religious commitment for the integrated human subjectivity. For both of them, the starting point is rather an establishment of one's will on the orthopraxis of the communally informed dao (the Way).

2. Confuciology as a heuristic device for a Confucian–Christian dialogue. Theology articulates a critical and coherent reflection on a faith in the theistic paradigm (*fides quaerens intellectum*). I use the term *confuciology* to designate an analogous type of systematic discourse for a faith in the Confucian paradigm. Confuciology designates an interpretative explication of the Confucian faith in a specific context. This term needs two further clarifications. First, the term is not a Confucian counterpart to Christology. Although confuciology includes an interpretation of the teachings of Confucius, it does not mean a specific discourse on the person of Confucius in the way that Christology exclusively involves the interpretation of the person and work of Jesus Christ. Second, I am fully aware that not only Daoism but also Confucianism has an inherent suspicion of and aversion to systematic discourse, because such a deliberation inevitably violates the natural flow of dao (*wú*

---

and Self-Cultivation: Essays in Confucian Thought (Berkeley: Asian Humanities Press, 1979), 89-90.

7. For this distinction, see Tu, *Centrality and Commonality*, 116-21.

8. For this discussion, see my dissertation, Heup Young Kim, "Sanctification and Self-Cultivation: A Study of Karl Barth and Neo-Confucianism (Wang Yang-ming)" (Ph.D. diss., Graduate Theological Union, 1992), 115-16, 135, 164, 221-23.

wéi). I argue, however, that it is necessarily a heuristic device for a dialogue with Christian theology. Without such an attempt of postmodern construction, a necessity Tu Wei-ming also proposed in terms of "the third epoch," Confucianism would be an easy prey to be swallowed up by scientifically armed, modern, heavy-duty theological systems.

In the words of George Lindbeck, confuciology is "to give a normative explication of the meaning" that Confucianism has for East Asian people as their cultural-linguistic matrix.[9] If theology is a thick description of the intratextuality of the Christian faith, confuciology is that of the Confucian faith. Confuciology describes intelligibly and thickly the stories of the Confucian ethico-religious persuasions within their own contexts. Analogous to theology (at least similar to Barthian-Reformed and liberation theologies), being secondary to the faith itself, confuciology explicates the rules of the game for understanding the cultural-linguistic matrix. It prevents an eclectic and fragmentary reading whose dangerous decontexualization jeopardizes and violates the integrity and inner coherence of the Confucian intratextuality. Hence, confuciology is a protective device to tell Confucian stories authentically and thickly in their own structures. Then, a Confucian–Christian encounter can be examined appropriately in the relation of and in the dynamic interplay between confuciology and theology.

3. The orthopraxis of radical humanization (*self-cultivation and sanctification*, respectively) as a point of contact. The focus of the Confucian project lies in self-cultivation, learning how to be fully human, or an integrated attempt to realize humans' intrinsic transcendental goal, "the achievement of a *radical* human-ity."[10] The point of departure of Confucian discourse is the concrete human situation of the living person here and now. As its crucial notion propriety (*li* [*lǐ*]) denotes, its main concern is a person's proper embodiment of the dao to a given ethico-religious context. The

---

9. George A. Lindbeck, *The Nature of Doctrine: Religion and Theology in a Postliberal Age* (Philadelphia: Westminster, 1984), 113.

10. Julia Ching, *Confucianism and Christianity: A Comparative Study* (Tokyo: Kodansha, 1977), 105.

prime locus of Confucian discourse, similar to that of liberation theology, is the shared orthopraxis of spirituality for its fundamental vision. Their visions are different: While liberation theology envisions an emancipatory spirituality for the fully shared society, confuciology embodies a sapiential spirituality for the anthropocosmic vision. Both of them, however, are a spirituality of the radical humanization of a living community here and now.

In addition, theology underscores the issue of radical humanization; as Hans Küng puts it, being a Christian means being radically human.[11] Protestant theologies understand this as a theme of sanctification, a corresponding human action to the gracious election to achieve the full humanity that was realized once and for all for the human race through the redemptive life-act of Jesus Christ. Reformed theology, particularly that of Barth, emphasized sanctification as a central doctrine (equal in value to justification), following Calvin's shift of gospel over law. Sanctification and justification are two expressions of an inseparable action of cosmic reconciliation. While justification is that from above, sanctification is the perspective from below.

My point at this juncture is twofold. First, radical humanization is a common issue of confuciology and theology (self-cultivation and sanctification), and this point of contact constitutes an appropriate locus to facilitate a Confucian–Christian dialogue. Second, the nature of this point of contact is primarily not a static concept or a psychological consciousness but a living person's dynamic engagement with a shared practice. The basic locus of the dialogue should be not a metaphysics, a psychology, or a philosophy of religion, though they are constitutive, but a spirituality of radical humanization. For their point of contact as well as their common ground first and foremost refers to the spiritual orthopraxis, an ethico-religious embodiment of each faith in a historical context.

Both theology and confuciology articulate descriptively and normatively the fabrics and intratextualities of their cultural-linguistic matrices. A Confucian–Christian dialogue can be formulated as

---

11. Hans Küng, *On Being a Christian*, trans. Edward Quinn (Garden City, NY: Doubleday, 1984), 555-57.

interplay of confuciology and theology. Descriptively, the interplay is more related to a secondary level, a reflective level to examine the practical encounter, than to a primary level. Normatively, the discourse elicits an *a posteriori* thematization of the ethico-religious and theological meaning for a community in the historic Confucian–Christian encounter. This enterprise, thus, consists in two stages: (1) a descriptive-comparative stage and (2) a normative-constructive stage.

Confuciology constitutes the main device for the first stage. Pointing out the methodological dangers of a simple juxtaposition of Confucian categories with those of other religions, Henry Rosemont Jr. proposed a method of "a concept cluster," the formulation of a conceptual framework for a more appropriate process of decontextualization and recontexualization.[12] In partial agreement with this method, confuciology involves the much wider scope of the historical horizon, a systematic explication of the Confucian intratextuality. Although it uses modern categories for the sake of communication, its purpose is to tell its story in its own categories, properly resisting impositions of other categorical schemes. Hence, this stage takes equivocity more seriously than univocity.[13]

In the second, normative-constructive stage, the locus is shifted to the concrete context—East Asian churches, that is, Christian communities in the historic collision of the two spiritual traditions. Those communities need a holistic articulation of the Christian faith in their given cultural-linguistic matrix, namely, Confucianism. Hence, this stage inevitably focuses on their univocities. However, the goal of finding those univocative dimensions is primarily toward an *a posteriori* articulation of the Christian faith in the context of the fusion of the two horizons, more concretely, the two

---

12. See Henry Rosemont Jr., "Why Take Rights Seriously," in *Human Rights and the World's Religions*, ed. Leroy S. Rouner, Boston University Studies in Philosophy and Religion 9 (Notre Dame, IN: University of Notre Dame Press, 1988), 168-69.

13. For this distinction, see Lee H. Yearley, *Mencius and Aquinas: Theories of Virtue and Conceptions of Courage,* SUNY Series, Toward a Comparative Philosophy of Religions (Albany: State University of New York Press, 1990), 188-91.

powerful stories of radical humanization. This enterprise refers not to an arbitrary deliberation of speculative comparison but to an imperative thematization of a Christian community for the holistic understanding of their faith. The result, however, will enhance the theology of the Christian community as a whole.

In this chapter, I will present a case study of this method. First, for the stage of descriptive-comparative study, I will briefly deal with two key confuciological and theological notions, *chéng* and *agapē*, represented by two paradigmatic thinkers, Wang Yang-ming (1472–1529) and Karl Barth (1886–1968). Second, for the normative-constructive stage, I will propose a new understanding of Jesus Christ for the East Asian churches, namely, a Confucian (Sage) Christology.

2. Chéng *(Confucian Sincerity): A Confuciology of Wang Yang-ming*

The Self-Directing Dao [Tao] (道; *the Way*)

Confucianism claims that humanity is the heavenly endowment. *The Doctrine of the Mean* (中庸; *Zhōng Yōng* [*Chung-yung*]) said, "What Heaven imparts to human beings is called human nature."[14] The primordial unity between humanity and Heaven (an East Asian expression of transcendence) constitutes the Confucian faith in the innate possibility (or perfectibility) for human self-transcendence.

In the context of this anthropocosmic vision, Confucianism addresses the mission of humanity in the world. Basically, however, Confucianism is suspicious of metaphysical and cosmological abstractions. As Confucianism is also called the learning to be human, its focus is rather on practical issues such as how to attain sagehood, the original humanity. Confucius tried to demythologize mythical cosmologies rampant in the ancient period of China and to reformulate the Confucian values in the new life situation. Therefore, Confucius emphasized the virtue of propriety (*li*), the

---

14. For a translation, see Chan Wing-tsit, *A Source Book in Chinese Philosophy* (Princeton, NJ: Princeton University Press, 1963), 95 (modified).

orthopraxis of Way (dao).[15] The crucial issue of Confucianism is not to obtain knowledge for the sake of theory but how to embody the wisdom of dao into a shared practice.

Although subtle and hidden, dao is already immanent in the original human nature. It is a self-directing spirituality that gives a sapiential direction in a specific context. Etymologically, it means a human head in movement. Dao does not signify a static concept but a dynamic human action in the right way. Herbert Fingarette said this well: "*Tao* is a Way, a path, a road, and by common metaphorical extensions it becomes in ancient China the right Way of life, the Way of governing, the ideal Way of human existence, the Way of the cosmos, the generative-normative Way (pattern, path, course) of existence as such."[16] As Fingarette further clarified, the Confucian freedom in the direction of dao does not mean a choice among many alternatives but a capacity to locate one's act within the orthopraxis of the dao, namely, *propriety* (禮; *lǐ* [*li*]).[17] According to *The Doctrine of the Mean*,

> To follow our original nature is called *Tao*. *Tao* cannot be separated from us for a moment. Cultivating *Tao* is called education. What can be separated from is not *Tao*. Therefore the profound persons are cautious over what they do not see and apprehensive over what they do not hear. There is nothing more visible than what is hidden and nothing more manifest than what is subtle. Therefore the profound persons are watchful over themselves when they are alone.[18]

To attain the ultimate human existence (sagehood) in the anthropocosmic vision, this passage said, one should be able to penetrate and perceive the direction of dao beyond its hiddenness and subtlety. The Confucian profound person is such a person who has developed the necessary skills of cautiousness and watchful-

---

15. See Herbert Fingarette, *Confucius—The Secular as Sacred* (New York: Harper & Row, 1972), chapter 1.

16. Ibid., 19.

17. See ibid., 22.

18. Chan, *Source Book*, 98 (modified).

ness over his or her anthropocentric proclivities through self-cultivation. These skills refer to two key notions of Neo-Confucianism, namely, *kyŏng* (敬; *jing* [*ching*]; mindfulness) and *chéng* (*ch'eng*]; sincerity).[19] Keum Jang Tae, a Korean Confucian scholar, delineated these terms:

> Mindfulness refers to an attitude of faith that attempts to attain the ultimate human existence through the purification and attention of the human mind-and-heart in its fullest self-awareness. Sincerity signifies a mystical experience that maintains and realizes one's unity with the ultimate human existence. That is to say, while mindfulness capacitates a human being to encounter, the transcendent dimension of its ultimate existence, sincerity enables a person to realize the mysterious union with the ultimate existence.[20]

Chéng [Ch'eng] (誠; *Sincerity*)

According to *The Doctrine of the Mean*, *chéng* (sincerity) enables a person to follow the direction of dao.

> Sincerity is the Way of Heaven. To think how to be sincere is the way of human being. One who is sincere is one who hits upon what is right without effort and apprehends without thinking. A person is naturally and easily in harmony with the Way. Such a person is a sage. One who tries to be sincere is one who chooses the good and holds fast to it.[21]

---

19. For *kyŏng* [*jing*], see Michael C. Kalton, *To Become a Sage: The Ten Diagrams on Sage Learning by Yi T'oegye,* Neo-Confucian Studies (New York: Columbia University Press, 1988), 212-24. Whereas the English word *sincerity* holds some negative connotations, *chéng* always refers to positive meanings such as honesty, genuineness, and truth. Etymologically, *chéng* means the completion, actualization, and perfection of words, or the unity of words and deeds.

20. Keum, *Problems of Confucian Thought*, 11 (my translation); see also 8-11.

21. Chan, *Source Book*, 107 (modified).

Sincerity refers not to an intentional deliberation but to an effortless, natural execution (*wú wéi*) of the Way, as it ought to be. Sincerity is the way to attain the true self, that is to say, an appropriate positioning of the self in the direction of dao. On a deeper level, sincerity entails the freedom and capability of the profound person to embody naturally the spark of dao in ethico-religious praxis.

Sincerity makes a person actualize the nature of one's own humanity to the utmost in the fullest moral sensitivity. *The Doctrine of the Means* said:

> Only those who are absolutely sincere can order and adjust the great relation of humankind, establish the great foundation of humanity, and know the transforming and nourishing operations of Heaven and Earth. Does a person depend on anything else? How earnest and sincere—a person is humanity! How deep and unfathomable—a person is abyss! How vast and great—a person is Heaven! Who can know the person except one who really has quickness of apprehension, intelligence, sageliness, and wisdom, and understands the character of Heaven?[22]

Hence, the *sage* is defined as the absolutely sincere person, capable of extending the task of self-realization to the cosmos as a whole through authenticating his or her true nature in the ontological unity with Heaven. Sincerity denotes both "the creative process by which the existence of things becomes possible, and the ground of being on which the things as they really are ultimately one."[23] It is the foundation of both self-realization and self-transformation. Sincerity empowers a person to fulfill the very definition of humanness as "a self-transforming and self-realizing agent."[24]

Focusing on this spirituality of humanness immanent in one's concrete self, the absolutely sincere person, the sage, participates in the universal transforming process of the cosmic creativity. This implies the vertical dimension of the Confucian concrete-universal

---

22. Ibid., 112 (modified).
23. Tu, *Humanity and Self-Cultivation,* 97.
24. Ibid.

approach. As the Mencian analogy of the sinking of a well implies, "the deeper one goes into the ground of one's own being, the closer one gets to the spring of common humanity and the source of cosmic creativity."[25] Mencius said, "For one to give full realization to one's mind is for one to understand one's own nature, and one who knows one's own nature will know Heaven."[26] Tu Wei-ming articulated this succinctly:

> Self-realization, however, is not a process of individuation; it is primarily a course of universal communion. The more one sinks into the depth of one's being, the more he transcends his anthropological restriction. Underlining this paradox is the Confucian belief that the true nature of man [human being] and the real creativity of the cosmos are both "grounded" in *sincerity*. When one, through self-cultivation, becomes absolutely sincere, one is the most authentic man [human being] and simultaneously participates in the transforming and nourishing process of the cosmos. To do so is to fulfill one's human nature.[27]

Rén (仁): *The Confucian Paradigm of Humanity*

The Confucian locus of mindfulness (an attitude of faith) and sincerity (a mystical experience) is *xīn* [*hsin*] (心; the human mind-and-heart). *Xīn*, a principle concept of the East Asian thought since Mencius, can be hardly grasped with the Greek philosophical framework that distinguishes body and soul as well as emotion and reason. It is not only cognitive but also affective and conative as well. In the Mencian sense, *xīn* refers not merely to psychology, epistemology, or physiology but also to the ontology of humanness. It is "an ontological basis for moral self-cultivation," which constitutes the morality and subjectivity of human life.[28]

---

25. Ibid., 87-88.
26. D. C. Lau, *Mencius* (Harmondsworth: Penguin Books, 1970), 182 (modified).
27. Tu, *Humanity and Self-Cultivation*, 99.
28. Tu, *Confucian Thought*, 70.

Focusing on this intrinsic possibility for self-transcendence, Wang Yang-ming identified the mind-and-heart with *li* [*lǐ*] (理; principle), the formative and normative principle of dao or built-in structure of the cosmic order.[29] Wang perceived the mind-and-heart as the human locus where "the embodiment of the Heavenly Principle" (天理: *Tiān lǐ* [*T'ien-li*]) eventuates (CSL: 7). Since *li* is a Neo-Confucian expression of transcendence, Wang's claim of *xīn jí lǐ* [*hsin chi li*] (心即理) signifies a Neo-Confucian soteriological leap that authenticates the human capacity to realize sufficiently the anthropocosmic reality inherent in human nature, that is, an immanent transcendence.[30]

The basic paradigm of humanity in the anthropocosmic vision is perceived by *rén* (benevolence), the cardinal Confucian virtue since Confucius. Etymologically, its Chinese character, composed of a graph that means human being and two strokes that mean two, denotes two human beings, or togetherness of human beings. Hence, *rén* is also translated as "co-humanity," co-human," or co-humanize."[31] Confucian anthropology is grounded in the axiom that *rén* (humanity) is *rén* (co-humanity). Since the first word, *rén*, is the Chinese gender-neutral term for a human being (*homo*), the axiom signifies that humanity is benevolent co-humanity. The immanent transcendent self-conceived in the everyday living situation does not mean a self-fulfilled, individual ego in the modern sense but a communal self or the togetherness of a self as "a center of relationship."[32]

---

29. *Li* refers to a built-in structure, pattern, or standard that holds the order of universe as a whole. *Li* and *Dao* are generally the same: *li* is more concrete, whereas *Dao* is broader. Wang Yang-ming, *Instructions for Practical Living and Other Confucian Writings,* trans. Chan Wing-tsit, Records of Civilization, Sources and Studies 68 (New York: Columbia University Press, 1963), 6-7 (hereafter CSL).

30. For the notion of immanent transcendence, see Liu Shu-Hsien, "The Confucian Approach to the Problem of Transcendence and Immanence," *Philosophy East and West* 22 (1972): 45-52.

31. See Peter A. Booderberg, "The Semasiology of Some Primary Confucian Concepts," *Philosophy East and West* 2, no. 4 (1953), 329-30.

32. Tu Wei-ming, *Centrality and Commonality,* 53.

Neo-Confucianism expands the notion of *rén* to the cosmic togetherness of the anthropocosmic vision. Zhang Zai [Chang Tsai] (1022–1077) offers this poetic description in the *Western Inscription*:

> Heaven is my father and Earth is my mother, and even such a small creature as I finds an intimate place in their midst. Therefore that which fills the universe I regard as my body and that which directs the universe I consider as my nature. All people are my brothers and sisters, and all things are my companions.[33]

Wang ontologized this anthropocosmic togetherness further in his doctrine of the Oneness of All Things:

> The profound person regards Heaven, Earth, and the myriads things as one body. Such a person regards the world as one family and the country as one person. As to those who make a cleavage between objects and distinguish between the self and others, they are small people. That the profound person can regard Heaven, Earth, and the myriads things as one body is not because one deliberately wants to do so, but because it is natural human nature of one's mind that one does so. (CSL: 272)

The profound person of *rén* perceives the ontology of his or her humanity in an organismic unity with Heaven, Earth, and the myriad things. This realization of oneself as a cosmic being-in-togetherness enables a person to make the cosmic spiritual communion with utmost "spiritual sensitivity and loving care."[34] *Rén* as the paradigm of humanity implies not only a manifested structure of human subjectivity but also a spiritual medium through which reconciliatory communion is made possible (see CSL: 272). Wang predicated *rén* as the "clear character" or the illustrious virtue (明德; *míng dé* [*ming-te*]) and the "loving people" (新民; *qīn mín*

---

33. Chan, *Source Book*, 497.
34. Tu, *Humanity and Self-Cultivation*, 157.

[*ch'in-min*]),[35] the two root-metaphors of *The Great Learning*. In terms of the substance–function relationship, the clear character defines the substance (the ontological structure) of humanity as a cosmic being-in-togetherness, while the loving people predicate its function (an ethico-religious realization). The "loving people," the function of *rén*, necessitates serious sociopolitical implications, by dynamically recovering the original structure of humanity as a cosmic being-in-togetherness. This love is basically prereflective and spontaneous, like the feeling of commiseration. Its execution should follow the order of this natural feeling of social relations, starting from one's nearest shared praxis and extending to the remotest. *The Great Learning* specifies the order of establishing and enlarging human relatedness through the extending networks of self, the family, the society at large, and the world (see CSL: 273-74). Wang also argues against an ideal concept of Mohist's universal love, because this concept, with a weak starting point, is vulnerable to the abuse of "leveling" natural affections and responsibilities (see CSL: 56-57). This stipulates the horizontal dimension of the Confucian concrete-universal approach, a spiral movement of creative transformation from the particular to the universal, from the inner to the outer, and from selfhood to the cosmos.

Liáng zhī (良知; *The Innate Knowledge of the Good*)
The Confucian Root-Paradigm

Wang's confuciology culminates in his doctrine of *zhì liáng zhī* [*chih liang-chih*] (致良知), meaning the extension of the innate knowledge of the good. *Liáng zhī* is Wang's term designating the innate faculty of the mind-and-heart to discern the Heavenly Principle and know the good. It refers to the prereflective and spontaneous feeling like the primordial human feeling of "alarm and commiseration"—one of the Mencian Four Beginnings of moral-

---

35. Rejecting Zhu Xi's revision of this word to "renovating people" (*hsin-min*), Wang argued for this original rendition. See CSL: 276. For the passage of *The Great Learning*, see Chan, *Source Book*, 86.

ity—when one sees a child about to fall into a well.[36] *Liáng zhī* is revelatory knowledge of the Heavenly Principle in human original consciousness, whose content is "true sincerity and commiseration" (CSL: 176).[37] It is the foundation of all knowledge and learning including the teachings of the sage (CSL: 150). It is the inherent moral standard to judge right and wrong, "the true secret" of the Confucian project of self-cultivation (CSL: 193). Tu Wei-ming rendered *liáng zhī* as "primordial awareness," that is, "an innermost state of human perception wherein knowledge and action form a unity" or the "'humanity of the heart' [which] creates values of human understanding as it encounters the world."[38] Hence, according to Wang, the whole Confucian project of radical humanization centers on the hermeneutics of *liáng zhī*.

Wang established *liáng zhī* firmly as the hermeneutical principle for the Confucian enterprise. The classics are valuable as paradigmatic records of the work of *liáng zhī* in the historical context, while sages are worthy as living paradigms of *"liang-chih* in action."[39] The stories of sages only as its "passing shadow" illustrate the trajectory of *liáng zhī*. Wang demythologized not only the authority of classics and sages but also even that of Confucius himself. He claimed that the true Confucian foundation lies not in the person and work of Confucius but in the revelatory action of *liáng zhī* (the *kērygma* of *liáng zhī*, if you will) in everyone's mind-and-heart (CSL: 159).[40] Wang's notion of *liáng zhī* shows a strong egalitarianism. *Liáng zhī* as the inner sage is naturally endowed in all people, whether a sage, worthy, or stupid. Every person has an innate power to become fully human through the extension

36. Mencius 2A:6. See James Legge, *The Chinese Classics* (1866; repr., New York: Paragon Books, 1966), 2:78.

37. See also Hitoyuki, "Wang Yang-ming's Doctrine of Innate Knowledge of the Good," *Philosophy East and West* 11 (1961): 41-42.

38. Tu, *Confucian Thought*, 32.

39. Philip Ivanhoe, *Ethics in the Confucian Tradition: The Thought of Mencius and Wang Yang-ming* (Atlanta: Scholars Press, 1990), 103. Also, see CSL: 23.

40. See ibid., 109.

of one's *liáng zhī* (see CSL: 194). Rejecting the distinction of the Cheng-Zhu school between human nature (性: *xìng* [*hsing*]) and mind-and-heart (*xīn*), Wang identified *liáng zhī* with *xīn*-in-itself (literally, the original substance of the mind-and-heart), the state of "the equilibrium before the feelings are aroused" (CSL: 136). This state of *xīn*-in-itself transcends any existential, ontic distinction of before and after, equilibrium and harmony, inner and external, or activity and tranquillity (CSL: 137). *Liáng zhī* as the *xīn*-in-itself refers to a primordial, ontological state of a dynamic being-in-itself. It is so bright and transparent like the "shining mind" and the "bright mirror" as to be identical with the Heavenly Principle (CSL: 139-40, 148-49; see also 152).

Furthermore, Wang equated *liáng zhī*-in-itself with the Great Vacuity (太虛; *Tài xū* [*T'ai-hsü*]), the ultimate source of creative transcendence. Like the Great Vacuity, *liáng zhī*-in-itself is absolutely self-transcendent (CSL: 220). The self-transcendent *liáng zhī* entails the creative spirit, which capacitates not only cosmic differentiations through permeating all things but also warrants them into the anthropocosmic identification. *Liáng zhī* substantiates the cosmic unity among diversities and the cosmic interpenetration through the work of its *ki* [*qì*] (氣; material force) (CSL: 221-22). In other words, *liáng zhī* is the foundation of achieving *rén*, humanity as a cosmic being-in-togetherness.

Liáng zhī as *xīn*-in-itself is also the life giving true self, the "subjectivity" of radical humanity.[41] As "the innermost and indissoluble reality" of the human, it is both "a self-generative 'intellectual intuition'" to empower a person to perceive the Heavenly Principle and "a self-sufficient 'anthropocosmic feeling'" to commission one to fulfill the mission of *rén*, to be a cosmic being-in-togetherness.[42] *Liáng zhī* as the intellectual intuition and the anthropocosmic feeling constitutes the most concrete-universal foundation for the Confucian faith. The concrete, transcendent possibility sufficiently generates the imperative of its universal extension. Through an extension of *liáng zhī* in the ever-enlarging circles of relatedness,

---

41. Tu, *Humanity and Self-Cultivation*, 138-61; also CSL: 80-81.
42. Tu, *Humanity and Self-Cultivation*, 156.

the bewildering self at the loss of equilibrium and harmony in the differentiated world can return to its true self. This is the Confucian concrete-universal way that implies the necessary identification of one's subjectivity and the cosmic ontological reality (the Unity of All Things).[43] In Wang's confuciology, hence, the whole Confucian learning is summarized in the doctrine of *zhì liáng zhī*, the extension of the innate knowledge of the good.

The foundation of *rén* (benevolent humanity), the substance of the Confucian persuasion, is *liáng zhī*, and *ai* (love), its function, is conceived of as a process of *zhì liáng zhī*. *Liáng zhī* as a built-in order of the Heavenly Principle also constitutes the root-paradigms of four other Confucian virtues. Wang said, "It [the order] is righteousness [義]. To follow this order is called propriety [禮]. To understand this order is called wisdom [智]. And to follow this order from beginning to end is called faithfulness [信]" (CSL: 223).

In Wang's confuciology, we find a positive articulation of the Confucian principle of reciprocity (恕), the single thread that binds all Confucius's teachings together.[44] Confucius said the negative golden rule, "Do not do unto others what you would not want others to do unto you."[45] Wang's affirmation does not betray the Confucian perception of reciprocity "as the human way par excellence."[46] Rather, Wang warranted *liáng zhī* as the self-transcendent source for a person to transform dynamically one's reciprocity into practice, not only in networks of human relatedness but also in the cosmic pool of ecological relationship. Wang's ontology of humanity as a cosmic being-in-togetherness presupposes reciprocity and mutuality among beings-in-encounter. Wang's doctrine of the Unity of All Things articulates the Confucian anthropocosmic vision that entails cosmic and ecological reciprocity. The original Confucian suggestion is not to propagate an evangelical faith of the religiously privileged by means of domination, coercion, or exploitation. On

43. Ibid., 159.

44. D. C. Lau, trans., *Confucius: The Analects* (Harmondsworth: Penguin Books, 1979), 74, 132.

45. Ibid., 135.

46. Tu, *Centrality and Commonality*, 103.

the contrary, the humble and modest principles of *rén* and reciprocity reject any "epistemological immodesty and moral *hubris*."[47]

3. Agapē *(Christian Love): A Theology of Karl Barth*

Election and Sanctification

An important theological paradigm shift in Karl Barth's work is the reversal of the traditional sequence of law and gospel to gospel and law, radicalizing John Calvin's idea.[48] Barth argued that Luther's doctrine of law and gospel results in a "dualist peril" and "anthropological narrowness" because of its dialectical separation of the two modes of the Word of God. Instead, he overcame the duality by reversing the sequence to subordinate law to gospel. The gospel does not reveal the ultimate reality of God's grace dualistically. Since law is the necessary form of the gospel, whose content is grace, it should be understood in the context of the gospel. This reversal—the triumph of Grace—constitutes Barth's radical revision of traditional dogmatics: in his new formulation, Christology precedes the doctrine of sin, and ethics (law) is subsumed under dogmatics (gospel).

Barth's doctrine of election saliently presents the paradigm shift. The sum of the gospel is God's gracious election of the human race as God's covenant partner. This loving attitude of God claims a corresponding human response toward God, which is sanctification. However, God's election as the Lord of the covenant already empowered us to be and become fully human, as God's covenant partners. In other words, if God's covenantal election is the ontological human condition, sanctification is the necessary human enterprise to realize this ultimate reality. In this context, the essence of a human being is conceived of as free self-determination

---

47. Robert E. Allison, "The Ethics of Confucianism and Christianity: The Delicate Balance," *Ching Feng* 33, no. 3 (1990): 168.

48. For Barth's reversal of gospel and law, see Eberhard Jüngel, "Gospel and Law: The Relationship of Dogmatics and Ethics," in his *Karl Barth, a Theological Legacy*, trans. Garrett E. Paul (Philadelphia: Westminster, 1986), 105-26.

in action. The meaning of being and becoming a Christian lies in the unified action of hearing (dogmatics) and doing (ethics). Hence, Barth included ethics as a part of dogmatics in each of the three major volumes of *Church Dogmatics*. In these deliberations, his focus shifts "from the commanding position of God to the commanded position of humanity," which enables his theology to make a strong political impact.[49] Sometimes, as Robert Palma noticed, Barth exercised even the freedom of a "bracketing off the theological dimension."[50] Barth "intermittently excludes the theological dimension" to ascribe what Hans Frei called Barth's "secular sensibility."[51]

From this vantage point, it can be argued that Barth's real focus is on sanctification. Since sanctification belongs to election in Barth's supralapsarianism, sanctification is prior to justification. Barth emphasized that Calvin, his main theological basis, was a theologian of sanctification. Furthermore, since only love, the virtue of sanctification, has its own hymn in the Bible, 1 Corinthians 13, he argues, it is more crucial than faith, the virtue of justification. He said that *agapē* is the Christian way that embraces faith and hope.[52]

Humanitas Christi: *The Christian Root-Paradigm*[53]

Humanitas Christi (the humanity of Christ): Barth conceived that the foundation of sanctification is the exaltation of Christ, metaphorically presented as the homecoming of the Son of Man in the parable of the prodigal son (Luke 15:11-32) (CD IV/2:21-25). Jesus

---

49. Jüngel, *Karl Barth*, 126.

50. See Robert J. Palma, *Karl Barth's Theology of Culture: The Freedom of Culture for the Praise of God* (Allison Park, PA: Pickwick, 1983), 10-14.

51. Ibid., 11, 13; also Hans Frei, "Karl Barth—Theologian," in *Karl Barth and the Future of Theology*, ed. David L. Dickermann (New Haven: Yale Divinity School Association, 1969), 8-9.

52. See Karl Barth, *Church Dogmatics*, vol. IV, pt. II, *The Doctrine of Reconciliation*, trans. G. W. Bromiley (Edinburgh: T&T Clark, 1958), 840 (hereafter CD IV/2).

53. For this topic, see CD IV/2:64.2, 3; also see Kim, "Sanctification and Self-Cultivation," 125-38.

Christ is both *vere Deus* (truly God) and *vere homo* (truly human). *Vere homo* refers to God's complete assumption of humanity. This *humanitas Christi* is the foundation of Christian anthropology. Christology, "the particular knowledge of the man Jesus Christ," offers the basis for understanding theological anthropology, including sin and the human condition (CD IV/2:27).

Sanctification conceived in the context of the exaltation of the humanity of Christ does not mean destruction or an alteration of humanity. The doctrine of *humanitas Christi* is related to election, incarnation, and resurrection and ascension, a theology of glory grounded in a theology of the cross. Since the humanity of Christ, both the electing God and the elected humanity, is the root-paradigm of God's gracious election, it is the root-paradigm of sanctification. The incarnation (*assumptio carnis*) of Jesus, God's becoming and being of human existence in totality, signifies ultimately the exaltation of human essence to divine essence. The resurrection and ascension are an inseparable, revelatory, and historical event in which the risen Christ manifests himself as the ultimate foundation of sanctification.

Barth's understanding of *humanitas Christi* entails the threefold concrete-universal act of God. First, *humanitas Christi* was the concrete-universal manifestation of God's election of the human race. Second, the incarnation of the Triune God in the particular person Jesus was the historical, and thus the most concrete, fulfillment of God's salvific love for the human race. Third, the event of resurrection and ascension of the particular humanity of Jesus has opened once and for all the ontological basis for the redemption of humankind and thus has established the universal foundation for the exaltation of the human race. Through the humanity of Christ in these events of election, incarnation, and resurrection and ascension, God has accomplished God's gracious will to humanity as God's covenant partner. Hence, the humanity of Christ is the revelation of God's most concrete-universal way of including humanity in his intratrinitarian history that established the ontological space of human sanctification. *Humanitas Christi* is God's revelation for the most concrete-universal paradigm of humanity.

Royal Man Christology: The most concrete-universal humanity was manifested in the life-act of the royal man Jesus (traditionally, the kingly office). The royal man Jesus, as both the root-paradigm of radical humanity and a mode of God's being, exhibits a revolutionary attitude "in a preferential option for the poor" against the exploitative established order. His life-act is the history of the Word in unity with deed (the unity of speech and act), which was dramatically expressed in his miracle stories. The life-act of the royal man Jesus reveals the paradigm of the unity of being and becoming, knowing and acting, and theology and ethics par excellence.

The cross of Jesus, the final negativity, paradoxically, constitutes all-embracing positivities, the resurrection. The cross, the most concrete point of the Christian faith, opens the new aeon of universal actualities. This dangerous memory of the Crucified, the most concrete point of the Christian faith, points to the inseparable, dangerous memory of the resurrection of the Crucified, the most universal point of the Christian faith.

Imago Dei: *The Christian Paradigm of Humanity*

The mature Barth gave up his early claim in his commentary on Romans that God is everything, and humanity is nothing.[54] The living God becomes the dialogical and ontological partner of humans in God's "sovereign togetherness" with humanity; God's deity with "the character of humanity" includes our humanity.[55]

In the doctrine of creation, Barth formulated the paradigm of humanity as (1) real human being in relation to God (vertical), (2) humanity in relation to others (horizontal), and (3) the whole person in relation to self (selfhood).[56] First, analogous to Jesus

---

54. Karl Barth, *The Epistle to the Romans*, 6th ed., trans. Edwyn C. Hoskyns (London: Oxford University Press, 1933).

55. See Karl Barth, *The Humanity of God*, trans. John Newton Thomas and Thomas Wieser (Atlanta: John Knox, 1960), 45-46.

56. See Karl Barth, *Church Dogmatics*, vol. III, pt. II, *The Doctrine of Creation*, trans. Harold Knight et al. (Edinburgh: T&T Clark, 1960), hereafter CD III/2.

Christ, who is from, to, and with God, a real human being is defined as a person with Jesus in the hearing of the Word of God, as a historical being in gratitude, and as subjectivity in pure spontaneity to the grace of God. Second, since Jesus is a human being with and for other human beings, a person is the cosmic being that exists absolutely with and for its fellow beings. In the paradigm of Jesus, humanity (*Menschlichkeit*) means a joyful co-humanity (*Mitmenschlichkeit*). This image of God, fulfilled in the *humanitas Christi*, signifies humanity as co-humanity, being-in-encounter, life-in-fellowship, or history-in-partnership. Humanity, as the image of God, analogous to intertrinitarian coexistence, coinherence, and reciprocity, means a plurality as being-in-togetherness or a being-with-others. Third, Jesus Christ is the paradigm of the whole person in the unity of soul and body. The human nature of the whole person is constituted by an interconnected unity of creaturely life (soul) and creaturely being (body).

4. The Direction (Weisung) of the Holy Spirit[57]

Barth conceived the direction of the Son as the basis of sanctification. The exaltation of Jesus as the royal man is its objective basis. Since the history of Jesus includes the history of all humanity, there is an ontological connection between the being of Jesus and all other beings (expressed in the Johannine writings in terms of abiding). Since this ontological reality that is the basis of the power of our conversion and our freedom is concealed, we need to recognize this ontological dignity to be and become radically and really human. Being and becoming a Christian is based on the operative power of transition from Jesus to us. This transitional power of being and becoming has characteristics of light, liberation, knowledge, peace, and life.

The New Testament testifies that this power is the work of the Holy Spirit. The Holy Spirit authenticates and sanctifies human

---

57. See CD IV/2, sections 64.4, 66; also Kim, "Sanctification and Self-Cultivation," 158-82.

beings as really human, and to be really Christian means to be radically human. The Three decisive historical factors are (1) the royal man is the controlling center; (2) the community is the goal; and (3) the power of transition links the royal man and the community. The Holy Spirit effects the transition from Jesus to human beings in the distinctive history of the Trinity that is history as partnership (God is never solitary but always has a partner). The history between the Father and the Son culminates in the concrete history of the Holy Spirit. The Holy Spirit is the basis of the riddle of the servant and the royal man Jesus in the dialectic between humiliation and exaltation. The dialectic is not a paradox, but the *doxa* (glory) of God in the trinitarian life, entailing the powerful Yes of resurrection over the No of the cross. The Holy Spirit calls forth our response of thankfulness and brings us real joy, underscoring the theologies of resurrection and glory. The Holy Spirit also gives direction (*Weisung*) with its twofold meaning, wisdom and way. *Weisung*, very similar to the Confucian notion of dao, directs, corrects, and instructs us to a concrete and sapiential way (on the march, not static) to becoming radically human.

Further, sanctification is realized in the relationship between the Holy One and the saints. Often, *de facto* we have not grasped our transformation (sanctification and conversion) that *de jure* has been realized in the Holy One. Sanctification *de jure* has come to humanity as an *a priori*, as the ontological connection with the Holy One. It is achieved *de facto*, however, by our participation in the body of Christ. A Christian is defined as a disturbed sinner by this *Weisung* of the Holy One. By a critical but totally free direction, sanctification entails discipleship, conversion, works, and the cross.

The commanding summons of Jesus to "follow me" binds persons to the One in practice, which demands simple obedience in response to the irruption of God's coming kingdom. Christian discipleship in the reign of God requires our resolute renunciation of possessions, honor or fame, fixed ideas, family, and the absoluteness of religion. Conversion means an awakening of human involvement in totality and a movement in faith in the opposite direction, to new humanity (renovation). New humanity, however, is still present with old humanity (*simul iustus et peccator*). Thus, like a falling out or a quarrel, conversion still finds the human existence in a twofold movement. It also entails social relationship with others. Conversion is a public matter, as a public person acts in the totality of his or her being. Sanctification also entails works in mutuality (God's praise of our works and our praise of God's works). We do good works in correspondence to God's good works and participate in God's works as His coworkers. Finally, the cross, as the limit and goal of our sanctification, reveals the most concrete form of fellowship between Christ and Christians. It involves persecution, sharing in tension, and temptations. However, it implies neither self-sought sufferings nor the end of our life, but our sanctification. The cross is penultimate and provisional, for its real goal is to bring human beings joy in the eschatological hope of the coming kingdom of eternal life.

Agapē, *Christian Love*[58]

Barth understood Christian love as a total human self-giving, in correspondence with faith as the reception of the total self-giving of God. *Agapē*, self-giving love, is the way and the act, distinguished from self-love (*eros*). Although both *agapē* and *eros* are related to human nature, *agapē*-love is in correspondence with real human nature, while *eros*-love is in contradiction. Vertically, *agapē* fulfills and transcends real human being in proper relationship with God, but *eros* falls short of it. Horizontally, *agapē* affirms and realizes radical humanity, but *eros* betrays or denies humanity (as cohumanity). Only through self-giving love (*agapē*) can we liberate ourselves from the vicious circle of destructive self-love (*eros*).

The foundation of Christian love (*agapē*) is faith in the self-giving love of God. Our love is a free action, but as a secondary love, responding to a primary love. God, who is love, forms the ultimate

---

58. For this topic, see CD IV/2:68; also Kim, "Sanctification and Self-Cultivation," 183-203.

basis of love in his triune mode of being. Divine love, as the external work of God (*opus Dei ad extra*) as well as the basis of human love, is an electing, purifying, and creative love.

Although it is exclusively grounded in the love of God in the trinitarian mode of being, our own action of love is equally significant. The act of love is new, free, sacrificial, and joyful. It is not merely a prolongation of divine love but a fully human act in return. This act of love has a twofold content: the love of God and Jesus (the first commandment) and the love of neighbors (the second commandment). First of all, Christians are those who love God and Jesus in the freedom of obedience to the command of Jesus: "You shall love the Lord your God with all your heart, with all your soul, and with all your mind, and with all your strength" (Mark 12:30). This vertical love of God is not a theonomistic conception but involves a real human act in continual subjection to the command. Second and equally, Christian love is the love of others, according to the other command of Jesus: "You shall love your neighbor as yourself" (Mark 12:31). This second commandment is as indispensable as the first. This commandment implies not an abstract universal love of humanity but a differentiated love in shared praxis. Thus, proximity is an important factor for its concrete realization. It always begins with specific fellow people in the context of salvation history. Neighbor, in the biblical sense, means a reciprocal witness on the horizontal plane.

There is no revelation of love without a gracious interrelating among people. Although, in the final analysis, the emphasis on particularity is practical and provisional, the circle of mutual love must be widened to universal extension. Therefore, Barth's conception of horizontal Christian love is congruent with the Confucian notion of the concrete-universal approach. Finally, Christian love is the culminating manner of Christian life. Love is not merely an effluence of God's own life but a real and concrete human act. Love, as the greatest among the manners of Christian life (faith, love, and hope), alone counts, alone conquers, and alone endures. In the last sentence of the *Church Dogmatics* IV/2, Barth said that "*agapē* is *the* Way" (IV/2:840).

4. Chéng *and* Agapē: *Thick Resemblances within Radical Differences*

A Confucian Turn by Barth

Barth's focal shift from the commanding position of God to the commanded position of humanity (sanctification) through the reversal of gospel and law resonates with the Confucian focal turn to the ethico-religious practice (propriety) of self-cultivation from cosmological postulations. Barth's doctrine of God's universal election coincides with the Confucian understanding of humanity as a heavenly endowment. Despite their different predications, obviously from their different perspectives, both Barth and Confucianism suggest a high ontology of humanity. Whereas humans' ontological possibility for self-transcendence is perceived as a heavenly endowment from the Confucian perspective from the below, it is conceived of as an elected being from Barth's Christian perspective from the above.

From this vantage point, Barth's theology shows intriguing similarities to Confucianism. Particularly with Wang's confuciology, Barth's theology presents thick resemblances. Both Wang and Barth challenged the established interpretive paradigms and made crucial paradigm changes, revolutionizing their traditions. Their paradigm changes share two converging goals: (1) maintaining a unified foundation of faith, guarding against dualism; and (2) dynamically opening up the possibility of human involvement in the process of realization. Wang's identification of mind-and-heart with principle (心卽理; *xīn jí lǐ* [*hsin chi li*]) is a radical plea for a return to the Mencian tradition that established the authentic foundation of Confucian persuasion in the mind-and-heart, correcting Chu Hsi's excessive emphasis on principle (格物; *gé wù* [*ko-wu*]). Barth's reversal of gospel and law establishes the unity of the two modes of the Word of God, overcoming the dualism of Luther's doctrine of God and the narrowness of his theological anthropology.

Whereas Wang thematized his doctrine of the unity of knowing and acting from the primordial nondualism in the structure of mind-and-heart (立志), Barth developed his doctrine of the unity of theology and ethics from the doctrine of election as the sum of the gospel (faith). Both of them held a positive vision of an ultimately transcendent reality (immanent-transcendence in Confucianism, grace Christian terms). Generally, while theology thematizes explicitly, placing this vision to the forefront (focusing on justification), confuciology brackets it off, placing it in the background (focusing on self-cultivation). Both Wang and Barth, however, lessened these differences. Wang constructed a dynamic confuciology of self-cultivation, further developing the Zhōngyōng-ian vision of Heavenly embodiment into human nature (*liáng zhī*). Barth brought the doctrine of sanctification to the forefront, thematizing the Christian vision of God's gracious election of the human race.

Both Wang and Barth affirmed the ontological unity of the human being. Both emphasize the unity of the inner and the outer dimensions of the whole person, the self-determined being. Both agree that true humanity embraces the unity of knowing and acting (in the Confucian sense) or hearing and doing (in the Christian sense), between ontological knowledge and ethical practice or between orthodoxy and orthopraxis. The unity so conceived constitutes both Wang's confuciology and Barth's theology to produce a most dynamic, radical social hermeneutics in their traditions. For both Wang and Barth, radical humanization does not mean merely individual piety but a collective process as teamwork of community (communal acts) with serious sociopolitical involvements.

The Root-Paradigm: Liáng zhī *and* humanitas Christi

Liáng zhī (the innate knowledge of the good), the foundation for self-cultivation, constitutes the center of Wang's confuciology. Likewise, *humanitas Christi* (the humanity of Christ), the foundation of sanctification, constitutes the center of Barth's theology. Both *liáng zhī* and the humanity of Christ refer to radical humanity—full, real, authentic, and true human subjectivity—the root-paradigm for radical humanization. These two central notions of Wang and Barth provided salient points of convergence and divergence.

Points of convergence include the following: (1) Both Wang and Barth took these root-paradigms as the hermeneutical principle for understanding their texts and traditions. Whereas Wang's confuciology is *liáng zhī*–centered, Barth's theology is Christ-centered. (2) Christ also can be understood as an innate knowledge of the good (*liáng zhī*) for Christians in relation to sin and evil. The knowledge of Christ reveals specificities of sin, just as *liáng zhī* illuminates those of evil. (3) Wang and Barth congruently affirm the inseparability of ontological knowledge and ethical practice. While *liáng zhī* manifests the proto-paradigm of the unity of knowing and acting, the life-act of Christ reveals the historical paradigm par excellence of the unity of logos and ethos, theory and praxis, and theology and ethics. (4) Both *liáng zhī* and the life-act of Christ manifest the most concrete-universal. Jesus Christ, the true God and the true humanity, is the most concrete-universal of the Christian faith. *Liáng zhī*, the immanent-transcendence of the Heavenly Dao in the human mind-and-heart is the most concrete-universal of the Confucian faith. (5) Both *liáng zhī* and the humanity of Christ as the most concrete-universal are self-transcendent, life-giving human subjectivity (true self).

Points of divergence include the following: (1) Whereas *liáng zhī* is based on the anthropocosmic vision of immanent-transcendence, the humanity of Christ is founded on a faith in the gracious election of God and salvation history.[59] (2) While Wang thematized *liáng zhī* as the immanent-transcendence of the Heavenly Principle in the human mind-and-heart, Barth articulated the humanity of Christ as the historical and personal incarnation of the divine *logos*. (3) Whereas *liáng zhī* is viewed as inner sage or incarnate wisdom endowed in every person's mind-and-heart, Jesus of Nazareth, a historical person, is comprehended as the assumption of the flesh (*assumptio carnis*) of the Triune God and Christ, the messianic figure. Wang focused on immanent potentiality, while Barth emphasized historical revelation. If *liáng zhī* is an *immanent-transcendence*, Christ is a *historico-transcendence*. (4) Whereas confuciology primarily focuses on ontological identification (e.g., the unity of all things), theology concentrates relatively on existential

---

59. The election of God through salvation history also has a dimension of immanent-transcendence. However, it is basically grounded in radical transcendence and focuses on its historical immanence.

differentiation (e.g., the problem of evil). (5) Thus, confuciology is strong in its all-embracing, anthropocosmic-sapiential articulation and relatively weak in dealing with the historical-existential problems of the human predicament, suffering, and death: theology is strong in dealing with existential-historical problems, while falling easily into an exclusivism, fundamentalism, or historical anthropocentrism.

The Paradigm of Humanity as Co-Humanity: Rén *and* Imago Dei

Liáng zhī and the humanity of Christ can be divided into two dimensions: vertical (transcendental) and horizontal (human-to-human). Vertically, they are divergent (roughly, immanent-transcendence versus historico-transcendence). Horizontally, however, they are congruent. The Confucian notion of *rén* and Barth's understanding of the image of God show remarkably a substantial point of convergence. Whereas the cardinal Confucian virtue, *rén*, is grasped as benevolent co-humanity, Barth understood *imago Dei*—the paradigm of humanity—as joyful *Mitmenschlichkeit*. Hence, both Barth and Confucianism arrived at the same conclusion that the ontological paradigm of humanity is benevolent or joyful co-humanity, being-with-others, or being-in-togetherness. They alike claim that humanity (*rén* or *Menschlichkeit*) means co-humanity (*rén* or *Mitmenschlichkeit*). Wang and Barth held a congruent understanding of what it means to be human: to be human means to realize a radical being-in-togetherness in one's totality in the unity of body and soul. Bracketing off the vertical dimensions, they are congruent: being a Confucian or a Christian means being radically human, which in turn means being co-human. This congruence constitutes a concrete, material point of convergence beyond their structural resemblances.

However, their divergent emphases of the root-paradigm—immanence and historicality—also affect their further formulations. Whereas Wang extended the notion of togetherness to the cosmic dimension, Barth focused on the meaning of co-humanity within the historical dimension. In this encounter, on the one hand, the Christian historical consciousness would challenge Neo-Confucianism to move beyond an innocent dream of anthropocosmic vision. On the other hand, the Neo-Confucian understanding of human being as a cosmic being-in-togetherness would be a corrective to evoke theology to move beyond its captivity of anthropocentric understanding of historical process, which, some say, is responsible for the present ecological crisis.

Zhì liáng zhī *and the Direction* (Weisung) *of the Holy Spirit*

Wang and Barth articulated a similar method of radical humanization. Both self-cultivation and sanctification point to radical humanization according to their root-paradigms, *liáng zhī* and Jesus Christ. Both Wang and Barth viewed these root-paradigms as radical subjectivity generating the spiritual power of our being and becoming radically, really, and fully human. Both agree that self-cultivation and sanctification are an enactment of radical subjectivity beyond the existentially dysfunctional state. Their foci, however, diverge. Whereas confuciology primarily looks into the human mind-and-heart, theology focuses on the sinful structure of human condition. While Wang emphasized the capacity of human effort through the sincerity of the will (immanent, internal power), Barth focused on the transforming power of the Holy Spirit (transcendent, external power). Hence, while Wang consummated the insights of self-cultivation in the precept of the "extension" of *liáng zhī*, Barth articulated sanctification as a participation in Christ under the direction of the Holy Spirit.

Nevertheless, Barth's insight of the direction (*Weisung*) of the Holy Spirit resonates with the Confucian notion of dao (the Way). Fingarette explained the dao:

> Thus there is no *genuine* option: either one follows the Way or one fails. To take any other "route" than the Way is not a genuine road but a failure through weakness to follow *the* route. Neither the doctrine nor the imagery allows for choice, if we mean by choice a selection, by virtue of the agent's powers, of one out of several equally real options. . . .

Put in more general terms, the task is conceived of not as a choice but as the attempt to characterize some object right or not. The moral task is to make a proper classification, to locate an act within the scheme of *li* (propriety).[60]

Likewise, Barth said,

He [the Holy Spirit] does not, therefore, make us an offer or give us a chance . . . [but] places us at once at a very definite point of departure, in a very definite freedom. . . . The Holy Spirit does not create the ghosts of a man [human being] standing in decision, but the reality of man [human being] concerning whom decision has already been made. . . . (CD IV/2:840)

Further, the *Weisung* does not put us "at a point or in a position" but sets us "on the way, on the march" (CD IV/2:376). This metaphorical language for a dynamic action in progress or process rather than a static status echoes an ideograph of the Chinese character dao that symbolizes a movement, process, or action. The Chinese word *dao* is an outstanding linguistic rendition of what Barth had in mind when he plays with the German word *Weisung*, which has a twofold meaning, way and wisdom. Dao designates precisely such a sapiential way of life to be and become really, radically, fully human. Furthermore, the Way—dao or *Weisung*—in both traditions refers primarily to orthopraxis, salient in the notions of Confucian propriety and Christian discipleship. We see here a good case that a Confucian notion illuminates theological material.

Chéng *(Confucian Sincerity) and* Agapē *(Christian Love)*

While *rén* is the cardinal virtue of the Confucian dao, *agapē* is the cardinal virtue of the Christian *Weisung*. Since *rén,* however, is a Confucian notion more related to human nature, it is more comparable to the Christian notion of *imago Dei*. *Agapē* refers to an existential fulfillment of the image of God in theology. In confuciology, *chéng* (sincerity) involves an existential effort to realize the

---

60. Fingarette, *Confucius*, 21-22.

transcendent humanity (*rén* or *liáng zhī* for Wang). If a Christian disturbed sinner is called a *loving* "hearer and doer" of the message of grace, a Confucian profound person is a *sincere* "digger" in the anthropocosmic vision. Hence, a comparison of *agapē* (Christian love) and *chéng* (Confucian sincerity) uncovers salient features of their differences and similarities.

Chéng and *agapē* are based on different perspectives. Whereas *chéng* is based on the Confucian all-embracing anthropocosmic vision, *agapē* is rooted in the divine–human covenantal relationship in the context of salvation history. While *chéng* focuses on an ontological dimension of humanity (as a self-realizing and self-transforming agent for cosmic equilibrium and harmony), *agapē* refers primarily to an existential dimension of humanity (as a self-giving and reconciling agent beyond the human predicament of alienation and separation). Hence, whereas *chéng* as the Confucian dao is more ontological (sincerity), *agapē* as the Christian dao is more existential (loving).

Nevertheless, both *chéng* and *agapē* refer to a realization of ontological reality into existential totality, or, in other words, a transformation of existential ambiguity by the ontological reality. *Agapē* converges with *chéng* in the claim of the inseparability of ontological knowledge and ethical action. *Chéng* and *agapē* congruently point to transcendent human subjectivity in the unity of being in becoming. Furthermore, similar to Confucianism, Barth advocated a concrete-universal approach for the horizontal execution of *agapē*. According to Barth, Christian love (*agapē*) does not refer to the abstract notion of undifferentiated, universal love but entails a concrete-universal realization of co-humanity through ever-expanding human relatedness, namely, through the channels of neighbors in salvation history.

5. Toward Christodao: A Confucian Christology

In this normative-constructive stage, the focus is shifted to East Asian churches in the world, Christian communities in the historic collision of the two spiritual traditions. These communities need a holistic grasp of the Christian faith in their given cultural-linguistic matrix (Confucianism) beyond the dialogue. This need inevitably forces us to focus on univocities between theology and confuciology. The main task of this univocative moment, rather, lies in an *a posteriori* articulation of the normative Christian faith for a community in a historic collision and/or fusion of two hermeneutical horizons, the two powerful stories of radical humanization. Primarily, hence, the normative-constructive enterprise refers not to an arbitrary deliberation of speculative comparison but to an imperative thematization of these Christian communities for the holistic understanding of their faith. Nevertheless, its theological implication will not be limited merely to these communities. A Christian constructive theology of Confucianism so conceived can make profound contributions to the world Christian communities as a whole by enhancing and improving theological categories and understandings.

The points of convergence between confuciology and theology discussed here may constitute feasible points of departure to thematize a Christian constructive theology of Confucianism. The center of Christian faith is Jesus Christ. I turn now to the question of how East Asian Christians can better understand the meaning of Jesus Christ in the Confucian-Christian context. Jesus Christ is without doubt the root-paradigm of humanity. If an East Asian Christian finds the unity of *rén* and *imago Dei* and of *chéng* and *agapē* in Jesus Christ, then thick resemblances between Confucianism and Christianity will be substantiated in a form of Christology. If an East Asian Christian apprehends Jesus Christ as the paradigm of the ultimately sincere humanity (sage) who has authenticated, once and for all, the Confucian faith in humanity's intrinsic possibility of self-transcendence, then the Confucian story enriches and illuminates the story of Jesus Christ. In Jesus Christ, a Confucian-Christian experiences the two stories of radical humanization encountered, collided, and fused with each other. From this vantage point, I will suggest five ways to understand the reality and meaning of Jesus Christ: (1) Christ as the Dao, (2) Christ as the sage, (3) Christ as the *chéng* par excellence (the most concrete-universal), (4) Christ as the unity of *rén* and *agapē*, and (5) Christ as the *liáng zhī*.

Jesus Christ as the Dao

First of all, the term "the dao (the Way) of Jesus Christ" is preferable to the term "Christology." Jesus called himself as the Way (dao [John 14:6]). The Greek *hodos* (the Way, also meaning path, road, route, journey, march, etc.) was an original name of Christianity (see Acts 9:2; 19:9; 22:4; 24:14, 22). Jürgen Moltmann was correct to avoid the term and instead use the title *The Way of Jesus Christ* in his book on Christology.[61] He explained that the metaphor of the way "embodies the aspect of process," "makes us aware that every human christology is historically conditioned and limited" and involves "an invitation" to follow "christopraxis."[62] He further said, "I am trying to think of Christ no longer statically, as one person in two natures or as a historical personality. I am trying to grasp him dynamically, in the forward movement of God's history with the world."[63]

If Christ is conceived of as the dao, the Confucian insight of dao can clarify and enrich even further than Moltmann's. Borrowing Fingarette's phrases, Jesus Christ as the Dao means "the right Way of life, the Way of governing, the ideal Way of human existence, the Way of the cosmos, the generative-normative Way (pattern, path, course) of existence as such."[64] The life-act of Jesus signifies the culmination of propriety (*li*) according to a self-directing orthopraxis of dao that Moltmann appropriately called christopraxis.

The parallelism between dao and Barth's notion of the *Weisung* of the Holy Spirit further illuminates the sapiential character of the self-directing dao. The freedom of Christian discipleship in the christopraxis and the outpouring power of the Holy Spirit converge with the freedom of propriety (*li*), which means not a choice among alternatives but a capacity to take part freely in the orthopraxis of the dao.

---

61. Jürgen Moltmann, *The Way of Jesus Christ: Christology in Messianic Dimensions*, trans. Magaret Kohl (San Francisco: Harper, 1990).
62. Ibid., xiv.
63. Ibid., xv.
64. Ibid., 19.

Jesus Christ as the Sage (Sage Christology)

To attain the freedom of the dao, Confucianism advocates mindfulness (*jìng*) and sincerity (*chéng*). In the humanity of Christ, the royal humanity, a Confucian-Christian finds a perfection of both mindfulness and sincerity. The humanity of Christ is the ultimate human existence that attained once and for all the attention and purification of the mind-and-heart in its fullest capacity of awareness. Jesus Christ, as both the true God and the true humanity, realized and maintained the ultimate human existence in the complete unity with Heaven. Jesus Christ is, in every aspect, the perfecter of sincerity. His works were not intentional deliberations but effortless, natural executions (*wú wéi*) of the dao, as they ought to be. Further, a Christian profound person finds Jesus as the absolutely sincere person, the true sage, who manifested the very definition of humanness as a self-transforming and self-realizing agent. Furthermore, a Christian sincere person apprehends Jesus Christ as the Sage-King who has fulfilled the complete normalization of humanity, fully restored its original goodness, and perfected the goal of self-cultivation, "Sageliness Within, Kingliness Without (內聖外王)."

Jesus Christ as the Chéng Par Excellence
(the Most Concrete-Universal)

In Christ the Sage-King, a Confucian-Christian sees that the concrete-universal way of the dao is extended to the fullest horizons. The Confucian story of benevolent humanity collides and is fused with the Christian story of the gracious God. The anthropocosmic drama is further substantiated and retold in an anthropo-theistic theater. Now, a Christian profound person grasps Jesus Christ as both the concrete-universal authentification of humanity in the anthropocosmic vision and the concrete-universal embodiment of the Triune God in the human history. The humanity of Christ is the concrete-universal action of God's gracious election for the human race. The incarnation of the Triune God in the particular person Jesus is the historical, and thus the most concrete, manifestation of God's salvific love for the human race. The most concrete point of the Christian faith is the dangerous memory of the Crucified One, while its most universal point is the dangerous memory of the risen Christ.

The life-act of Jesus the Sage-King, as the single foundation of Christian theology and ethics, radically manifested the unity of ontological knowledge and ethical action. It is the history of a Word in unity with deeds, as the proto-paradigm of "human being as the doer of the Word." In his life-act, there is no distinction between logos and ethos, or speaking and action. Such a unity of word and deed resembles the etymological connotation of the Chinese character, *chéng*.[65] In the life-act of Jesus the Sage-King, a Christian sincere person perceives the historical manifestation of the *chéng*-sincering par excellence. In the miracles of Christ, the person finds examples of the process of divine-human sincering in the cosmic history. In the event of his crucifixion and resurrection, the person discovers a consummation of the concrete-universal drama of divine-human sincering in the history of the Trinity with the world. Hence, sincerity in a Confucian-Christian sense means a faith in Jesus Christ.

Jesus Christ as the Paradigm of Humanity in the Unity of Chéng and Agapē

Jesus Christ is a human being with and for other human beings. His life-act was the full manifestation of *imago Dei*, meaning co-humanity, being-in-togetherness, being-in-encounter, life and history-in-partnership. A Confucian-Christian fascinates with the remarkable parallelism in the notions of *image Dei* and *rén*. A Christian profound person discovers the root-paradigm of humanity (*rén*) in the humanity of Christ as the image of God. A Christian sincere person is challenged by Christ as the perfecter of *agapē*, a radically affirmative attitude of love through a self-giving, an action consummated on the cross. However, the Christian attitude

---

65. The Chinese character *chéng* consists of two graphs that mean word (or speech) and accomplishment (action); etymologically, it denotes sincere actualization of one's word. Hence, I also translate *chéng* in the gerund form "sincering" to emphasize its dynamic and active dimension.

of self-giving *agapē*-love is also challenged by the Confucian attitude of self-critical reciprocity. An excessive attitude of Christian love without a necessary self-reflection and humility entices an epistemological immodesty and an ethical hubris.[66]

Moreover, traditional Western theologies tend to remain under the captivity of the anthropocentric interpretation of history. Grounding the unity of *chéng* and *agapē* in the humanity of Christ, a Confucian Christology can recover the epistemological humility and ethical modesty and overcome anthropocentrism by ecological and cosmic implications of the anthropocosmic vision. Christ the Sage is envisioned as the root-paradigm of humanity as a cosmic reconciled being-in-togetherness. The Confucian model of reciprocity and mutuality in the anthropocosmic interaction fosters the liberation of humanity and nature from the Western models of domination and exploitation.[67]

Jesus Christ as the Ultimate Embodiment of Liáng zhī

Finally, a Confucian-Christian grasps that Jesus Christ, the divine-human *chéng*-sincering par excellence, is the historical and personal incarnation of immanent-transcendence in the human mind-and-heart. Manifesting the unity of *chéng* and *agapē*, Jesus Christ is the ultimate embodiment of the innate knowledge of the good (*liáng zhī*). Jesus Christ fully reveals the pure and good knowing that not only naturally discerns good and evil but also radically uncovers specificities of sin and evil and the misery of the human condition.

Further, a Christian profound person perceives that Jesus Christ as the root-paradigm of radical humanization is the historical consummation of *zhì liáng zhī*, the omega point of the extension of the *liáng zhī*. In Jesus Christ, the true God and the true humanity, the ontological connection of Heaven, humanity, and all things has been fully reestablished, and human subjectivity has been completely identified with the ontological reality (*Tiān lǐ*).

---

66. See Allison, "Ethics of Confucianism," 168.
67. See Tu, *Centrality and Commonality*, 102–7.

In a Confucian Christology, hence, the two concrete-universal stories of *chéng* and *agapē* are fully encountered. A Confucian Christology elicits the two encountered stories to move beyond dialogue and to be transformed into a new holistic story of inclusive human being, profound human subjectivity, the novel paradigm of radical humanity (radicalizing and theologizing the Confucian axiom "Sageliness Within, Kingliness Without") in a new context, the eschatologically anthropocosmic vision in the new aeon (toward *Christodao* and *theodao*).

CHAPTER SIX

Imago Dei *and* Tiān mìng: *John Calvin Meets Yi T'oegye*

Korean Christianity is distinctive in the fact that, among tradition-ally Confucian societies, Korea is both the most Christianized (at least in population) and the most Confucianized (at least in form) country. Hence, a Confucian–Christian dialogue is crucial for Korean society and constitutive of doing Korean Christian theol-ogy for the twenty-first century. A dialogue between the teachings of Yi T'oegye (1501–1570)[1] and John Calvin (1509–1564) is par-ticularly significant in this context, because their legacies have had the most far-reaching influences in the Korean formation of Confu-cianism and Christianity.

On the one hand, Korean Neo-Confucianism was firmly estab-lished by T'oegye, and his school of the Way (道學) played decisive roles in the trajectory of Korean Confucianism. On the other hand, Presbyterianism (or the Reformed tradition), founded by Calvin, has flourished exceptionally ever since it was introduced into this

---

Adapted from my article *"Imago Dei and T'ien-ming*: John Calvin and Yi T'oegye on Humanity," originally published in *Ching Feng* 41, nos. 3-4 (1998): 275-308. It was reprinted in *Christ & the Tao* (Hong Kong: Christian Conference of Asia, 2003), 89-120.

1. This is the honorific name of Yi Hwang (李滉), but he has been more widely known as T'oegye (退溪). For a brief introduction to his life, see Michael C. Kalton, "Introduction," in Yi Hwang, *To Become a Sage: The Ten Diagrams on Sage Learning by Yi T'oegye*, trans. Michael C. Kalton, Neo-Confucian Studies (New York: Columbia University Press, 1988), 14-28 (hereafter *Diagrams*).

country. The Korean Presbyterian Church has been not only the largest in total membership but also culturally and socially the most active among all the Christian denominations in Korea. Within the history of a little more than a century, furthermore, it has grown to be the largest in membership among all the Reformed churches in the world, even surpassing the size of the American Presbyterian churches, which made a major contribution to planting the church in Korea. In Korea, the Reformed tradition has achieved a miracle, perhaps the most successful mission in its entire history.[2]

Calvin and T'oegye, two contemporaneous figures of the sixteenth century, lived in two radically different worlds, namely, Christendom and Confucianism. Nevertheless, their lives and thoughts present remarkable similarities that, I think, illuminate some important clues for the great success of Presbyterianism in Korea. Interestingly, both of these figures wrote seminal treatises to crystallize their traditions: Calvin's *Institutes of the Christian Religion* (1559)[3] and T'oegye's *Ten Diagrams of Sage Learning* (1568).[4] Moreover, both of these writings were originally written to explain the essences of their religions to their kings. Calvin wrote the *Institutes* to defend his religion to Francis I; T'oegye drew the *Ten Diagrams* to educate Sŏnjo.

Christianity and Confucianism originated from two radically different religious visions, which I call "theohistorical" (salvation his-

---

2. In fact, Korean people are not unfamiliar with this sort of massive religious structuring. In the Chosŏn Dynasty (1392–1910), Neo-Confucianism had permeated society in an even more systematic and pervasive way so that it had built Chosŏn culturally and socially as the most Confucianized society in the history of East Asia. See Tu Wei-ming, *Confucianism in an Historical Perspective*, Occasional Paper and Monograph Series 15 (Singapore: Institute of East Asian Philosophies, 1989), 35; and James H. Grayson, "The Study of Korean Religions & Their Role in Inter-Religious Dialogue," *Inculturation* 3, no. 4 (1988): 8.

3. John Calvin, *Institutes of the Christian Religion*, ed. John T. McNeill, trans. Ford Lewis Battles, 2 vols., Library of Christian Classics 20, 21 (Philadelphia: Westminster, 1960) (hereafter *Inst.*).

4. *Sŏnghak Sipdo* (聖學十圖). For an excellent English translation, see *Diagrams*.

tory) and "anthropocosmic" (the unity of humanity and cosmos).[5]
Since the two paradigms have divergent foci (roughly, theism and
humanism), their *a priori* dimensions such as the Christian God
and the Confucian Heaven are not adequate starting points for a
genuine dialogue. Rather, since Christianity and Confucianism
meet each other in the common issue of humanity ("the common
quest for the *Tao* of full humanity"), humanity is a more legitimate
point of departure for a practical and productive dialogue.[6]

The Confucian–Christian dialogue I formulated previously
between Wang Yang-ming and Karl Barth demonstrates thick
resemblances between Confucianism and Christianity on the issue
of humanization—how to be fully human—despite their radical
differences.[7] This Confucian–Christian dialogue I am now suggesting between Calvin and T'oegye also presents striking resemblances, even thicker than those between Wang and Barth. In what
follows, I will juxtapose some of the "similarities-in-differences"
that I find striking in a dialogue between Calvin and T'oegye on
the theme of humanity.[8]

1. *Original Humanity:* Imago Dei *and* Tiān mìng [T'ien-ming] (天命)

Calvin and T'oegye both believe that human beings are relational
to and inseparably intertwined with the transcendent grounds of
being (namely, God and Heaven). Hence, their anthropologies are

---

5. See Heup Young Kim, *Wang Yang-ming and Karl Barth: A Confucian–
Christian Dialogue* (Lanham, MD: University Press of America, 1996), 176.

6. Ibid., 138-39.

7. Ibid., 175-78.

8. Interestingly, T'oegye not only knew but also emphasized the use of
the comparative method of the "sameness-in-difference" or the "difference-
in-sameness," in his famous Four-Seven Debates with Ki Taesŭng. T'oegye
said, "Approaching what is unified one must recognize differentiation, and
approaching what is differentiated one must see the unity" (*T'oegye chŏnsŏ*
[The Complete Works of T'oegye] [Seoul: Songgyungwan Taehakkyo, 1985],
A, 16.10b; hereafter TGCS). See also Sasoon Yun, *Critical Issues in Neo-
Confucian Thought: The Philosophy of Yi T'oegye*, trans Michael C. Kalton
(Seoul: Korea University Press, 1990), 44.

basically relational and transcendental. The Christian doctrine of *Imago Dei* (the image of God) and the Neo-Confucian concept of *Tiān mìng* (Heavenly endowment) reveal saliently this characteristic of a relational and transcendental anthropology. Calvin and T'oegye both define humanity as a mirror or a microcosm to image and reflect the glory and the goodness of the transcendent ground of being. Moreover, they are remarkably similar in understanding attributes of the goodness endowed in original humanity. Calvin described these attributes as wisdom, virtue, justice, and holiness: in short, integrity and rectitude. T'oegye expressed the attributes of the original nature as benevolence (*rén* 仁), righteousness (*yì* 義), propriety (*lǐ* 禮), and wisdom (*zhī* 智): in short, sincerity (*chéng* 誠) and principle (*li* 理). If the idiosyncratic differences between God and Heaven are bracketed, the understandings of Calvin and T'oegye on ontological humanity seem to be almost interchangeable.

Relational Anthropology

The knowledge of humanity and the knowledge of God are the two basic themes of Christian theology. In fact, Calvin was very explicit in asserting that anthropology is as important as theology.[9] The *Institutes* is written not only for the true doctrine of God but also for the true doctrine of humanity as the subject of faith. Brian Gerrish said well, "Nothing less than the whole of the *Institutes* is required to set out his doctrine of man,[10] just as the work *as a whole* presents his doctrine of God."[11] In Calvin's theology, hence, anthro-

---

9. In the very beginning of the *Institutes*, Calvin stated, "Nearly all the wisdom we possess, that is to say, true and sound wisdom, consists of two parts: the knowledge of God and of ourselves. But, while joined by many bonds, which one precedes and brings forth the other is not easy to discern" (*Inst.* 1.1.1 [35]). See the important book of T. F. Torrance, *Calvin's Doctrine of Man* (London: Lutterworth, 1949).

10. I fully recognize the importance of using inclusive language. For citation, nevertheless, I will follow the texts as they are.

11. Brian Gerrish, "The Mirror of God's Goodness: A Key Metaphor in Calvin's View of Man," in *Readings in Calvin's Theology,* ed. Donald K. McKim (Grand Rapids: Baker Book House, 1984), 108.

pology and theology are relational, "inseparably intertwined," and "mutually condition each other."[12]

The Confucian understanding of humanity is also closely related to Heaven. It is not too much to say that, in the confuciology of T'oegye, the relationship of Heaven and humanity is more important than that of *li* (principle) and *ki* [*qì*] (氣; material force), a subject for which T'oegye is famous. In fact, the Four-Seven Debates, "the most celebrated and important controversy in Korean Neo-Confucian history,"[13] began with T'oegye's revision of the *Diagram of Heavenly Endowment* drawn by Chŏng Chi-un (1509–1561), which defines humanity as a being that illuminates and reveals Heaven (Heavenly endowment). T'oegye's understanding of humans' intimate relationship with Heaven is not so much mechanistic or metaphysical as personal, using the metaphor of a wider family.[14] This familial relationship is well expressed in the *Western Inscription* of Chang Tsai (1020–1077): "Heaven is my father and Earth is my mother." Because of this significance, T'oegye included this *Western Inscription* as the second diagram in his *Ten Diagrams*.[15]

Imago Dei *and* Tiān mìng

Just as Genesis states that the first two human beings were created in the image of God (Gen. 1:27), *The Doctrine of the Mean* says, "What Heaven imparts [*Tiān mìng*] to man is called human nature."[16] Just as the doctrine of *imago Dei* is the center of Calvin's theological anthropology, the teaching of *Tiān mìng* is the heart of T'oegye's Neo-Confucian anthropology. Both doctrines state very explicitly that humanity is relational to and inseparably intertwined with its transcendent ontological ground.

---

12. Benjamin A. Reist, *A Reading of Calvin's Institutes* (Louisville: Westminster John Knox, 1991), 9; Gerrish, "Mirror of God's Goodness," 108.

13. *Diagrams*, 23.

14. Keum Chang-tae, *T'oegyeŭi sarmgoa cholhak* [The life and Philosophy of T'oegye] (Seoul: Seoul National University Press, 1998), 136.

15. *Diagrams*, 50.

16. *A Source Book in Chinese Philosophy*, trans. Wing-tsit Chan (Princeton, NJ: Princeton University Press, 1963), 98.

In the confuciology of T'oegye, the *Diagram of Tiān mìng* refers to an epistemological process of knowing the origin of creation through created human beings and natural things (i.e., a perspective from below), while the *Diagram of T'aegŭk [Tài jí] (the Great Ultimate;* 太極) explains the metaphysical process of creation from the origin (i.e., from above).[17] Similarly, the theology of Calvin also has a twofold structure; the doctrine of *imago Dei* is certainly a perspective from below, if the doctrine of the Triune God is a perspective from above.

Calvin called the *imago Dei* "a heavenly image" or "celestial image," a precise translation of *Tiān mìng*. He favored using the metaphor of a mirror, a reflection, to explain the image of God.[18] While the whole of creation is a theater that vindicates the glorious work of God, the human being is "distinguished from the mute creation by his ability to reflect God's glory in a conscious response of thankfulness" like the brightest mirror.[19] According to the *Diagram of Tiān mìng*, likewise, while the myriad things in the cosmos are made of *Tiān mìng*, human being is the only species that illuminates and discloses the goodness of Heaven in a sufficient purity and transparency like a brilliant mirror.[20]

Further, Calvin and T'oegye are strikingly similar in their understanding of original humanity. Just as original humanity (性; *xìng* [*hsing*]), a Heavenly endowment, was perfect, the image of God implanted in original humanity implies "the perfection of our whole nature . . . as appeared when Adam was endued with a right judgment, had affections in harmony with reason, had all his sense sound and well regulated, and truly excelled in everything good."[21] Calvin called this perfect condition of humanity *integrity*: "The integrity with which Adam was endowed is expressed by this word [*imago*] . . . truly referred his excellence

17. Keum, *T'oegye*, 130.

18. See Gerrish, "Mirror of God's Goodness," 107-22.

19. Ibid., 114.

20. See Keum, *T'oegye*, 123, 127.

21. John Calvin, *Commentaries on the first book of Moses: called Genesis,* trans. John King (Grand Rapids: Eerdmans, 1948), 94-95 (1:26).

to exceptional gifts bestowed upon him by his Maker."[22] T'oegye called this perfect condition sincerity, which includes four "constant characteristics of the *Tao* of Heaven": origination, flourishing, benefiting, and firmness (元亨利貞; *yuán hēng lì zhēn* [*yüan, heng, li, chen*]).[23]

Calvin also called the original order of humanity "rectitude" (*rectitudo*). The image of God contains not only external goodness (*bonum adventium*) but also internal goodness (*bonum interim*): "The likeness must be within, in himself. It must be something which is not external to him, but is properly the internal good of the soul."[24] Calvin described the characteristics of this internal goodness as "wisdom, virtue, justice, and holiness."[25] The school of *Hsing-li*, to which T'oegye faithfully attached himself, identifies original humanity (*xìng*) with principle (*lì*). Since Heavenly endowment is identified with *lì*, humanity is viewed in unity with Heaven through the same *lì*. Corresponding to the four constant characteristics of the Dao of Heaven, Neo-Confucianism designates four attributes of original humanity as benevolence (*rén*), righteousness (*yì*), propriety (*lǐ*), and wisdom (*zhì*). These four beginnings strikingly resonate with Calvin's characterizations of the internal goodness of original humanity: wisdom, virtue, justice, and holiness.

Furthermore, for Calvin, the creation of both Adam and Eve according to the image of God means that the human being is basically a "social animal"[26] and that humans are created to "cultivate mutual society between themselves."[27] The etymological meaning of *rén* is co-humanity (two humans). Hence, long before Karl Barth, Calvin already accepted fully the Confucian equation that the root-paradigm of humanity is co-humanity, or being-in-togetherness.[28]

---

22. *Inst.* 1.15.3 (1:188).

23. See the third and seventh diagrams (*Diagrams*, 66-69; 143-49); also Keum, *T'oegye*, 131.

24. *Inst.* 1.15.4.

25. *Inst.* 2.1.5; 3.3.9; 3.18.1; 3.20.42.

26. Calvin, *Comm. on Gen.* 2:18; 2:21-22; *Inst.* 2.2.13; 2.8.39; 3.7.6.

27. Calvin, *Comm. on Gen.* 2:18; also see Torrance, *Calvin's Doctrine of Man*, 43.

28. See Kim, *Wang Yang-ming and Karl Barth*, 43-46, 86-90, 158-60.

Confucius said that reciprocity (*shù*) is a consistent principle of Confucianism. Calvin also underscored that the *imago*-relation implies especially the "sacred bond and mutual reciprocity" that a person has with God, fellow human beings, and natural things.

For Calvin, moreover, the "express image of God" is Christ, the Son of God who faithfully obeyed the Father until the crucifixion on the cross. Calvin regarded filial piety as "the subject basis of the image."[29] Hence, not only in Confucianism but also in Calvin's theology, the paradigm of humanity is described as a filial relation of the Son to the Father in Heaven through the story of the Trinity.

Calvin advocated that, by the *imago*-relation, a person could participate in the order of God. To be truly human refers to recovering the whole humanity (integrity) and original order (rectitude). Calvin said, after all, "regeneration is nothing else than the restoration of the same image."[30] Likewise, T'oegye affirmed that, by the endowment-relation, a person could participate in the principle of Heaven. To be fully human means recovering the whole human nature (*chéng*) and the original cosmic pattern (*li*). Except for the idiosyncratic differences between God and Heaven, the teachings of Calvin and T'oegye on original humanity seem to be strikingly similar and almost interchangeable.

2. Existential Humanity: The Fallen Nature and the Human Mind

Calvin and T'oegye are similar in perceiving the mind-and-heart (*xīn*) as the primary locus of original humanity. They agreed that the mind-and-heart in reality, however, is so ambivalent and vulnerable that it functions ambiguously against its original goodness. Accordingly, both of them made a distinction between original humanity with the original goodness (ontological humanity) and actual humanity in ambiguity and ambivalence (existential humanity). In theology, it is expressed as a sharp distinction between original humanity first created by God and actual humanity after the Fall.

---

29. Torrance, *Calvin's Doctrine of Man*, 77.
30. Calvin, *Comm. on Gen.* 1:26.

In confuciology, it is indicated as a dichotomy between the mind of Dao (道心; *Dào xīn*) and the human mind (人心; *rén xīn*). Consequently, how to recover and restore the original goodness immanent in ontological humanity beyond the ambivalent and dualistic nature of existential humanity becomes the primary subject matter for both of them. This primary project of humanization, that is, a learning how to restore true and full humanity, is expressed in the doctrines of sanctification and self-cultivation (sage learning), respectively.[31] It is true that Calvin defended the doctrine of original sin and rigorously scrutinized the negative reality of corrupted humanity, whereas T'oegye carefully investigated the phenomenon of mind-and-heart. If we look deeper into their thoughts, however, we can find that the differences in their analyses of human reality are not so thick but subtle. As T. F. Torrance pointed out correctly, the doctrines of original sin and total depravity should not be understood independently but as corollaries to the doctrines of grace and Christology. T'oegye's view of human mind-and-heart is not so romantic; he experienced four bloody purges of Confucian literati, in one of which his beloved brother was killed. Moreover, Calvin and T'oegye converge in a comprehension of humanity's existential ambiguities as arising from a distortion and perversion of original goodness, rejecting the ontological status of evil.

Ambivalent about the Human Condition

Calvin did not make a radical dichotomy between mind (soul) and heart (body). Rational portraits of modern Calvinism are excessive and incorrect from the vantage point of the historical Calvin.[32] Calvin said, "the chief seat of the divine image is in his mind and heart where it was eminent."[33] He seems to be very much in agreement

---

31. For T'oegye, self-cultivation as the prime learning of Confucianism can be attained through the learning of the Way, which is also called sage learning.

32. See the important biography of Calvin by William J. Bouwsma, *John Calvin: A Sixteenth Century Portrait* (New York: Oxford University Press, 1988).

33. Calvin, *Comm. on Gen.* 1:26.

with Confucianism in a belief that the *locus* of a human's transcendental relationship lies not in the mind (reason) alone, differentiated from the body, but in the mind-and-heart, a psychosomatic totality. The mind-and-heart (*xīn*) is a unique East Asian notion that transcends the body-and-soul dualism. T'oegye is famous for his insightful analysis of the nature and phenomenon of the mind-and-heart (see *Diagrams* 6-8).

Calvin described twofold knowledge of humanity corresponding to the twofold knowledge of God as Creator and Redeemer. In the *Institutes*, he first treated what original humanity was like when created (*Inst.* 1.15), and then what the human condition looks like since the Fall (*Inst.* 2.1-5). Gerrish summarized: "The existence of man in the design of God is defined by thankfulness, the correlate of God's goodness; the existence of man in sin is defined by pride or self-love, the antithesis of God's goodness."[34] Deeply conscious of the dualistic nature of ontological humanity and existential humanity, Calvin rigorously investigated the depth and complexity of the human psyche long before Sigmund Freud. Calvin's famous doctrine of depravity was formulated to explain such an ambivalent human condition, while remedying the problem of theodicy.

Calvin's discussion of humanity continued in the sections on Christology (the perfect humanity) and Christian life, on which he spent many more pages. Since the restoration of humanity "has dogmatic precedence even over the doctrine of the original state,"[35] it is not too much to say that humanization (sanctification) is the main agenda for Calvin's anthropology.

T'oegye perceived that the mind-and-heart as the master of the self is the nucleus of humanity, and the problematique of the mind-and-heart was the central issue of T'oegye's thought. Although he did not, like Calvin, speak of the doctrine of depravity, as a person who experienced four bloody literati purges, T'oegye fully recognized the ambivalent vulnerability of the human mind-and-heart

---

34. Gerrish, "Mirror of God's Goodness," 108.
35. Ibid.

in reality.[36] To explain this ambiguity, he developed further subtle Neo-Confucian distinctions between the mind of Dao and the human mind, before it is aroused and after it has been aroused, between principle (*li*) and material force (*ki* [*qì*]), and between original humanity (*xìng*) and feelings (*qíng*).

In the unity with the body, the mind-and-heart functions freely in the universe with no limitation of time and space. However, this capacity before it is aroused can be disturbed after it has been aroused. The substance (*tǐ*) of the mind-and-heart before aroused is called original humanity, and its function (*yòng*) after aroused is recognized as feelings.[37] The title of his *Diagram 6* is "The mind-and-heart unites *li* and *ki*, and governs nature and feelings." The subtleties of their distinction and the nuance of their balance are the basic issue in his famous Four-Seven Debates with Ki Taesŭng (1529–1592).

The Fallen Nature and the Human Mind

As Torrance argued, Calvin's doctrine of human depravity was composed not for a dogmatic purpose but for a didactic purpose in the context of the doctrine of grace. "Calvin's doctrine of the fall of man and sin is a corollary of the doctrine of grace in forgiveness and salvation."[38] Later Calvinist theologies, however, unfortunately turned Calvin's didactic devices into dogmatic procedure and produced the doctrine of the fall and of human depravity without the context of grace. Interpreting grace as God's answer to human depravity is in fact an insult to the Creator. Torrance said:

> In actual fact, he [Calvin] refused to advance any doctrine of man, apart from God's original intention of grace in creating in the image of God, and apart from God's supreme act of grace in Jesus Christ for our salvation. Within these two

---

36. See Kalton, "Introduction,"in *Diagrams*, 9-19. In 1550, T'oegye's brother Yi Hae died from the severity of a beating he received.

37. For the terminology of *t'i-yung* (*ch'e-yong*), see *Diagrams*, 211-12.

38. Torrance, *Calvin's Doctrine of Man*, 19.

brackets, and only within these two brackets, does Calvin give us an account of man's fallen nature and his sin. Never does he attempt to give a philosophical account of man's depravity.[39]

When Calvin said that a human being is completely despoiled of the spiritual image, it does not mean that the gifts naturally endowed are polluted or destroyed ontologically. "Sin does not mean an ontological break with God, for Calvin does not hold a doctrine of evil as the privation of being." Even after the Fall, a human being is still a rational creature with a mind and a will that can reflect the image of God. Although we are utterly deprived of God's glory in rectitude, righteousness, and love, our natural gifts still remain. Although grievously impaired, we can see God's workmanship in our mind-and-heart that reflects God's image and distinguishes between good and evil. In the mind-and-heart, there still remains "a spark of knowledge," "a portion of light," or "a seed of religion."[40]

Calvin's doctrine of justification by faith alone also does not deny the existence of natural goodness in fallen humanity. But the righteousness with which sinners are clothed is not their own but is of Christ Himself, "the very image of God." "The more he presumes upon the relic of the *imago Dei* within him, the deeper he gets into the abyss of darkness and corruption and death. If the light that is in him is darkness, how great is that darkness!"[41]

Torrance emphasized repeatedly that Calvin's doctrine of total perversity must be interpreted in the context of his doctrine of the dynamic relation of human and God. "Total perversity thus means that man's personal being, grounded by grace in a continuous relation with the living God, has been perverted into an existence in which he is continually turned away from God, so that all that he does in the exercise of his God-given gifts is against God."[42] Hence, the human being has lost all rectitude (the divine order in creation) and is governed by a perverted order (*Inst.* 1.15.7). The

---

39. Ibid., 20.
40. Ibid., 83, 101.
41. Ibid., 105.
42. Ibid., 106.

whole order of creation has been perverted as a consequence of the Fall of humanity.

Sin cannot destroy the image of God but can pervert the whole (*Inst.* 1.15.1; 2.1.9). "The total perversion of the mind or the reason means that the whole inclination of the mind is in the direction of alienation from God."[43] Calvin called the perverse motion in the mind *concupiscence*,[44] that is, the "wantonness and prurience of the human mind" (2.12.5). He also described concupiscence as "the violent lawless movements which war with the order of God," as "a perpetual disorder and excess apparent in all our actions," or as an "inordinate desire" (3.3.12). According to Torrance, "*concupiscentia* is diametrically opposed to the *imago Dei* which reflects the order of God in creation. It is through this *unorderly dealing* that the creation is perverted, and God's glory diminished."[45] Concupiscence resonates with selfish desires, a Neo-Confucian notion "diametrically opposed" to *Tiān mìng*, which will be explained later.

T'oegye viewed feelings as the function that issues from the substance of original humanity in the mind-and-heart.[46] Since the mind-and-heart is also a unity of *li* and *ki*, the issued feelings are of two kinds. The one that exposes purely the *li* of original humanity is called the four beginnings, namely, commiseration, modesty and deference, shame and dislike, and approving and disapproving. The other, in which the *li* of original humanity is perturbed by the physical disposition, is called the seven feelings, namely, joy, anger, grief, fear, love, hate, and desire.

After the series of debates with Ki Taesŭng, T'oegye changed his position to conclude that the four beginnings are what *li* issues and *ki* follows, whereas the seven feelings are what *ki* issues and *li* rides on it.[47] In other words, *li* issues primarily in the four beginnings,

---

43. Ibid., 116.

44. See *Inst.* 2.1.8; 3.3.11, 12.

45. Torrance, *Calvin's Doctrine of Man*, 124 n. 1.

46. For this view, T'oegye used the *Diagram of Ch'eng Lin-yin* (1279–1368). See *Diagrams* 6-a.

47. See *Diagrams* 6-c.

while *ki* does principally in the seven feelings. This demarcation is precisely to discern and establish a boundary line with the possibility of evil by the concrete grasp of the foundation of goodness.

T'oegye suggested the substance and function of the mind-and-heart in terms of the empty and spiritual and the knowing and perceiving. The empty and spiritual signifies the numinous capacity of knowing and perceiving when the mind-and-heart is empty by the invisible *li*. The empty and spiritual substance of the mind-and-heart appears as the knowing and perceiving (*Diagram 6-b*). He defined the spiritual and intelligence (神明) as a totality that unites the substance and function of the human mind-and-heart (*Diagram 8*). The spiritual and intelligence of the mind-and-heart is basically the same as those of Heaven, and the mind-and-heart possesses the spiritual and intelligence of Heaven.

Based on the *Diagram of the Mind-and-Heart of Ch'eng Lin-yin*,[48] T'oegye further classified six kinds of the mind-and-heart, namely, the original mind, the naturally good mind, the mind of the infant, the mind of the great person, the mind of Dao, and the human mind. The naturally good mind is the "goodness endowed from Heaven." The original mind is the "originally inborn goodness." The mind of the infant is pure and has no falsehood. But the mind of the great person is not only pure and has no falsehood but also is conversant with all kinds of circumstances. In contrast to the naïve mind of the infant baby, the mind of the great person reveals the mature and accomplished mind of the sage. This distinction entrenches the need of self-cultivation.

The polarity of the human mind and the mind of Dao is especially important. It uncovers the original source of the mind-and-heart and entails the foundation of human morality and the practice of self-cultivation. Whereas the human mind issues from the form of material force, the mind of Dao is based on the natural endowment,

---

48. Ch'eng said, "The 'mind of the infant' is the 'naturally good mind' before it has been disturbed by human desires; the 'human mind' is the mind that has been awakened to desire. The 'mind of the great man' is the 'original mind' which is perfectly endowed with moral principle; the 'mind of the Tao' is the mind that has been awakened to moral principle"(*Diagrams*, 160).

though they are mutually interrelated rather than clearly divided.[49] While the human mind consists in the impartiality of one's body, the mind of Dao reveals the commandment of Heaven. The former can be united with the latter only after a hearing of the commandment of the latter. Nevertheless, since sages also possess the human mind, we must distinguish between the human mind before falling into evil and human desires that reveal the state of evil.[50]

T'oegye delineated the phenomenon of good and evil arising with the issuance of the mind-and-heart in terms of *li* and *ki*. "That which *li* exposes and *ki* adjusts accordingly is good: that which *li* is hid by the hindrance of *ki* is evil."[51] On the one hand, the good arises when *li* becomes predominant in the mind-and-heart and *ki* adjusts itself obediently. On the other hand, the evil arises when *ki* becomes predominant and *li* is concealed by the blocking of *ki*. *Li* as the source of good is a pure goodness, whereas *ki* as the source of evil is a condition in which good and evil divide. *Li* refers to the standard for human living, that is, the Heavenly principle that was endowed in original humanity and still is immanent in the mind-and-heart. *Ki* implies the physical disposition, a basis in which human mind and body consist. A person actualizes the good when the Heavenly principle is disclosed brilliantly in one's being beyond the physical disposition, whereas one falls into evil when the Heavenly principle is concealed by the physical disposition. Hence, T'oegye's doctrines of *li* and *ki* do not refer essentially to a system of metaphysical speculation but signify a moral principle of self-cultivation to preserve and disclose the Heavenly principle and to restrain human desires beyond the physical disposition.

In the *Explanation of the Diagram of Tiān mìng*, T'oegye said, "The will makes the mind-and-heart arise, embraces and impels the feeling to the left or to the right, or to follow the justice of the Heavenly principle, or to the partiality of human desires. The distinction of good and evil is made from this. This implies the so called 'the

---

49. TGCS, 39.24.
50. TGCS, 40.9.
51. TGCS, 25.20.

incipient wellsprings divide good and evil.'"[52] The division of good and evil appears more vividly in the will, issuing spontaneously from the mind-and-heart, than in the feeling, issuing responsively. The good is an innate thing, because it originates from the pure goodness of nature, whereas evil is a secondary thing arising by the blocking of the physical disposition. T'oegye denied the actuality of evil, following Cheng-i's definition that evil is "what surpasses or is unattainable."[53]

The division of good and evil involves the subtlest beginning of issuance, that is, the incipient wellsprings. A distinction of good and evil and a choice of good should be made from the point when the willing and the knowing begin to arise. The division of good and evil, however, does not denote such an opposition as *yin* and *yang*, which arise to divide from the Great Ultimate (*T'aegŭk*). Evil does not originate from original humanity and cannot be an ontological substance equal to the good. According to T'oegye, evil is not an ontological being but an existential thing that arises from the disturbance of the physical disposition. Therefore, T'oegye and Calvin are same in a perception that evil is not an innate or original being.

3. The Restoration of Original Humanity: Sanctification and Self-Cultivation

For both Calvin and T'oegye, reverence (*pietas* and *kyŏng*) is the central concept that permeates their thoughts. For T'oegye, without doubt, *kyŏng* is the cardinal concept of self-cultivation that involves a personal and corresponding relationship with the Lord of Heaven (*Shàng dì*). For Calvin, *pietas* is "the shorthand symbol for his whole understanding and practice of Christian faith and life."[54] For both of these thinkers, reverence includes both fear

---

52. TGCS, 8.18.
53. TGCS, 37.34.
54. Ford Lewis Battles, "True Piety According to Calvin," in McKim, *Readings in Calvin's Theology*, 192.

and love (*mysterium tremendum et fascinans*) toward the ultimate ground of being and has a doctrinal precedence to knowledge (*doctrina* and *li*). T'oegye's overarching methodology of sage learning is the "dwelling in the reverence and investigating the principle." It is not too much to say that, though the object of investigation is different, Calvin holds structurally the same methodology, as faith-seeking-understanding (*fides quaerens intellectum*) is the classical definition of theology. Whereas *li* is the object of investigation for T'oegye (confuciology), Jesus Christ (the Word) is the object of faith for Calvin (theology). Furthermore, they converge in a belief that these objects of investigation are also the transcendent grounds of being that enable us to attain radical humanity with original goodness. For *li* and Jesus Christ refer to the perfect manifestations of *Tiān mìng* and *imago Dei*. T'oegye also articulated this task in terms of the "re-embodying Heaven and progressing along the Way," whereas Calvin explained it as restoring the original image of God through the faith in Christ and walking under the direction of the Holy Spirit. They are similar in arguing for reverence as the inner means and righteousness as the outer means in order to achieve sanctification and self-cultivation. In a nutshell, sanctification is the realization of Christ (the perfect image of God) through hearing the Word (theology), and self-cultivation is the embodiment of *Tiān mìng* through investigating *li* (confuciology). If Christ (the Word) is identified with the principle (*li*), the structure of humanization in Calvin's theology and T'oegye's confuciology will be basically the same; both of them point to sage learning.

Calvin's Doctrine of Sanctification (Pietas)

Since the Christian gospel speaks of human salvation in total terms, Calvin claimed, the doctrine of human depravity must be stated also in total terms. This logic applies also to the doctrine of the *imago Dei*. The gospel tells us that we can be restored to a being in the image of God only by going outside of ourselves to Christ, who is "the expressed image of God." The revelation of grace inescapably infers that Christ (cf. *li*) is our righteousness (*yi*), wisdom (*zhī*), and *imago Dei* (*Tiān mìng*), whereas a fallen human being is quite bereft of the image of God.[55]

Knowing God and being in the image of God are closely interrelated. But we cannot use the image as a means of knowing God, because the image is only a reflex of the glory of God. We should not indulge in a speculative imagination to know God: "All knowledge of God, apart from His revelation, is a vast abyss that swallows up our thoughts in the thickest darkness. God is Himself the Author of all our knowledge of Him, while His Word is both the standard and the warrant of its Truth."[56] Calvin's emphasis on the Word signifies that "*all our knowledge of God is essentially analogical, i.e., through a revelation which accommodates itself to the humble capacity of the human mind.*" Nevertheless, "*The relation between God and the analogical element is not ontological but essentially sacramental.*"[57] These analogical and visible elements have validity only in relation to the Word and the Spirit to convey the Truth.[58] They are only symbols made to point beyond themselves.[59] Any remnant of light formerly possessed cannot serve "as a *predisposition* for faith or as an analogical point of contact for the true knowledge of God."[60] The only preparation a person can do is to deny and empty oneself "objectively through the Cross, subjectively in *metanoia*."[61]

Calvin affirmed the inseparability of the doctrines of justification and sanctification. They are a twofold fruit of the same faith:

> Why, then, are we justified by faith? Because by faith we grasp Christ's righteousness, by which alone we are reconciled to God. Yet you could not grasp this without at the same time grasping sanctification also. . . . Therefore Christ justifies

---

55. Torrance, *Calvin's Doctrine of Man*, 86.
56. Ibid., 128.
57. Ibid. Italics are original.
58. *Inst.* 4.14.5; 4.19.7.
59. *Inst.* 4.14.12; 4.19.7.
60. Torrance, *Calvin's Doctrine of Man*, 147.
61. Ibid., 129. See *Inst.* 3.7.1.ff.; 3.8.1ff.

no one whom he does not at the same time sanctify. These benefits are joined together by an everlasting and indissoluble bond, so that those whom he illumines by his wisdom, he redeems; those whom he redeems, he justifies; those whom he justifies, he sanctifies. (*Inst.* 3.16.1)

While justification is the external imputation of righteousness, sanctification is the inner process of continual struggle under the direction of the Holy Spirit toward the restoration of the *imago Dei.* The purpose of sanctification is the restoration of a lost order through the restoration of the image of God in us. The work of Christ is precisely for this restoration of us to the original rectitude (*lǐ*) by regenerating the image of God in Christ: "Christ is the most perfect image of God; if we are conformed to it, we are so restored that with true piety, righteousness, purity, and intelligence we bear God's image" (*Inst.* 1.15.4). Christians are no other than those who are elected and called to order and fulfill this harmonious structure of God's order through their participation.[62]

Calvin put a special emphasis on the term *pietas* (reverence or piety). *Pietas* is both "the predominant category of Calvin's spirituality" and "the shorthand symbol" for Calvin's whole understanding and practice of Christian faith and life.[63] Calvin attested that human beings are created for reverence. God has planted the awareness of divinity in our mind-and-heart and surrounded us with irresistible signs for the order of God. Reverence is "the attitude of a man being integrated within God's order: a pious person is one who has taken his place within God's order."[64]

In the *Institutes*, Calvin defined *pietas* as "reverence joined with the love of God which the knowledge of his benefits induces" (*Inst.* 1.2.1). Reverence is the root of love, and *pietas* takes a higher position than *caritas* (love), the cardinal Christian virtue. *Pietas* means

---

62. See "Christian Life" in *Inst.* 3; also Gerrish, "Mirror of God's Goodness," 108.

63. Lucian Joseph Richard, *The Spirituality of John Calvin* (Atlanta: John Knox, 1974), 114; Battles, "True Piety," 192.

64. Richard, *Spirituality of John Calvin*, 114.

the reverence of God (the first commandment), and *caritas* implies our just living among our neighbors (the second commandment). Calvin, like Confucians, believed that filial obedience is the foundation of reverence. The first step to reverence is none other than "to know that God is a father to us" (*Inst.* 2.6.4). "*Pietas* bespeaks the walk of us adopted children of God the Father, adopted brothers and sisters of Christ the Son."[65] Ford Lewis Battles put the interrelationship among the terms related to *pietas* in the following diagram.[66]

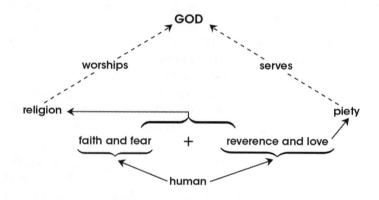

T'oegye's Teaching of Self-Cultivation
(敬; Kyŏng; Jìng [Ching])

The basic methodology of T'oegye's sage learning is "dwelling in the reverence" and "investigating the principle." These two methods consist of the two inseparable sides of one sage learning, mutually serving each other as "the outside and the inside" or as "the root and the branch." If investigating the principle refers to an epistemology of knowing (*zhī*), the dwelling in the reverence implies a doctrine of self-cultivation (*xíng*).

"Investigating the principle" is to know and perceive *li* in every-

---

65. Battles, "True Piety," 196.
66. Ibid., 193.

thing and every event in one's life. It means a realization of *li* that is immanent in things as their order and principle by the ability of knowing and perceiving, a function of the mind-and-heart. Since *li* is the substance of the mind-and-heart, we can know and perceive *li* latent in things: "*Li* and *ki* conjoin as the mind-and-heart, and it possesses as it were unfathomable emptiness and spirituality such that if things or affairs approach it is able to perceive them."[67]

The Great Learning suggests a specific method to investigate the principle of things, that is, the "investigation of things" and the "extension of knowledge." T'oegye explained that the investigation of things is a process of learning in which, investigating *li* in depth, the mind-and-heart grows to attain knowledge. Before the debates with Ki Taesŭng (1527–1572), T'oegye held an epistemological position that the function of knowing and perceiving in the mind-and-heart actively performs the investigation of the principle of things. After hearing Ki's argument that "*li* of itself approaches," however, he changed his position to accept that *li* manifests itself actively and that the mind-and-heart also waits passively for this approach of *li*.

T'oegye rejected Wang Yang-ming's doctrine of the unity of knowing and acting. Instinctive and sensual knowledge, based on physical nature, can be attained without effort. However, since moral knowledge is grounded in the principle of righteousness, it cannot be obtained without learning and practice. For this reason, T'oegye distinguished acting from knowing and proposed that knowing and acting mutually advance and reciprocally support each other "like two wheels or two wings."[68]

Kyŏng is the center of T'oegye's teaching of self-cultivation. In the *Ten Diagrams*, he said, "these ten diagrams all take mindfulness as essential."[69] *Kyŏng*, as the master of the mind-and-heart,

---

67. TGCS, A, 25.25b; trans. Yun Sasoon, *Critical Issues in Neo-Confucian Thought: The Philosophy of Yi T'oegye*, trans. Michael C. Kalton (Seoul: Korea University Press, 1990), 33.

68. TGCS, A, 21.25b; trans. from Yun, *Critical Issues*, 30.

69. *Diagrams*, 87. Kalton translated *kyŏng* (敬; *jìng* [*ching*]) as "mind-

is the nucleus by which the mind-and-heart is controlled and converged. In the "Diagram of the Study of the Mind-and-Heart," Cheng Fuxin explained (*Diagrams*, 8):

> In sum, the essence of applying one's effort is nothing other than a matter of not departing from constant mindfulness [*kyŏng*], for the mind is the master of the entire person and mindfulness is the master of the mind. If one who pursues learning will but thoroughly master what is meant by "focusing on one thing without departing from it," "becoming properly ordered and controlled, grave and quiet," and "recollecting the mind and making it always awake and alert," his practice will be utterly perfect and complete, and entering the condition of sagehood likewise will not be difficult.[70]

"Focusing on one thing without departing from it" bespeaks of the state when the mind-and-heart is so concentrated and attentive as to be fully mindful. The structure of *kyŏng* involves the correspondingly harmonious relations among action and tranquillity, substance and function, and in and out. When the mind-and-heart is not yet aroused (or in tranquillity), "grave and quiet" becomes the substance of *kyŏng*. When the mind-and-heart has been aroused (or in action), "becoming properly ordered and controlled" becomes the function of *kyŏng*.

For the practical method of *kyŏng*, T'oegye paid special attention to quiet sitting and combined the grave and quiet mind with a quiet posture of body. The learning of *kyŏng* cannot be achieved at one time. It begins from the state of self-conscious attempts of "recollecting the mind and making it always awake and alert" and arrives at the state of perfection where one freely identifies one's mind-and-heart with the principle of the *Dao*.[71]

---

fulness." For an explanation of the term *kyŏng*, see Kalton, "Appendix," in *Diagrams*, 212-14. However, I translate it as "reverence" to compare with Calvin's term *pietas*.

70. *Diagrams*, 162.

71. T'oegye said that in this state of perfection one can attain the "true news."

In the polarity of the mind of Dao and the human mind, T'oegye summed up the method of self-cultivation in terms of "blocking human desires and preserving Heavenly principle":

In general, although the study of the mind-and-heart is complex, one can sum up its essence as nothing other than blocking [self-centered] human desires and preserving the principle of Heaven, just these two and that is all. . . . All the matters that are involved in blocking human desires should be categorized on the side of the human mind, and all that pertain to preserving the principle of Heaven should be categorized on the side of the mind of the Tao.[72]

The purpose of *kyŏng* lies in attaining harmoniously corresponding relationships with other people and Heaven in the practice of everyday life. This learning leads us finally to obtain sagehood in the unity of Heaven and humanity, transcending the polarity of the mind of *Dao* and the human mind. T'oegye advised the king:

The practice of this kind of reverent fear and mindfulness is nothing extraordinary; it is simply part of everyday life, but it can bring about the "perfect equilibrium [of the mind before it is aroused] and perfect harmony [after it is aroused]," establish [heaven and earth] in their proper positions and accomplish the nurture [of all things]." Virtuous conduct is simply a matter of proper human relationships, but through it the wondrous unity of Heaven and man is attained.[73]

Sanctification and Self-Cultivation

Christianity and Confucianism are normally contrasted: Whereas theology is based on the infusion or the imputation of the external and transcendental substance (the divinity of Christ), confuciology focuses on the revitalization of the dynamic relation with the

---

72. *Diagrams*, 169.
73. *Diagrams*, 36.

internal and immanent source (*li*) through the practice of learning. To put it in their terms, whereas theology underscores justification (for salvation), confuciology focuses on self-cultivation (for sagehood).

The comparison of Calvin's theology and T'oegye's confuciology, however, discloses that such a simple distinction does not say the whole truth. On the contrary, the differences between Reform Christianity and Neo-Confucianism represented by Calvin and T'oegye are not so thick but thin and subtle. Although they use different terms, Calvin and T'oegye agree fully in recognition that the restoration of ontological humanity (*imago Dei* and *Tiān mìng*) requires both external and internal means.

Calvin articulated this in the doctrines of justification and sanctification. In his theology, justification refers to the external imputation of righteousness, and sanctification means the inner process of continual struggle under the direction of the Holy Spirit toward the restoration of the *imago Dei*. T'oegye's teaching of "dwelling in the reverence" and "investigating the principle" consists in a similar structure. In his confuciology, investigating the principle refers to an epistemology of knowing the principle, and dwelling in the reverence implies a practice toward the embodiment of original humanity (*xing*), that is, *Tiān mìng*. T'oegye also used other expressions such as "investigating the principle and perfecting the nature" and "re-embodying Heaven and progressing along the Way."[74] These expressions also resonate with Calvin's doctrines of justification and sanctification.

T'oegye's doctrine of "blocking human desires and preserving Heavenly principles" also has a thick resemblance with Calvin's doctrine of sanctification.[75] Calvin's doctrine of sanctification

---

74. *Diagrams*, 144; Keum, *T'oegye*, 141.

75. William Theodore De Bary characterized the teaching of "blocking human desires and preserving Heavenly principle" as a Neo-Confucian moral "rigorism" and differentiated it "from the more exclusively negative focus of western Puritanism" (*Diagrams*, 169; see also De Bary, *Neo-Confucian Orthodoxy and the Learning of the Mind-and-Heart*, Neo-Confucian Studies [New York: Columbia University Press, 1981], 67-185). This distinction

would be described in a comparable way, namely, blocking the sinful human desires in the power of the Holy Spirit and preserving the *imago Dei* restored by the faith in Jesus Christ. For Calvin, the whole purpose of sanctification is to restore a lost order through the restoration of the image of God in us. In fact, the work of Christ denotes nothing other than this restoration of the original rectitude (*li*) by the regeneration of the image of God in us.

Calvin and T'oegye are similar in delineating the corresponding relationship of reverence (*pietas* and *kyŏng*) and righteousness (justice and *i*). On the one hand, Calvin said, "Piety and justice express the two tables of the law; therefore of these two attitudes the wholeness of life is constituted."[76] For Calvin, reverence implies our basic relationship to God (the first commandment), while justice (love) does that for our fellow human beings (the second commandment). On the other hand, T'oegye said, "We must make the inside of the mind-and-heart upright by reverence and the outside straight by righteousness," while maintaining both reverence and righteousness.[77] For T'oegye, *kyŏng* refers to the inward disposition (tranquillity), and *i* to the outward (activity). Both Calvin and T'oegye further suggested expanding this outward relationship to nature (cosmos).

Both thinkers put a special emphasis on dwelling in reverence (*pietas* and *kyŏng*). Calvin took the doctrine of sanctification as seriously as Karl Barth, who called Calvin "a theologian

---

may be true in a comparison of Neo-Confucianism and Puritanism but not wholly true in a comparison of Calvin and T'oegye. The bipolar structure of this Neo-Confucian teaching does contain a positive side, whereas Puritanism is excessively concerned with sin and evil. As we have seen already, however, the theology of Calvin also consists in a bipolar structure of two inseparable doctrines of justification and sanctification. In fact, this emphasis on sanctification is a point at which Calvin's theology departs radically from Luther's theology.

76. Calvin, *Commentary on Luke* 2:25, cited from Richard, *Spirituality of John Calvin*, 117.

77. TGCS, 36.15.

of sanctification."[78] Likewise, T'oegye is called "a philosopher of *kyŏng.*" Moreover, the teachings of Calvin and T'oegye converge in the common quest of full humanity by the investigation of the original rectitude or principle. Their objects of investigation are radically different, that is, Jesus Christ (the Word) for Calvin and the Great Ultimate (*li*) for T'oegye. Their expressions for the ground of being (transcendental relationship) are also different, that is, God (*imago Dei*) and Heaven (*Tiān mìng*). Nevertheless, if these *a priori* dimensions are bracketed, Calvin's doctrine of sanctification entails basically the same mode as T'oegye's teaching of self-cultivation, dwelling in reverence and investigating the principle. As we have discussed already, furthermore, except for the idiosyncratic differences between God and Heaven, the teachings of Calvin and T'oegye on original humanity (*imago Dei* and *Tiān mìng*) are strikingly similar and almost interchangeable. Hence, it is not too much to say that Calvin's theology and T'oegye's confuciology show striking similarities within the radical differences of their axiomatic presuppositions. Calvin and T'oegye, who lived almost at the same period of history but in two radically different worlds, are extraordinarily comparable partners for dialogue.

4. *Ecological Vision of Reverence:* Pietas *Meets* Kyŏng

Calvin and T'oegye had a similar view of humans' relationship with nature. With the doctrines of the image of God and the Heavenly endowment, both of them denied the qualitative differences between humanity and nature. In the narrow definition, only humanity can function as the true mirror of their transcendental ground of being. In the wider definition, nevertheless, humans and things are equivalent to the common image of God and the common Heavenly endowed nature. T'oegye explained their differences in terms of "physical disposition." A human being consists of upright and transparent *ki*, whereas things are composed

---

78. Karl Barth, *Church Dogmatics,* vol. IV, pt. II, *The Doctrine of Reconciliation,* trans. G. W. Bromiley (Edinburgh: T&T Clark, 1958), 510-11; also Kim, *Wang Yang-ming and Karl Barth,* 76.

of concealed and opaque *qì.* Hence, the posture of human bodies is upright (toward Heaven), that of wild animals is horizontal (parallel to the Earth), and plants grow vertically in a reverse direction. Calvin also agreed that "the upright posture of the human body is at least an outward token of the divine image."[79] Finally, Calvin and T'oegye converge in a similar vision that the transcendent (God and Heaven), the human, and the cosmos are closely interrelated (in terms of the *imago Dei* and the *Tiān mìng).* From this vantage point, Calvin and T'oegye seem to agree in advocating a theanthropocosmic (the transcendent, human, and nature interrelated) vision. In this view, human beings are not so much vicious conquerors of the universe or the sole independent subjects of history in the linear cosmos as interdependent co-spectators to witness the glorious cosmic drama of God or ecological keepers to harmonize the wonderful trajectory of Heaven in the theanthropocosmic theater.

According to Calvin, there are no "qualitative differences" between human beings and natural things, because they are created in the same image of God. Hence, the wider definition of *imago Dei* includes not only human beings but also natural things. Since all creatures are the works of God, all things in the cosmos, small or large, possess the image of God, a capacity to reflect the glory of God. The narrow definition of *imago Dei,* however, comprises only human beings who can perform the true function of creatures like a clear mirror: "While the entire created order reflects God's glory as in a mirror and in this sense 'images' of God, man is distinguished from the mute creation by his ability to reflect God's glory in a conscious response of thankfulness."[80] This is related to the outward physical appearances among creatures. Calvin admittedly cited a phrase of Ovid's *Metamorphoses,* "while all other living things being bent over earthward, man has been given a face uplifted, bidden to gaze heavenward and to raise his countenance to the stars."[81]

---

79. Gerrish, "Mirror of God's Goodness," 113.
80. Ibid., 114.
81. Ovid, *Metamorphoses* I. 84ff.; Calvin cited in 1.15.3.

God's commandment to humanity for the "dominion over the earth" does not endorse the right of control and domination to abuse and exploit nature for our own benefits. On the contrary, it implies our obligation to take good care of the cosmos, as a steward of the wonderful garden of God. A person can exercise one's just dominion over the earth, only when "his dominion over the world becomes part of the way in which he as man images the glory of God."[82] Gerrish summarized well:

> Man's being points beyond him to the source of his existence and of the existence of all that is. He was fashioned as the point of creation at which the overflowing goodness of the Creator was to be "mirrored" or reflected back again in thankful reverence. This is the condition from which he fell, no longer the voice of God; and it is the condition to which, through hearing the Word of God in Jesus Christ, he is restored. For all Calvin's persuasion that man has a privileged standing in the world, his cosmos is not man-centered: man has his place as spectator and even agent of the manifestation of God's glory, in which alone the cosmos has its final meaning. It may well be that, when demythologized, such an austere view of the dignity and finitude of man takes no profounder relevance than Calvin ever dreamed of, as Western man moves out of the tight little world of the Middle Ages into the immense, mysterious cosmos of the modern astronomer.[83]

Battles also agreed with this point: "[Calvin] enunciated a principle of Christian stewardship of nature and of style of living that speaks of our present ecological crisis. Before the great technological advances of recent centuries, before the present age of extraterrestrial exploration, Calvin knew the planet Earth was what we today call a 'closed eco-system.'"[84] In the sixteenth century, Calvin already mentioned "peace, justice, and preservation of the creation": "Moreover, that this economy and this diligence, with

---

82. Torrance, *Calvin's Doctrine of Man*, 25.
83. Gerrish, "Mirror of God's Goodness," 122.
84. Battles, "True Piety," 203.

respect to those good things which God has given us to enjoy, may flourish among us; let everyone regard himself as the steward of God in all things which he possesses. Then he will neither conduct himself dissolutely, nor corrupt by abuse those things which God requires to be preserved."[85]

T'oegye included not only humanity but also nature and the cosmos in his revised *Diagram of Tiān mìng*. He also delineated that humanity and nature are made of the same *Tiān mìng*, an endowment from Heaven. In this Neo-Confucian cosmology, Heaven, humanity, and nature (cosmos) are closely interconnected through the same principle and original nature. But the differences between humanity and nature are not in quality but in function. They are different because they consist in different "physical dispositions." Whereas nature is composed of a concealed and opaque physical disposition, human beings are endowed with an upright and transparent physical disposition. Hence, only human beings possess a capacity of "knowing and perceiving" and morality.

The *Diagram of Tiān mìng* explains the postural differences among humans, animals, and plants. The posture of the human body is square and upright toward Heaven, because human beings possess a transparent and pure physical disposition. That of animals and beasts is horizontal and parallel to the Earth, because their capacity of "knowing and perceiving" is opened toward only one direction. But plants and trees grow vertically in a reverse direction, because their capacity of "knowing and perceiving" is completely blocked. Summarizing this as "humanity and things are similar in nature but different in material," Keum put this relationship in the following diagram.[86]

---

85. John Calvin, *Comm. on Gen.* 2:15, trans. John King, 2 vols. (Edinburgh: Calvin Translation Society, 1847–50), 1:125; cited from Battles, "True Piety," 203.

86. See Keum, *T'oegye*, 178.

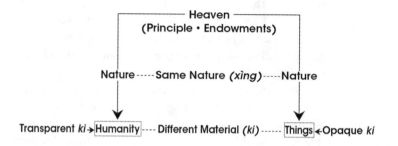

Of course, Calvin did not know the concept of *ki* and "physical disposition." However, if Heaven were identified with God, the principle and the endowment with Christ and the image, Calvin would have agreed with this diagram. After all, Calvin and T'oegye seem to have a similar vision of the relationships among the transcendent (Heaven or God), humanity, and the cosmos. Furthermore, unlike that in Chinese Neo-Confucianism, T'oegye's concept of Heaven includes a personal dimension, as he criticized the doctrine of mechanic correspondence of Heaven and humanity (Dong Zhongshu) but advocated the personal corresponding relationship between Heaven and humanity.[87] This personal corresponding relationship contains the way of faith and reverence for the Lord on High. Pushing one step further, Keum argued that T'oegye's concept of Heaven involves a bipolar expression of "reverence and fear" and "benevolence and love," analogous to Rudolf Otto's idea of the holy, *mysterium tremendum et fascinans*.[88] If the interpretations of Lee Sang-eun and Keum Jang-tae are accurate, T'oegye's concept of Heaven would have a notable affinity with the Christian notion of personal God.

The external and internal practices of *kyŏng*, "the single, consistent thread which runs through"[89] the life and thought of T'oegye,

87. See Lee Sang-eun, "Life and Scholarship of T'oegye," in *Lee Sang-eun sŏnsaeng chŏnjip* [The Complete Works of Master Lee Sang-eun: Korean Philosophy], vol. 2 (Seoul: Yemoonseowon, 1998), 135.

88. See Keum, *T'oegye*, 136. Cf. Battles's diagram, above.

89. *Diagrams*, 34.

points to its climax; that is to say, "Behave as if you were present before the Lord on High." After all, we need not be merely a contingent frame of reference but an absolute ground of being such as Heaven or God in order to maintain the mind-and-heart fully in respect of other people and genuinely in love of myriad things. We must realize the ultimate reality that we are present in front of the Lord on High (cf., *coram Deo*). The Neo-Confucian doctrines of *Tiān mìng*, the endowment from Heaven, and *Tiān lǐ* (*T'ien-li*), the Heavenly principle, already disclose this transcendent and ontological ground of original humanity.

At this point also, we find a common thread that connects the whole thinking of Calvin and T'oegye. We need the ultimate ground of all beings—whatever we name it, whether God or the Lord on High. The just and righteous relationship among all beings can be truly realized only when it is based on a proper relationship with this ultimate ground of being. Calvin and T'oegye called this attitude and effort to make the mind-and-heart in this proper relationship "reverence" (*pietas* or *kyŏng*). We must treat neighbors and nature in reverence and thanksgiving as much as we are facing God or the Lord on High. Reverence is not only the way toward God but also the way to establish a proper relationship with other people and natural things. Hence, Calvin and T'oegye placed a doctrinal precedence in the concept of reverence. This attitude of reverence has profound implications for us in today's ecological crisis. Summarizing T'oegye's ecological vision in terms of the reverence of Heaven, the benevolence of people, and the love of things, Keum placed their relations in the following diagram:[90]

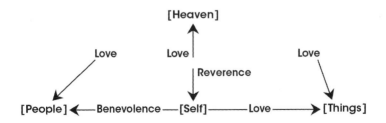

90. Keum, *T'oegye*, 184.

Finally, Calvin's doctrine of *imago Dei* (*pietas*) and T'oegye's teaching of *Tiān míng* (*kyŏng*) converge in a similar vision that the transcendent (God or Heaven), humanity, and the cosmos are closely interrelated. Calvin and T'oegye seem to agree in advocating a theanthropocosmic vision. "The Admonition for the Studio of Reverence," which T'oegye included as the ninth in his *Ten Diagrams* exhorts, "Select the ground and tread so carefully to turn around (not to step into) an anthill."[91] From this vantage point, human beings are not so much vicious conquerors of the universe or the sole independent subjects of history in the linear cosmos. But, according to Calvin and T'oegye, they are interdependent co-spectators to witness the glorious cosmic drama of God or ecological keepers to harmonize the wonderful trajectory of Heaven in this theanthropocosmic theater.

---

91. Cf. *Diagrams*, 178.

CHAPTER SEVEN

The Korean Face of Jesus Christ: Ryu Yŏng-mo's Christodao

Introduction

In chapter 3, I argued for *Christodao* rather than traditional *Christo-logy* or modern *Christo-praxis* as a more appropriate paradigm for the understanding of Jesus Christ in the new millennium. This christological paradigm shift solicits a radical change of its root-metaphor, from *logos* (Christ as the incarnate logos) or *praxis* (Christ as the praxis of God's reign) to *dao* (Christ as the embodiment of the Dao, the "theanthropocosmic" Way) with a critical new interpretation.[1] First of all, *Christo-logy* has been taken as the orthodox view but now becomes very problematic, and Christopraxis can serve as a necessary corrective but still within the limit of a dualistic end of the former.[2] Christodao utilizing

---

Adapted from Heup Young Kim, "The Word Made Flesh: Ryu Yŏungmo's Christotao: A Korean Perspective," in *One Gospel—Many Cultures: Case Studies and Reflections on Cross-Cultural Theology*, ed. Mercy Amba Oduyoye and Hendrik M. Vroom (Amsterdam: Rodopi, 2003), 129-48. Reprinted with permission. It was reprinted in *Word and Spirit: Renewing Christology and Pneumatology in a Globalizing World*, ed. Anslem K. Min and Christotoph Schwöbel, Theologische Bibliothek Töpelmann 158 (Boston: De Gruyter, 2014), 113-30.

1. As a composite adjective of *theos* (God), *anthropos* (humanity), and *cosmos* (universe), literally, *theanthropocosmic* refers to the interrelation of God, humanity, and the cosmos.

2. See Jürgen Moltmann, *The Way of Jesus Christ: Christology in Messianic Dimensions*, trans. Margaret Kohl (San Francisco: HarperSanFrancisco, 1990), 38-72.

the holistic metaphor of dao can overcome this vestige of Greek dualism remaining between Christology and Christopraxis. Furthermore, for East Asian Christians, the christological adoption of dao is as inevitable and legitimate as that of logos for the Western church in the fourth century.

I argued that, in fact, this adoption has been operative since the beginning of Korean Christianity. As an example, I introduced briefly the thoughts of Dasŏk Ryu Yŏng-mo (柳永模, 1890–1981).[3] Although unpopular, Ryu Yŏng-mo is a most innovative religious thinker in the history of Korea. He was a guru, a towering teacher of very important Korean Christian leaders of the last generation. His most famous disciple was Ham Sŏk-hŏn (咸錫憲, 1901–1989), who also became a guru of Korean minjung (people's) theology and movement.[4] Ryu's religious insights also deeply influenced significant intellectuals in other religious traditions in Korea such as Neo-Confucianism, Daoism, and Buddhism.

Ryu entered into the Christian faith as a Presbyterian at the age of fifteen (1905), though he later declared himself to be non-ortho-

---

3. Ryu's literary name is Dasŏk 多夕, which means, literally, "so many nights." This name symbolically shows his Daoist inclination (namely, night rather than day, vacuity rather than substance, non-being rather than being, and so on). The most important primary source for the study of Ryu's thought is the photocopies of the diaries that he wrote from 1956 to 1975, but they are very difficult even for Korean scholars to comprehend due to his recondite writing style and very innovative usage of Korean language: see *Dasŏk-ilji* 多夕日誌 [The Diaries of Dasŏk], 4 vols. (Seoul: Hongikje, 1990), here abbreviated DI. Fortunately, his faithful student Kim Heung-ho recently published a complete commentary, which has become a crucial aid for the study of Ryu: *Dasŏk-ilji Gong-bu* [The Study of Dasŏk's Diaries], 7 vols. (Seoul: Sol, 2001), here abbreviated KDI. There are two other important resources of Ryu's lecture notes that his students had dictated: See Park Young-ho, ed., *Dasŏk-ŏrok* 多夕語錄 [The Analects of Dasŏk]: *Ssial-ŭi-maeari* (Seoul: Hongikje, 1993), here abbreviated DU; and Kim Heung-ho, ed., *Jesori* [The Genuine Voice from the Self]: *The Sayings of the Honorable Ryu Yŏng-mo* (Seoul: Poongman, 1985), here abbreviated JS.

4. See Ham Sŏk Hŏn, *Queen of Suffering: A Spiritual History of Korea*, trans. E. Sang Yu (London: Friends World Committee for Consultation, 1985).

dox (DU: 287). Perhaps this Korean religious genius was ahead of his time, as was Søren Kierkegaard (1813–1855) in nineteenth-century Europe. The Korean Calvinists in his time, extremely loyal to their learning from fundamentalist and exclusivist missionaries, could in no way appreciate Ryu's provocative foresight, which would be prepared rather for twenty-first century Christians in the highly global and multireligious world. Indeed, he was a precursor of intertextual interpretation, multifaith hermeneutics, and comparative theology.[5] Deeply embedded in East Asian scriptures, he developed an intriguing interpretation of Christian faith in the light of East Asian thoughts. Simply, he read the Christian Bible seriously along with Confucian, Daoist, and Buddhist scriptures. He made an interesting suggestion for this multiscriptural reading: "regard all the scriptures of East Asian religions as the Old Testament" (DU: 82).[6]

Whether Ryu was a religious pluralist is an open question, and his followers are divided on this issue. It is clear, however, that his interest was not so much in an epistemology of religious pluralism as in a constructive hermeneutics of his faith in and through (not out of!) the plurality of those traditional, indigenous religions. Kim Heung Ho, one of the few living disciples of Ryu and probably the most reliable interpreter of Ryu's thought, argued that Ryu was first and foremost a Christian, a serious follower of Jesus Christ. One

---

5. Ryu said, "After Confucianism, Buddhism, and Christianity illuminate each other, they also know themselves better" (DU: 365). For an example of comparative theology, see Fancis X. Clooney, *Theology after Vedānta: An Experiment in Comparative Theology,* SUNY Series, Toward a Comparative Philosophy of Religions (Albany: State University of New York Press, 1993); for multifaith hermeneutics, see Kwok Pui-lan, *Discovering the Bible in the Non-Biblical World,* Bible and Liberation (Maryknoll, NY: Orbis Books, 1995), esp. 57-70.

6. Ryu partially supports the theory of preparation and fulfillment; he regarded Christianity as a New Testament that has completed all the truth revealed in Asian religious thoughts, so to speak, Asian Old Testaments. His cross-cultural Asian hermeneutics would be summarized in the following statement: "Putting the essence of Western culture in the backbone of Asian culture, I tried to explain the former [Christianity] in and through the latter [East Asian religions]" (KDI 2:176).

way in which he differed from other Korean Christians is that he freely employed scriptural resources of our indigenous religions in order to understand the Christian Bible better and more properly in his context. Having been with us for more than a millennium, these East Asian scriptures have profoundly influenced, shaped, and been deeply embedded in our modes of life and thought (just as the Bible has for Westerners). By reading the Bible in and through these indigenous scriptures, Ryu could conceive of his new faith in Jesus Christ more clearly, intelligibly, and practically.

In this chapter, I will continue to explicate Ryu's insights into Jesus Christ. They may portray a salient example of Korean contextual Christology, so to speak, the Korean face of Jesus Christ (or Christodao). Christians in the contemporary world, which is highly global and pluralistic, may need to hear these fascinating Christian thoughts in a new key. I will try to present his thoughts in his own words as much as possible by literal translations rather than a systematic interpretation, so as to make him speak for himself. Ryu's Christodao can be categorized in seven "configurations of basic insights" as follows:

1. Jesus is the filial son (孝子): a Confucian Christology.
2. Jesus is the Rice (*bap*): a Sacramental Christology.
3. Jesus is the Flower: an Aesthetic Christology.
4. Jesus is the Seed: an Anthropological Christology.
5. Jesus is the Spirit (靈): a Pneumatological (*Ki* 氣) Christology.
6. Jesus is the Dao (道): a Cosmic Life Christology.
7. Jesus is the Being in Non-Being (無極而太極): an Apophatic Christology.

1. *Jesus Is the Filial Son* (孝子): *A Confucian Christology*

Famous for an impeccable tradition of maintaining genealogy, Korea has been and still is the most Confucianized society in the world. Almost every family in Korea keeps a genealogy that records names and the kinship of all their ancestors and relatives since the origin of their clan (for the period of about one and half millennia). From this strong Confucian vantage point, first and foremost, *Jesus is a filial son.*[7] Filial piety (孝) is a well-known cardinal Confucian virtue. However, it is a big mistake of popular Confucianism to understand filial piety simply as a blind obedience to parents; Confucian filial piety ultimately means a faith in God, the true Father.

According to Ryu, Jesus could become the Christ because he has accomplished fully the loving relation between father and son (父子有親), one of the five Confucian moral rules (五倫). Our yearning for God the Father is in fact an unavoidable inclination of original human nature:

> Human yearning for God the Father cannot be prevented. For it is the relationship between father and son. . . . Father and son cannot be two [父子不二]. This refers to the loving relationship between father and son [父子有親]. The longing for God the Father, the beginning and the truth, is an unavoidable human nature [人間性]. That entails the true meaning of what is to be human. (DU: 165)

Therefore, the Christian expression to give the glory to God implies achieving the original nature given to us by the Father. Confucianism, however, has gone astray. It has forgotten the true object of filial piety, God the Father, but instead emphasizes the ancestor worship excessively: "Forgotten filial piety toward God since long time ago, people regard it as treating one's father as the Heaven. . . . [However,] God the Father should take precedence over one's parents. Confucianism that relied heavily on the mandate of the Heaven [天命] completely forgets the Heaven [忘天]. This is the reason why Confucianism is so enervated" (DU: 227, 230, 254).

Further, *Jesus is the Only-Begotten Son* (獨生子). Ryu interpreted this Johannine expression in a special way (John 3:16). The title "Only Son" does not imply so much a royal prerogative as a special mission given to him by God. In fact, the cross-bearing and the crucifixion of Jesus consummate the filial piety of the only-begotten son: "Jesus did not come from God in order to receive all

---

7. See KDI 6:319. In contrast to Luther's German theology of Reformation, Ryu called his a Korean "theology of filial piety" (KDI 2:223-24).

lavish hospitalities. The one who will ascend into the Heaven [on the contrary] ought to bear the cross. His death is nothing but to accomplish the mission given to him as a son" (DU: 216). Since we are also children of God, we also have the similar mission in the world as God's children. "Jesus taught people in the world to give. This world is the world to give [rather than to receive]." (DU: 71)

Furthermore, *Jesus is the Profound Person* (君子), the ideal Confucian personhood. The profound person in Chinese literally means a son of the king. Since God is the true king, Jesus, the only-begotten son of the king, is none other than the profound person. Religious exclusivism is wrong. For, first of all, you have to know others in order to know yourself better. And all religions, after all, converge in the common quest for full humanity, that is, the goal of a profound person: "Christians regard Confucianism as heretic and Buddhism as idol worship. Buddhists denounce Jesus and Confucianism. . . . [However] if a person does not know others, one does not truly know oneself either. If one wants to become a profound person, one should also know the other profound persons" (DU: 57).

The primary goal of Confucianism lies in attaining full humanity or sagehood through becoming a profound person. Hence, *rén* (仁; benevolence or co-humanity), the cardinal virtue of Confucianism, involves an ethico-ontology of "being togetherness."[8] The Confucian project of a profound person culminates in the achievement of this co-humanity through the sacrifice of oneself (殺身成仁). The crucifixion of Jesus on the cross is a perfect example of both the profound person who achieves this sacrificial act (DU: 320) and "the only-begotten son" who accomplishes his filial duty (DU: 125). In this sacrificial act of Jesus on the cross to realize co-humanity, Ryu found a true meaning of Christ: "Christ is the one who regards serving God and the human race as [the goal of] his life [生命]. Christ is the one who lends oneself to serving so as to show people of all races how to live eternal life as Christ. Therefore, isn't it natural for a person to honor and praise Christ sincerely?" (DU: 39).

---

8. See Heup Young Kim, *Wang Yang-ming and Karl Barth: A Confucian–Christian Dialogue* (Lanham, MD: University Press of America, 1996), 43-46.

2. *Jesus Is the Rice* (Bap): *A Sacramental Christology*

Ryu was famous for eating one meal a day (一食). For him, this was a serious ritual practice that embodies his Christian piety in everyday life: "The climax of the worship toward God is eating one meal a day. For it is the way in which the spirit draws nourishment from the body and also the way in which I may dedicate my body as a living form of worship" (DU: 52). Eating has a deeper spiritual meaning than a simple nutritional intake: "A meal signifies a sacrificial offering [祭物]." Since our bodies are "God's temple," to eat means to dedicate an offering to God who "lives in" us (1 Cor. 3:16). "Therefore, eating a meal is tantamount to a worship or a Mass. Regarding that it is I who eats is something like stealing the offering. To eat a meal means to love God" (DU: 186-87; JS: 129).

Jesus's sacrifice on the cross consummates this sacrament of eating. At this point, Ryu developed a fascinating insight that, on the cross, *Jesus becomes rice:*[9] "Jesus sacrificed himself on the cross. To sacrifice oneself means to become a meal. To become a meal signifies that a person becomes rice that can be cooked as food. To become rice implies that it has been ripened. It comes to maturity and becomes a ripe fruit" (DU: 187).

Hence, every meal should be regarded as the sacrament of the Eucharist: "The worship when Jesus was sacrificed by being nailed on the cross and shed blood is really our food to eat and drink. Eating with the acknowledgment that this is the Eucharist. We must have a daily meal as the Eucharist, not as an appetite to eat [食慾]" (DU: 100). "I eat a meal to imagine rice as the flesh of Jesus and water as the blood of Jesus. It is not true that this [kind of imagination] is required only during the Mass or the Lord's Supper. But whenever I eat rice, I suppose as if I were eating Christ, and then I receive some news" (DU: 223).

After all, he suggested, is not the purpose of life to become rice? That is, to ripen so as to be used and dedicated as a sacrificial food (DU: 187; JS: 130). Rice as human life is the fruit of the Holy Spirit,

---

9. Cf. John 6:48, 51. In Korean, rice *(bab)* has the multiple connotation of a grain, a meal, and food.

which Ryu identified with four Confucian virtues of full humanity: co-humanity, righteousness, propriety, and wisdom (仁義禮智). Full humanity as rice is what we ought to attain to be dedicated to God. "Human life is rice, fruit of the Holy Spirit [to be borne] to serve God. This fruit of the Holy Spirit means to become fully human or to attain true humanity [人格]. True humanity is what is to be devoted to God. True humanity signifies benevolence (or co-humanity), righteousness, propriety, and wisdom, that is, the original nature of human being. We should dedicate this original nature to God" (JS: 133).

> The purpose of eating, hence, is to attain true humanity. Based on a passage of *The Doctrine of the Mean*, Ryu defined this process of humanization as the tao [率性之謂道] (DU: 187, JS: 131). From this vantage point, Ryu conceived of Jesus as true humanity, the perfect embodiment of the Tao, who has accomplished four Confucian virtues once and for all. In his East Asian Christian thought, furthermore, the Word does not mean so much a doctrine as an expression of true humanity: "the Word is nothing other than an expression of true humanity. We are offering true humanity through the Word" (JS: 133). True humanity as universal sacrament, hence, entails the Word of the Holy Spirit, the salvific energy of the cosmos: "What special nourishment can the universe and humanity get from the rice of human life? It is the Word. In the rice of human life, there is the Word. There is the Word of the Holy Spirit and the Father. There is the Word of the Holy Spirit, the cosmic power to save the human race." (DU: 188, JS: 132)

3. *Jesus Is the Flower* (kkot-pi): *An Aesthetic Christology*

Ryu metaphorically imagined that red flowers are the blood of nature and that human blood is the flower of nature.[10] From this

---

10. In Korean, the two words "being red" (*pi*) and "blossoming" (*pinda*) are phonetically related. Ryu employed this relation to establish his suggestion.

image, Ryu surmised that "flower is blood." Applying this to the bloodshed of Jesus on the cross, Ryu conceived an intriguing Christology of salvific blood-flower (*kkot-pi*):

> Since flower is red like blood, it is called that flower blossoms. Flower is the blood of nature, and human blood is the flower of nature. Flower is blood, and blood is flower. This flower of blood or blood of flower is the blood Jesus shed on the cross. The flower-blood of Jesus shed on the cross is the blood of flower [花血]. In a word, it is the spilled blood of the righteous. No matter how evil the world is, the blood of flower spilled by the righteous can cleanse it. (DU: 165-66; cf. JS: 156)

Based on the natural phenomenon that flower blossoms at the end of life [of the plant], furthermore, he established another basic insight that "flower is the end."[11] And he developed an aesthetic Christology of the cross; that is, the crucifixion is the blossoming of cosmic flower:

> The present is both the end and a flower [*kkŭt-kkot*]. God is alpha and omega as well as the beginning and the end. The first character of the Chinese word *the present* [現在] connotes "blossoming like a flower," and the second "the end of God." The end of life is death, which means both the end and a flower. Seeing the cross where Jesus was crucified is just like observing the blossoming of a flower. Any death is solemn and holy. [Then, how solemn and holy] the death of a young person [who died] with the bloodshed of flower is! It is the blossoming of a far more sublime flower. (DU: 204, JS: 149)

Trees produce fruits after the fall of flowers. Analogously, Ryu applied this natural phenomenon to Christology. If the crucifixion of Jesus is the falling of the cosmic flower, then the resurrection is the bearing of cosmic fruit (花落能成實):

---

11. Again, Ryu pointed out the phonetic resemblance between the two Korean words "end" (*kkŭt*) and "flower" (*kkot*).

Jesus regarded death as the falling of flower. To blossom flower is [to manifest] the truth, and to fall petals of flower is the cross. The cross is a symbol of the truth over death. Believing the cross means believing the truth. This refers to the state where death has been swallowed up by life, in other words, when the spirit has overcome the body. (DU: 166, JS: 157)

Watching the blossoming of the azalea, a popular Korean mountain flower that blossoms in the early spring, Ryu contemplated this flower Christology and lamented poetically, "The azalea falling beforehand, taking the burdens of others! The one who was hanged on the cross would have been a blossom of this azalea!" (JS: 64). "The azalea to be crucified on the cross is to bear the burdens of the human race!"(JS: 66).[12]

4. *Jesus Is the Seed* (Ssi): *An Anthropological Christology*

Ryu envisioned Jesus as the cosmic seed. He propounded an agricultural analogy of the Trinity: Jesus is the seed; God is its tree; and the Spirit is the life that includes both the seed and the tree:

> The life of Jesus and the life of God are one in terms of the life of the Spirit [ŏl].[13] If the spirit of Jesus is the seed, then that of God is its tree. Where does a seed come from? It [obviously] comes from its tree. A tree is the source of its seeds. Jesus comes from God. And when a seed sprouts, it again becomes a tree. This means the return to God. (DU: 148)

Here, Ryu's thought is clearly trinitarian, not so much unorthodox as he confessed.[14] The spirit of Jesus is the seed of God, that

---

12. Using this symbolic expression, Ryu would have lamented pains and the suffering of Korean people during the period of Japanese occupation. Also see KDI 5:536-37, 6:133-34, 7:13-14.

13. The Korean word ŏl connotes both "soul" and "spirit" in English. In this essay, however, this term will be translated as "spirit," as Ryu stated that "ŏl [靈] is the Holy Spirit" (JS: 125).

14. Ryu also underscored the meditation of the Trinity (念參); see KDI 7:558-59.

is, the spirit of eternal life. Ryu explicated *perichoresis* in light of this seed Christology: "When Jesus said 'whoever sees me sees him who sent me' [John 12:45], the 'me' here refers to God's seed (spirit) in him. To believe in God's seed in me, the Word (logos), or the one whom God sent is salvation and eternal life [John 12:50]" (DU: 351). "To give the only son [John 3:16] means to give us the seed of God [1 John 3:9]" (DU: 277).

With the support of these Johannine passages, Ryu claimed that it is not only Jesus but also all of us who possess the seed of life from God as only sons. The only difference between Jesus and us lies in the fact that Jesus is the first ripe fruit of the seed, a paradigm we should follow and produce. Jesus is the Christ who once and for all has accomplished the purpose to be God's seed (DU: 341):

> Not only the spirit of Jesus but also the spirit of every human being is the seed. To tell this [truth] is [the purpose of] religion. In other words, in terms of the spirit, both Jesus and "I" are the same seeds of God. *If Jesus is the first ripe fruit, I also ought to become a ripe fruit.* I should believe in Jesus, God, and me. In terms of the life of the spirit, all of them are [the same] one life. To believe in the spirit of [true] "I" is to believe in Jesus and God. Jesus and "I" are the same seeds that have come from God. (DU: 148; cf. JS: 167)
>
> Jesus has come in order to make us realize our true selves. To believe in Jesus means to know that I am an immortal life. I must realize that I am a seed from the Heaven. If Jesus is a seed, then I am also a seed. (DU: 149)

The deeper objective of Christology, as we have seen repeatedly, lies in its anthropological implication, that is to say, a realization of our true selves. At this point, Ryu developed an anthropology of inner seed in dialogue with Confucianism. God's seed in us is the inner seed, the true life, which Ryu identified with the Confucian notions of moral power (*dé* 德) or the innate knowledge of the good (*liáng zhī* 良知): "Jesus taught us that the inner seed in me, God's seed, is the true life. Therefore, first and foremost, I should follow the inner seed in me. That inner seed is the true life of Jesus as well as my true life" (DU: 308).

Our true subjectivity is not so much our physical appearances as this inner seed, the spirit. Ryu made a profound suggestion that our true subjectivity is related to *ki* (氣), the cosmic spiritual energy. In Confucian terms, my true self, my inner seed, or my real life, is nothing other than the *ki* of natural greatness (浩然之氣):

> The thing that comes from the womb of my mother is not I. But the inner seed is I. The spirit [精神] is I. The inner self is I. The outer self (the body) is only a handful quantity of soil or of ash. However, the inner self can build the kingdom of the Heaven. It is the limitlessly great and limitlessly powerful I. It is I in the *ki* of the natural greatness. I in the natural greatness of *ki* is the body of *ki* [氣體] and the spiritual body [靈體]. To live in the real life is to cultivate this spiritual body. . . .
>
> A handful of soil is not I. But the *ki* of the natural greatness that covers the earth and the entire universe is I. It is too vigorous and too immense [至剛至大] to be measured and compared with anything. That is I, my true self. (DU: 192)

The goal of Christology, after all, lies in this anthropology, the realization of true I: "The I of Jesus is after all your I" (DU: 272). Jesus as the inner seed is not a being totally other but a personification of true humanity hidden but latent in us: "Jesus is both the budded and the resurrected I" (JS: 93). What Confucianism calls original nature (性) has been fully revealed and completely recovered in and through Jesus Christ, which he called the primordial revolution: "Original nature that Confucianism speaks of signifies the one 'whom He [God] has sent' (John 6:29). . . . By the recovery of this original nature, [Jesus] has accomplished the primordial revolution."[15]

---

15. DU: 371. This primordial revolution, however, not only implies an individualistic character formation but also contains a serious social dimension. From the notion of seed (*ssi*), Ryu originated the insight of *ssi-al* (literally, seed-egg, that is, the locus of the cosmic spiritual force), which he identified with minjung (the mass of people). In fact, Ham Sŏk-hŏn took over this insight to develop his famous thought of *ssi-al*, which became the foundation for minjung theology. Hence, it is a mistake to view Ryu's thought merely as a personal approach that lacks liberative aspects.

5. *Jesus Is the Spirit* (靈):
A Pneumatological (Ki 氣) Christology

As we have already seen in the previous section, Ryu's anthropological Christology is profoundly pneumatological:

> The Holy Spirit is the Christ, the Holy Spirit is the Word, and the Holy Spirit is my true self. It [the Holy Spirit] witnesses no other than Christ and my true self. By receiving the spirit of the truth, I could attain the "I" of the truth being liberated from the physical "I," even from death. The reason why we should receive the Holy Spirit is to obtain eternal life. Eternal life means to become the Son of God through the Holy Spirit. It would be as if one were returning to the Father like the prodigal son in Luke 15. (DU: 199)

At this juncture, Ryu played with the Korean word *breathing* (*sum*). Beyond the ordinary physical breath (*mok-sum*), he asserted, it has a spiritual dimension, the breathing of the Word (*mal-sum*) that bears a phonetic resemblance to the Word in Korean (*mal-ssŭm*). From this line of thought, he formulated an interesting pneumatology of logos, which may overcome the dualism between logos and spirit:

> The breathing of the Word [mal-ssŭm = mal-sum] is the end of breathing and the life after death.[16] To breathe the Word is to live eternal life. To think about the Word is to think about eternity, and the Word is none other than God. To breathe the Word is to believe and live in God. The breathing of the Word is to set the fire of truth in us. It sets fire on firewood in us. . . . The Word is written in the mind-and-heart of truth. . . . The flame of eternal life is flaring in our mind-and-heart. The Word of God is burning. . . . A human being is a holy brazier where the Word of God is burning. . . . If one cannot breathe the Word of God, the person is not worth being called a human. (DU: 205)

---

16. *Mal-sum* also connotes the end of breathing.

Ryu postulated that the Holy Spirit is comparable to the "illustrious virtue" (明德), a key notion in the Great Leaning (大學), one of Confucian four books: "the Holy Spirit is the illustrious virtue. The illustrious virtue should be manifested" (DU: 215). Further, he identified the Holy Spirit with the *ki* 氣, a crucial East Asian notion very similar to *pneuma*: "The Holy Spirit is nothing other than energizing and circulating the *ki*" (DU: 365). He explained:

> The Chinese word *ki* pictures clouds in the Heaven. It describes that clouds are moving with the wind. . . . The wind that makes clouds moving or the power that makes the wind moving is *ki*. . . . *Ki* is the foundation of creating and forming [生成] myriad things. . . . I view the Holy Spirit also as a metaphysical wind. As a wind, it is a movement of *ki*. It is the Tao that enables me to be connected with the *ki* flowing down from the Absolute Top. (DU: 369)

Furthermore, Ryu propounded an East Asian version of Jesus's prayer:[17]

> For me, to breathe is to take the breath of the Holy Spirit. In this way, I can embody the truth. All of these [after all] are based on prayer. Prayer is an awakening, and the Holy Spirit is the power. In this power of the Holy Spirit, we breathe and gush out. This is an illumination. (DU: 184)

6. *Jesus Is the Dao* (道): *A Cosmic Life Christology*

According to John 14:6, Ryu comprehended Jesus as the Dao, the way of the truth toward life in God.[18] Christ is *the* brightest *way* on which we can walk safely (*the truth*) to attain unity with God (*the life*). It coincides with the goal of Confucianism, the unity of Heaven and humanity. Ryu elucidated:

> Then, what are "the way [道], the truth [眞理], and the life [生命]" Jesus envisioned? He seems to understand them as

---

17. Ryu said, "Our Lord is the Lord Breathing" (KDI 2:607-8).
18. See KD 1:508-9. Ryu described Christ also as "the high way [*hang-gil*]" toward the Heaven (KDI 7:534).

follows. The way refers to ascending again to the Heaven after having descended from the Heaven to the earth. The truth is to walk brightly along the way, and the life means that the Father and the Son become one as the brightest light.[19] The Son of Man came from the Heaven and returned to the Heaven. There is no brighter way than this. Going straight along this way without error is the truth. And finally meeting with God is the life. Compare this to the railroad! The railroad is the way, the train is the truth, and the arrival is the life. (DU: 167, JS: 157-58)

As we already have seen, Jesus is ultimately the true "I."[20] The way, the truth, and the life, after all, refer to this true "I":

The way is eternally coming and eternally going. However, "I" come and go on the way. If I come and go on the way, I become the way. Just as a silkworm's cocoon makes thread and as a spider spins a web, I produce the way. The "I" of the Spirit, endowed by God, is the way, the truth, and the life [and Jesus is the enlightened one who realized this fact]. (DU: 43-44)

These statements may sound strange. Nevertheless, this is an ingenious East Asian interpretation of Paul's passage, "it is no longer I who live, but it is the Christ who lives in me" (Gal. 2:20). From Ryu's East Asian perspective, this passage virtually means that the Christ who lives in me is the true "I" (true humanity). Then Confucian insights on true humanity such as the mind-and-heart (*xīn*), original human nature [性], and the principle (*li*) can be utilized as profound resources to formulate Christology, more precisely, Christodao, some examples of which we have already seen. He said, hence, "The way toward God resides only in one's mind-and-heart [心]" (DU: 52). Moreover, Ryu equated the dao with the

---

19. Ryu argued that "being glorified" in John 13:31-32 means "being brightened." As they are the same bright light, God the Father and Jesus the Son can be united.

20. Ryu also described the true I as "the Heavenly I" that has opened the true way of life to us through "the cross Jesus has borne" (KDI 7:545).

Neo-Confucian notion of *li* (the principle) and the Buddhist notion of *dharma*:

> The way is absolutely necessary for us to move forward. Without the way, we cannot move an inch. The entire spaces [空間] exist to provide the way. The space between an atom and a neutron or that between molecules exists for the sake of the way. . . . This way implies precisely the principle [理]. The tao refers to the way. The statement that vacuity [虛空] is the truth should be understood from this vantage point. *Dharma* [法] in Buddhism also refers to the principle, the way. (DU: 170-71)

Ryu reminded us that a deeper meaning of dao lies in emptiness or vacuity. "No matter how beautiful flowers are, it is only the emptiness that really reveals the beauty of flowers" (JS: 288). In truth, the non-being (emptiness) is more fundamental than the being (a flower): "When people watch flowers, they normally focus only on flowers, but they do not pay even a slight glimpse to the emptiness in the outside of flowers. In fact, it is the emptiness that enables the existence of those flowers" (DU: 241).

At this point, the East Asian root-metaphor of dao departs from its Western counterpart, logos, as it saliently appears in medicines and paintings. Whereas Western paintings focus on things, East Asian paintings pay more attention to the empty space, which, we believe, is more profound:[21] "Westerners do not seem to know the non-being [無]. Although they are efficient, it is only with respect to the being [有], but it is not so well with respect to the remoteness and the greatness [遠大]" (DU: 309). Further, he formulated a fascinating theological insight into the Vacuity:

> I long for the Absolute Vacuity [絕對空]. What would happen to me after I die? There is nothing. Only the Vacuity without

---

21. See Heup Young Kim, "Response to Peter Lee, 'A Christian-Chinese View of Goodness, Beauty, and Holiness,'" in *Christianity and Ecology: Seeking the Well-Being of Earth and Humans*, ed. Dieter T. Hessel and Rosemary Radford Ruether (Cambridge, MA: Harvard University Press, 2000), 357-63.

anything can be the truth. What is really fearful is the vacuity. This is the truth. This is God. Without the vacuity, there is neither the truth nor an existence. How can the universe exist without the vacuity? There is nothing to exist without the vacuity. All the spaces between things, qualities, cells, molecules, atoms, and neutrons are part of this vacuity. Since there is vacuity, there is existence. (DU: 161)

Boldly declaring that God is the Absolute Vacuity, furthermore, Ryu suggested an intriguing Daoist-Buddhist-Christian apophatic theology:

If our life blossoms and expands limitlessly, it will arrive at the Vacuity [空, the Absolute (絶大)]. That is to say, living eternal life. The Vacuity is the foundation of the first beginning of life and everything. It is God. I also believe in the personal God. Although God is personal, it does not refer to such a personality that we have. Being personal denotes the first beginning of everything. God transcends both the being and the non-being [有無]. In the search of God, we cannot satisfy with materials. Since we cannot satisfy with things that exist, we search for God who is not. Therefore, God is the Being in Non-Being. (DU: 285)

7. *Jesus Is the Being-in-Non-Being* (無極而太極): *An Apophatic Christology*

Ryu upheld a mysticism of the One (*hana*): "After all, there is the only (absolute) One" (DU: 19). "All problems are ultimately related to the (absolute) One. . . . [T]hey are how to live authentically as the (absolute) One" (DU: 40). He identified this Absolute One with God the Lord: "The One is the Lord, and the Lord is the One" (DU: 45). Moreover, God in Korean (*Hana-nim*) literally means the One (*hana*) and the Lord (*nim*). Ryu conceived this absolute oneness of God at the pinnacle of Daoist and Neo-Confucian cosmogony: "God is the one and the absolute. The Non-Ultimate is the Great Ultimate [無極而太極]. There is only God" (DU: 186). "Non-Being [虛無] is the Non-Ultimate [無極], and Being [固有] is the Great

Ultimate [太極]. The Non-Ultimate and the Great Ultimate are one, and the one is God. The Great Ultimate of Being [有] cannot be conceived without the conception of the Non-Ultimate of Non-Being [無]. Hence, they are one" (DU: 240).

From this vantage point, finally, as we noticed at the end of the last section, he expressed a novel East Asian definition of God, namely, *God is the One who is "the Being in Non-Being"* (*Ŏpshi-gyeshin-nim*):[22] "We should not call in vain the name of God who is the Being in Non-Being" (DU: 269). "Since God is the One who is Being in Non-Being, we cannot see God" (DU: 275).This Being-in-Non-Being has been historically manifested in the crucifixion (the Non-Being) and the resurrection (Being) of Jesus Christ. Hence, he is both the Non-Being (the Non-Ultimate 無極; Vacuity 空) and Being (the Great Ultimate 太極; Form 色). "God is the Being in Non-Being. Although God is not, God is: Although human beings are, they are not" (DU: 371). Likewise, Jesus is the Being in Non-Being, the One who "Is" in spite of "Is-Not." Whereas we are those of non-being-in-being, he is the One of Being-in-Non-Being. Whereas we are the "forms" that are "none other than emptiness" (*Heart Sutra*), he is the "emptiness" that is "none other than form":[23] "I am who is but who is not [色卽是空]: The one is who is not but who is [空卽是色]" (JS: 68).

From the vantage point of the supreme cosmogonic paradox of Dao, Ryu "understood the cross as both the Non-Ultimate and the Great Ultimate. . . . Jesus is the One who manifested this ultimate [paradox] in Asian cosmology. Through the sacrifice of himself, He achieved genuine humanity [*rén*]. That is to say, by offering himself as a sacrifice, He saved the human race and opened the kingdom of God for humanity."[24] In Christ, the Non-Ultimate and the Great Ultimate become one. In the historical scene, this is revealed as

---

22. God is also "the Father who is the Being in the Non-being [Ŏpshi-gyeshin-*abba*]" (KDI 3:386).

23. Kim Heung-ho, *Jesori*, 68.

24. Kim Heung-ho, "Yu Yŏng-mo's View of Christianity from the Asian perspective," in *Dasŏk Ryu Yŏng-mo,* ed. Park Young-ho (Seoul: Sungchun Institution, 1994), 299.

the affectionate and filial relation between father and son. Seeing the blossom of the flower of Jesus on the cross, Ryu envisioned the glorious blossom of the cosmos, a new cosmogony. For "the cross implies a rush into the cosmic trajectory [Dao], the resurrection means a participation in the revolution of the cosmic trajectory, and the sitting on the judgment seat in the right-hand side of God entails a lighting up of the world."[25]

Conclusion

Ryu was not a systematic theologian and never wrote a theological treatise. Nevertheless, his insights of Jesus Christ present a splendidly innovative Christology in a crude form. In a nutshell, Jesus is the embodiment of the Dao. That is to say, Christ is the filial son (a proto-paradigm for loving human relationship), rice (cosmic sacrificial food), blood-flower (the cosmogonic flower), the seed of life (true humanity), the Spirit (the breathing of life, *ki*), and the Being-in-Non-Being (the supreme paradox of the Great Ultimate and the Non-Ultimate). Characteristically, his Christodao (Christ as the Dao) is Confucian, sacramental, aesthetic, anthropological, pneumatiological, cosmic, and apophatic (Daoist).

Naturally, Ryu's formation of Christodao reflects the complex history of three great world religions in Korea, namely, Confucianism, Daoism, and Buddhism. If Jesus Christ is the embodiment of the Dao, then, the teachings of all these religions converge at this point. Jesus is the perfect accomplishment of the Confucian project of the profound person, that is, to attain full humanity. Jesus is the perfect historico-cosmic manifestation of both the Daoist and the Buddhist visions, the dynamic power of the Vacuity and the Absolute Nothingness (in the paradox of weakness and reversal).

Ryu's religious propensity, however, seems to incline more to the Confucian and Daoist side than the Buddhist. For him, christology is a perfection of Daoist cosmology and Confucian anthropology. From this Confucian-Daoist vantage point, he conceived of Christ as the one who has achieved not merely a historical revolution but

---

25. Ibid., 301.

also the cosmogonic revolution, a transformation of the theanthro-pocosmic trajectory of Dao through the paradoxical change of the Non-Ultimate and the Great Ultimate (i.e., crucifixion and resurrection).

Since the goal of Christology is, after all, anthropology, Ryu's Christodao is positively anthropological (Confucian). Nevertheless, it also contains a profoundly apophatic dimension in naming God, the Ground of Being (Daoist). This apophatic aspect of Christodao will bear great fruit in the future. If the Confucian side of Christodao refers to the *yang* dimension of East Asian Christology, the Daoist side will present the *yin* dimension. As I predicted elsewhere, this *yin* dimension of Christodao is particularly important for Christology in the third millennium, as we are in the time when the *yang* Christ is going and when the *yin* Christ is coming.[26] After all, Christ is "the one who comes eternally" (DU: 341).

Are these insights a product of syncretism? This would be an important question to some, but it misses the point. For we cannot make such a clear-cut division between Christianity and our indigenous religions as some fundamental Christians mistakenly claim. If Christian faith has something to do with the totality of our lives, it should also have something to do with our indigenous traditions that have shaped and deeply permeated our modes of life. For Ryu, these insights are not so much the products of speculative synthesis as the results he attained after his serious reading of the Bible along with our indigenous scriptures, which have molded our worldviews and preunderstandings of life continuously. Through this intertextual interpretation (or multifaith hermeneutics), his understanding of Christian faith is much more meaningful, relevant, and practical. In fact, all his writings and dairies were written for this purpose, in order to make the biblical texts reach and arise some feeling to the mind-and-hearts of the Korean people.

Obviously, Ryu was a serious and sincere reader of the Bible, but he also was honest with and took seriously his own cultural-linguistic context. He tried to hear it, faithfully, as a message,

---

26. See chapter 3 above.

directed to [the Korean] people in the situation in which they are living. He would probably be a more serious and responsible reader of the Bible than so-called orthodox Presbyterian Christians, and so would be more a Reformed Christian than they are (if not in orthodox doctrines, in terms of *sola scriptura*). Every morning he performed a ritual: As soon as he woke up, he chose the biblical texts of the day. Reading repeatedly, he memorized and meditated on them until he could attain some enlightenment. Then he wrote a summary of the texts in a Chinese poem, in a manner similar to that of great Buddhist and Confucian scholars in Korea in the past. These poems constituted the most important contents of his famous diaries. He explained this meditative biblical hermeneutics, metaphorically comparing it to a chicken's production of eggs. He read, memorized, and meditated on the Word of God as diligently as a chicken eats and digests food. Then he gave birth to his own enlightenment as a chicken produces eggs every day.

Are these insights acceptable to other Korean Christians in the church? It is another difficult question. Korean Christians are still more willing to accept Western forms of Christology, aculturationally imported and mechanically transmitted. For Ryu, however, they are too foreign, dogmatic, abstract, irrelevant, and impractical to be the ultimate frame of reference for his whole being. Simply, they bypass the necessary process of self-appropriation in and through personal particularity and communal locality. Genuine universality must encompass genuine particularity. Understanding the gospel universally (the Word) presupposes first and foremost understanding it locally (the flesh). The confession of Christ without one's own particularities or contextualities is superficial, vague, incomplete, and unsatisfactory. The goal of Christology is rather to discern the meaning of human life and accountable actions and to respond to the command of the Spirit of Christ working here and now among diverse particularities and idiosyncrasies. For Ryu, therefore, existential and ethical concerns are far more important and immediate than a dogmatic speculation about Jesus Christ. At this juncture, it is also worth remembering that Ham Sŏk Hŏn, the guru of the Korean minjung movement was a disciple of Ryu and that Ham's well-known social thought of minjung (*ssi-al*), which deeply influenced minjung theology, in fact originated from Ryu.

Christodao, living in the Dao (Way) of Christ, is not merely a thinking of Christ but an eating, drinking, and breathing of the Spirit of Christ (the Word) in and through our whole bodies and the whole networks of communities. Living in the Way (Dao) of Christ calls us to move one step further beyond just conceiving the Word, that is to say, giving birth to our own "eggs" from the conception of Christian faith. For East Asian Christians, the adoption of East Asian ethico-religious metaphors is as legitimate a theological process of "owning up to one's own metaphors" in order to produce our own eggs as Euro-American Christians have done with respect to Greek-Western philosophical and secular metaphors for the formation of their theologies.[27] For this constructive theology, Ryu Yŏng-mo provided us with a marvelous example. Finally, confessing Jesus as the embodiment of the Dao is none other than an East Asian way of saying "the Word made flesh." [28]

---

27. See chapters 1 and 2 above.

28. For more on Ryu's theology, see Heup Young Kim, *Kaontchiggi: Dasŏk Yŏng-moŭi Global Hanguk Sinhak Sŏsŏl* [*Introduction to A Global Korean Theology of Dasŏk Yŏng-mo*] (Seoul: Dongyŏn, 2013).

CHAPTER EIGHT

Multiple Religious Belonging as Hospitality: A Korean Confucian-Christian Perspective

It is good that you should take hold of the one, without letting go of the other; for the one who fears God shall succeed with both. (Eccl. 7:18)

"Multiple religious belonging" has become a significant issue in today's theological discussion. From the vantage point of a Korean theologian, however, discourses on this issue continue to center on Western Christian perspectives, mainly dealing with it as a Western phenomenon. Most theologians and scholars in the discussion presuppose Christian faith, taking for granted Christian identity, with the rest of the world religions defined as "others." Excited by this new possibility of religious and spiritual explorations, they seem to enjoy a new, daring freedom of religious choice. Their reflections, however, remain on an academic, scholarly, epistemic, and speculative level, while keeping a safe hermeneutical distance from what they call "other religions."

Adapted from Heup Young Kim, "Multiple Religious Belonging as Hospitality: A Korean Confucian-Christian Perspective," in *Many Yet One? Multiple Religious Belonging*, ed. Peniel Jesudason Rufus Rajkumar and Joseph Prabhakar Dayam (Geneva: World Council of Churches Publications, 2016), 75-88.

Yet the attitude of Western theologians and scholars toward multireligious belonging looks odd and naïve to Christians who come from the so-called other religions. In order to attain a religious belonging to Christianity, many of them underwent processes in relation to their own traditions and communities, which of course has significant religious implications. Some have had to become deserters and betrayers of their beloved families and communities. It has happened not only in Korea but also in Asia as a whole that Christians from non-Christian traditions have had to leave their own traditions, cultures, religions, rituals, symbols, metaphors, communities, and sometimes even countries.

For example, a main reason for the recent visit (the first visit in Asia) of Pope Francis to South Korea (August 14-18, 2014) was to beatify 124 Koreans who were martyred by the last Korean Confucian dynasty (Chosŏn; 1392–1910), because of their new Christian faith. These Korean martyrs sacrificed their lives in order to belong to the Roman Catholic Church, which, unfortunately, at that time, demanded that they abandon their core societal ritual (ancestor rite). In that highly Confucianized society, this abolishment was regarded as a terribly humiliating and dangerously offensive act that implied an undeniable rejection of their native traditional and communal belongings. Likewise, in Asia, religious belonging was (and in some places still is) not a simple matter of free choice but a struggle of life and death (if not physically, then mentally and socially). In my case, it required a heartbreaking separation from my native belongings (the community of our family members and relatives and the Confucian tradition), which have been kept for more than one and a half millennia with clearly written records of genealogy.

> The most dramatic incident happened at the funeral of my beloved mother. Using my status as the eldest son of my family, which is in fact a Confucian authority, I succeeded in performing her funeral in a Christian style instead of the traditional Confucian one. This act, of course, involved an evangelical motive to make use of this event as an opportunity to proclaim the Good News to these stubborn Confucian relatives, in accordance with the evangelical teaching of the charismatic

Korean Church I attended in New York City. The result of this change was tragic. My relatives became outraged and received my obvious betrayal of their impeccable tradition as an offensive act. After the funeral, my eldest uncle, the most respected person in my clan, privately summoned me and said with a mournful face: "I don't care what kind of faith you have. But never had I expected that you would be the one who broke up our impeccable tradition of a thousand years like this!" This remark struck me like a thunder and made me realize that there was something wrong with my understanding of the new faith in an either-or dualism. In fact, this was the moment I committed myself to the study of Christian theology.[1]

To people like us, what are these Western scholars saying under the name of multiple religious belonging? Are they now telling us that, in fact, we did not have to leave our native belongings? If so, it is not only naïve but also irresponsible, as if killing us twice.

In this chapter, therefore, as a theologian from a non-Christian (Confucian) background, I will elaborate a different viewpoint on the issue of multiple religious belonging. In Korea, hostility continues to be the rampant attitude of the Christian faith, taught by Western missionaries as an exclusively monotheistic religion. In this context, Western discourses on "multiple religious dialogue" could be viewed as ambiguous, impractical, hypothetical, and abstract ideas for religious tolerance. For us, furthermore, our traditional, non-Christian religions are not "other" religions but "our" own religions, whereas, contrary to the Christian West, Christianity was in fact (and still is) the "other" (and a foreign) religion. In order to move beyond prevailing religious hostility and the ambiguous, scholarly religious tolerance (epistemology), multiple religious belonging must find more advanced theological bases. I would like to suggest that Christ's unequivocal command for hospitality can be a viable solution with an understanding of the Protestant principle of *coram Deo* (no religious belonging in front of God), the

---

1. Heup Young Kim, *Christ & the Tao* (Hong Kong: Christian Conference of Asia, 2003), v-vi (edited).

dual belonging of the cosmic Christ, and the trinitarian hospitality (the Oneness in multiple identities).

1. *Multiple Religious Belonging as Hostility: The Korean Context*

Upon being elected as the mayor of Seoul on May 31, 2004, the former president of South Korea, Lee Myung-bak, solemnly proclaimed, "I declare that the City of Seoul is a holy place governed by God; the citizens in Seoul are God's people; the churches and Christians in Seoul are spiritual guards who protect the city. . . . I now dedicate Seoul to the Lord!"[2] Immediately, this statement, steeped in a heavy overtone of Christian mentality, brought out bitter outrage among not only believers in other religions but also many people in this highly multireligious society. After this incident, the president would have to make repeated open apologies to secure the presidency.

The last South Korean premier nominee, Moon Chang-keuk, had to withdraw his own candidacy on June 24, 2014, because of past comments on Korean history based on an old missionary perspective of salvation history and Christian triumphalism.[3] He proclaimed:

> At the end of the Yi Dynasty [Chosŏn], expecting to eat and play for free was apparently embedded in our bloodstream. But [Western] missionaries came to our country and changed all that. After converting from laziness to Christianity and deciding to live according to the will of God, we changed.[4]

In this manner, he denounced his native Korean people and traditional Korean (East Asian) religions as inferior, lazy, corrupted,

---

2. Sunny Lee, "A 'God-given' President-Elect," *Asia Times*, February 1, 2008, http://www.atimes.com.

3. Song Sang-ho, "Park Remarks Haunt Moon: P.M. Nominee Expresses Regret; Opposition Party Demands Withdrawal," *Korea Herald*, June 12, 2014, http://koreaherald.com.

4. "S Korea's PM Nominee Praises God's Will," *Zoom in Korea*, June 13, 2014, http://zoominkorea.org.

and only redeemable by the Christian faith that Western missionaries brought in. You can imagine how people of the traditional religions responded to this statement!

Nonetheless, both Lee and Moon are not uninformed laypeople, but prominent elders of two very prestigious Presbyterian (officially ecumenical) churches in Korea. Unfortunately, these two famous, powerful—and, to a certain degree, exemplary—Protestant Christian leaders in Korea manifested the reality of the prevailing exclusive and hostile attitude against their own traditional religions according to what they were taught by Western Christian missionaries. It may not be unfair to say that this hostile and self-abnegating attitude taught by Western missionaries is still prevalent not only in Korea but also in Asia as a whole. The Congress of Asian Theologians (CATS) once reviewed Christian mission in Asia:

> The modern missionary era in Asia . . . was to a great extent, a dismal phase with hostile, aggressive, and even arrogant attitude to the other faiths. The local cultures and religious traditions of Asia were often looked upon as inferior ones that had to be replaced by Christianity and western cultural traditions. The missionary praxis, in general, was one of converting and baptizing people of other religions and extending the churches at the cost of the social, cultural and religious values that constituted their inherent sense of dignity and identity.[5]

In fact, religious belonging was not a popular concept in Korea (generally in East Asia) before Christianity introduced a rigid system of church membership. For much longer than the history of Protestantism (over a millennium), three great East Asian religions—Confucianism, Daoism, and Buddhism—had existed together in a relatively harmonious relationship. Before Christianity came, it can be said that Korean people and society accepted a loose concept of multiple religious belonging. Even though they were associated with different traditions, they regarded one another as fellow sojourners

---

5. Danile S. Thiagarajah and A. Wati Longchar, eds., *Visioning New Life Together among Asian Resources: The Third Congress of Asian Theologians* (Hong Kong: Christian Conference of Asia, 2002), 294 (edited).

walking on this road (everyday life) to the truth, and they respected one another for mutual learning. Unlike the religious history of the Christian West, there was no serious bloodshed, conflicts, and warfare, as there remained a relatively peaceful harmony among multiple religions. In fact, it was none other than the expansive Western Christianity that broke up this peaceful harmony and equilibrium among multiple religions, calling them "others," and instead brought in daunting hostility and deadly antagonism among religions, pursuing a militant crusade for membership.

The fierce demonstrations of those fundamental Korean Christians outside the BEXCO convention center in Busan, South Korea, during the 10th General Assembly of the World Council of Churches (October 30–November 8, 2013) was not an unusual event but would be understandable if the situation were properly considered. The WCC's interfaith openness to other religions directly implies an existential threat to the protesters' Christian identities (or belonging), which they have striven to attain through rigorous self-denial of their native belongingness, including their native religious traditions. They, in fact, honestly confess and testify to the reality of Christians in Korea (and perhaps in Asia as a whole) who are still in a struggle with their own religious identities, suffering traumas experienced in the process of self-degradation by hostile and fundamentalist Western missionaries who were ignorant of Korean (and Asian) traditional religions. If multiple religious belonging is discussed without proper consideration of these catastrophic mistakes by Western Christian missionaries in Asia, it would be nothing more than a naïve and irresponsible armchair talk of Western theologians and scholars, with a shameful amnesia regarding Asian mission history.

2. Multiple Religious Belonging as an Absurd Religious Tolerance (Epistemology)

I understand that it is from an honest intention after deep experiences in and appreciations of Asian religions through interreligious encounters and dialogues that Western theologians and scholars claim double or multiple religious belonging (freedom to belong to "other mansions") such as Christian-Buddhist, Christian-Hindu,

Christian-Confucian, and so on. Nevertheless, I doubt that Western scholars ever move beyond hypothetical, methodological, or comparative levels based on an epistemology of religion, whether it is inclusivim or religious pluralism. I wonder whether they are really free from the prolonged (conscious and unconscious) presupposition (of Christian religious imperialism) that Christianity is the ultimate (or "primary") religion and that others are penultimate (or secondary) religions.

About two decades ago, I advocated "a dual religious citizenship." Personally identifying as a Confucian-Christian, I pointed out the limits of Western theologians active in interreligious dialogue. Without alluding to most Western theologians at that time, even the liberal pluralist John Hick warned of crossing the Rubicon of dual religious citizenship: "One can only center one's religious life wholeheartedly and unambiguously upon one of them . . . but not more than one at once."[6] Classifying dual citizenship in three categories—cultural, ethical, and religious—the progressive inclusivist Hans Küng also concluded, "As much as cultural and ethical dual citizenship is possible and ought to be made possible even anew, a religious dual citizenship in the deepest sense of faith should be excluded—by all the great religions." He cautioned, "*Christian inculturation, not dual religious citizenship*, must be the watchword!"[7]

For us Asians, this was indeed an odd watchword. Although knowing well the East Asian situation, even Küng, a most open-minded European theologian toward great world religions, could not transcend an epistemic dualism in the either-or mode of thinking that was inherited through Western Christianity. He wrote, "Therefore, even with every cultural and ethical possibility for integration, the truth of every religion extends to a depth that ultimately challenges every person to a yes or no, to an either-or."[8] The genius of the Nicene Creed regarding the Trinity (not *either* one

---

6. John Hick, *An Interpretation of Religion: Human Responses to the Transcendent* (New Haven: Yale University Press, 1989), 373.

7. Hans Küng and Julia Ching, *Christianity and Chinese Religions*, trans. Peter Beyer (New York: Doubleday, 1989), 282. Italics in original.

8. Ibid., 281.

or three, but *both* one *and* three) and the Chalcedonian Christology lie in the fact that the Church Fathers enabled the Christian faith to overcome Greek dualism (*either* divinity *or* humanity) to declare christological dual belonging (*both* heavenly *and* earthly). Nevertheless, the Western church has not fully grasped this great wisdom of the ancient ecumenical church but, turning the clock back, has maintained ecclesiastical and epistemic intolerance of *the other*, anachronistically returning to an Arian monotheism ("only one!") and a pre-Constantinian confessional complex ("either-or").

For East Asian Christians, dual or multiple religious citizenship or belonging is not an epistemic and speculative issue but a hermeneutical and existential problem. For example, for us, Confucianism is a historical reality (perhaps ontologically given by the grace of God's creation). We have no hermeneutical distance to put aside and objectify Confucianism, giving it the status of the "other" religion. As Chinese Confucian scholar Tu Wei-ming stated, "East Asians may profess themselves to be Shintoists, Taoists, Buddhists, Muslims, or Christians, but by announcing their religious affiliations seldom do they cease to be Confucians." For us Koreans, and for some East Asians, in this way Confucianism is not one of the other religions but our own religion. If an assertion of multiple religious belonging still keeps a hidden presupposition that Christianity is the ultimate religion and others penultimate, it seems to us nothing more than a nice way of expressing an absurd religious intolerance or an upgraded strategy of mission and evangelism in disguise, such as Karl Rahner's "Anonymous Christian." Western theologians and scholars in the generations following those pioneers in inter-religious dialogue, such as Hick and Küng, do not seem to progress much further. Although they have gone one step forward with an explicit proposal of "multiple religious belonging," they still insist that one should transparently identify the primary religion to which one belongs. They argue that this distinction is necessary to make the discussion theologically proper and logically coherent. What a strange multiple religious belonging this is! It is nonsense, exposing an insufficient understanding and commitment to Christian theology. Moreover, what they consider "logical coherence" is rather based on the Western mode of thinking, that is, monism, possibly reinforced by exclusive monotheism. This is, in fact, neither a Christian logic nor a proper Christian doctrine of God. The mystery of Jesus Christ is based on his dual belonging and the Christian God has triune (multiple) identities. Even though they argue it is logical, it is logical only in the "either-or" mode of Western monistic and substantial thinking. The East Asian "both-and" mode of relational thinking such as *yin-yang* has no problem in logically including dual identities.

A sophisticated type of multiple religious belonging is called "asymmetrical belonging," which "involves belonging primarily to one religion while also identifying with another."[9] It is also self-contradictory to set up an unnecessary boundary: "It is, indeed, only insofar as one is moved or inspired by a teaching or practice in another religion that one will seek to incorporate it in one's own religious life and in the life of one's primary religion of belonging."[10] Nevertheless, this type refers not so much to a dual or multiple religious belonging as to an intrareligious dialogue. Furthermore, if it refers to Christianity as primary and others as secondary, it cannot be viewed as a position fully free from religious imperialism and arrogance. Whether consciously or unconsciously, there underlies an implicit cultural and philosophical imperialism: It is permissible for Western Christian scholars to belong to Western cultural and philosophical traditions that have religious implications; however, it is prohibited, in the name of Christianity, for Asian Christians to belong to their own Asian cultural and philosophical traditions such as Confucianism. Notwithstanding, I claim that I, as a Confucian-Christian, am both fully Christian and fully Confucian, rejecting the primary–secondary or the full–partial distinction. I also argue that this position has authentic and strong theological bases.

---

9. Catherine Cornille, "Multiple Religious Belonging," in *Understanding Interreligious Relations*, ed. David Cheetham, Douglas Pratt, and David Thomas (Oxford: Oxford University Press, 2013), 327.

10. Ibid., 336.

3. Christological Foundations for
Multiple Religious Belonging

The Dual Belonging of Jesus Christ

A fundamental axiom of Christianity is a belief that Jesus Christ is *both* fully God *and* fully human as expressed in the Nicene Creed (325 C.E.). Christianity is based on a faith in the dual belongingness of Christ; it is not based on a philosophy or logic of "either-or" monism (either divine or human, either Christianity or another religion, etc.). If we have to choose a Christian logic, in fact, it is not an "either-or" logic of Western monism (or dualism), but rather closer to a "both-and" logic of East Asian holism, such as *T'aegŭk* (Tài jí [*T'ai-chi*]), consisting of both *yin* and *yang* in complementary opposites. From the vantage point of the person of Christ, the latter is much more proper.[11] Thus, a dual (or multiple) belonging has a logical and theological basis in Christology (the person of Christ). Imitating Christ (fully dual belonging of Christ), Asian (Korean) Christians can be both Christian and Asian (Korean) at the same time, as fully as European Christians can be both Christian and European.

The Chalcedonian Christological Formula

The four adverbs of the christological formula in the Chalcedonian Creed (451 C.E.) present significant implications. The duality of both full divinity and full humanity coexists in the person of Christ Jesus "without confusion, without change, without separation, and without division." This coexistence in the unity of duality (or multiplicity) while retaining differentiation entails an ontological and theological basis for a Christian theology of dual (or multiple) religious belonging and a paradigm for Christian anthropology. Analogously to Christ's dual belonging, for example, Asian Christians can be both fully Christian (in relation to divinity) and Asian (as human) with their own religious traditions, in unity while retaining duality and differentiation ("unconfusedly, unchangeably, undividedly, and inseparably") at the same time.

---

11. See chapter 3, above.

The Dual Citizenship of Christian Anthropology

The Christian Bible identifies Christians as "aliens and exiles" in the world (1 Pet. 2:11) and propagates that Christians have dual citizenship; they belong to both Heaven and Earth (Phil. 3:20). The eschatological existence of Christians refers to their ultimate citizenship, which belongs to Heaven. Nevertheless, they also have an earthly existence that bestows freedom and the right to embrace and embody their own religious traditions endowed by birth, following the paradigm of Christ's full incarnation in humanity, which embraced and embodied Judaism, the religion of his mother and father. Hence, in Christian anthropology, there is a basis for Christians to have freedom to belong to their own native religious, cultural, and philosophical traditions, which eventually bring forth dual or multiple belonging.

4. Multiple Religious Belonging as Hospitality

Hospitality is the foundation of Christian faith and an unconditional command of Christ, as expressed in the parable of the sheep and goats (Matt. 25:31-46). Henri Nouwen said, "If there is any concept worth restoring to its original depth and evocative potential, it is the concept of hospitality."[12] Christine Pohl also claimed, "Hospitality is the lens through which we can read and understand much of the gospel, and a practice by which we can welcome Jesus himself."[13] A key Greek word for hospitality in the Christian Bible, *philo-xenia*, etymologically means "Love strangers!" Christ made it stronger, "You should treat them as me" by saying "whatever you did for one of the least of those brothers of mine, you did for me" (Matt. 25:40). I said at the 7th Congress of Asian Theologians:

> [Hospitality] relativizes every Christian doctrine and articulation of metaphysical, ideological, and systematic thought.
> In terms of the social location, strangers are more important

---

12. Henri Nouwen, *Reaching Out: The Three Movements of the Spiritual Life* (Garden City, NY: Doubleday, 1975), 66.
13. Christine D. Pohl, *Making Room: Recovering Hospitality as a Christian Tradition* (Grand Rapids: Eerdmans, 1999), 8.

theologically than others. The notion of Christian hospitality demands Christians to pay a preferential option to the poor, strangers, the alienated, the disabled, those in prison, and so on. In this cosmic age, this preferential care for strangers should be further extended to embrace and embody God's transcendent agapeic love toward the world, including human nature, other lives, and the eco-system on the earth.[14]

Of course, this list of hospitality toward strangers should include those in other religions as well. A key aspect of practicing hospitality is to abandon the prestige, rights, and powers of being a host. The Christian mission of the West, however, went in the opposite direction, taking over the mission field to be the host in the land, although they were guests in the land, as it is told in the stories of Thanksgiving and Apartheid. An African Christian leader stated, "When the [European] missionaries came to Africa they had the Bible and we had the land. They said 'Let us pray.' We closed our eyes. When we opened them we had the Bible and they had the land."[15] This is not the Christian way of hospitality Jesus taught us but a crafty way of invasion, conquest, colonialization, and exploitation in the name of Christian mission.

The "will to become host" or "will-to-host" would be a main cause for the original sin of Western imperial Christianity. Without forsaking the will to *host*, it inevitably leads to *host*-ility, in opposition to *hospital*-ity. As long as Western Christians do not give up their persistent (but many times hidden) presupposition that their religion is the host and other religions are guests (in need of their surveillance), they should be subject to a hermeneutics of suspicion, regardless of any good intentions they suggest. Western discourses on multiple religious belonging should pass through this scrutiny because many of them yet seem to retain a Christian (or ecclesiastical) will-to-host, as it is manifested in the idea of "asymmetrical" or "primary" distinction. Such notions of multiple religious

---

14. Heup Young Kim, "Embracing and Embodying God's Hospitality Today in Asia," *CTC Bulletin* 28, no. 1 (December 2012): 5.

15. Adrian Hastings, *The Church in Africa, 1450–1950* (Oxford: Clarendon, 1996), 485.

belonging could be an updated version of cunning Western Christian imperialism and religious colonialism, namely, *host*-ility in disguise, which is even more dangerous. It can involve humiliation and an exploitation of wisdoms of other great religions, by subjugating them as flowery additions at their academic dining table. Previously I have written:

> God is the only unconditional host. The nucleus of the Christian story is that the sovereign host-God emptied Godself completely to become a vulnerable human-guest and a stranger in this world. . . . This is a key to understand the mystery of Jesus, *i.e.,* God's hospitality *par excellence.* The theme of Embracing and Embodying God's Hospitality Today in Asia would be ultimately summarized in the question, "What would Jesus do to strangers and others in Asia if he came in this age of migration, globalization and science today?" What would he do and how would he welcome immigrant workers, multicultural marriages, refugees, the disabled, prisoners, people in other religions, other beings on this susceptible planet, possible extraterritorial (ET) guests from outer space, beings which come into existence by manipulations of science and technology, and so on? In the Asian context, furthermore, the hospitality list should include not only those in the present and the future but also those in the past, particularly ancestors.[16]

This list of Asian Christian hospitalities of course includes our own (forcedly rejected, hence almost forgotten) religious metaphors, which profoundly implies multiple religious belonging.[17]

5. Trinitarian Hospitality: The Ontological Foundation for Multiple Belonging

The Christian notion of hospitality is ultimately based on the immanent and the economic Trinity and their *perichoresis.* I further wrote:

---

16. Kim, "Embracing and Embodying God's Hospitality," 12.
17. See chapter 1, above.

Hospitality is the triune welcome of humanity in the life of the Trinity (the immanent Trinity). The triune God sent their only son to embrace humanity, which is an economy of the Trinity. The Incarnation of Jesus Christ is an embodiment of the Triune hospitality for the world. The Crucifixion of the God-man Jesus was the climax of the drama of divine hospitality. The blessings and joy of the Resurrection indicate the gifts to be received by the person who condescends, crossing boundaries, limitations, differences, and idiosyncracies, to execute hospitality to others including strangers. The *perichoresis* (the Father in the Son and the Son in the Father) notes the prototype of humanity as co-humanity, being-in-fellowship, being-in-togetherness, or being-in-between. Hospitality as an active participation in the process of radical humanization is an act of copying this Triune coinherence (*perichorsis*) on our existences.

Creation is a masterpiece of God's hospitality to beings in the universe. Through Jesus Christ, God opened the door to enable us to enter into the life of the Triune immanence. The Economic Trinity is a supreme act of divine hospitality welcoming humanity in the world. The Trinity embodied divinity in humanity and embraced humanity in divinity in and through the anthropocosmic drama of Jesus Christ, which is the mystery of salvation. And it is in fact the ultimate foundation and source for hospitality. As Christian mission is ultimately the mission of God (*Missio Dei*), hospitality is finally not a human, ecclesiastical, religious deed but an infused reflection of God's love in us. "God is already working in the lives of the people who come and in the lives of those who welcome them."[18] Doing hospitality does in fact signify embracing and embodying God's hospitality, by participating in the magnificent, gracious cosmic drama of the Trinity. The living God becomes the dialogical and ontological partner of the human, which Barth called "God's

---

18. Pohl, *Making Room*, 187.

sovereign togetherness with man."[19] God's deity, which already has "the character of humanity," "includes" our humanity.[20]

Without any doubt, this trinitarian hospitality should include Asian religions (our own, forcedly rejected, hence almost forgotten, religious metaphors), and provide an ontological basis for multiple religious belonging (as the Triune Godhead). Analogous to the relationship of the immanent Trinity, interrelationship among multiple religions should not be "asymmetrical" but rather "symmetrical," not similar (*homoi,* subordinational) but rather the same (*homo,* or equal).

The Western either-or logic of substance metaphysics cannot fully grasp the mystery of the trinitarian paradox of one nature (*una substantia*) and three persons (*tres hypostaseis*). In light of the *yin-yang* way of complementary opposites, however, this one-and-three paradox is no longer a problem but is reconciled within the both-and logic of relational thinking.[21] In fact, the "one and two" and the "one and three" principles are the foundation of East Asian ontocosmology of Dao (*Dàodéjīng:* 42) or the Great Ultimate (*T'aegŭk* [*Tàijí*]). This relational ontology of change is contrasted with the essentialist ontology of being in the West. In this relational ontology, multiple religious belonging is not only acceptable but also constitutes the very meaning of abundant life, always in both change (being in becoming) and exchange (*perichoresis*).

6. Further Thoughts: The Paradox of Multiple Belonging and None Belonging

Remembering the tragic mission history of Western religious imperialism, discourses on multiple religious belonging need to begin with *metanoia* in order to be free from Western propensities to subdue or

---

19. Karl Barth, *The Humanity of God,* trans. John Newton Thomas and Thomas Wieser (Atlanta: John Knox, 1960), 45.

20. Kim, "Embracing and Embodying God's Hospitality," 8-9.

21. See Heup Young Kim, "The Tao in Confucianism and Taoism: The Trinity in East Asian Perspective," in *The Cambridge Companion to the Trinity,* ed. Peter Phan (Cambridge: Cambridge University Press, 2011), 293-308.

colonize things in their mission fields, namely, the will-to-host, perhaps an original sin of Western imperial Christianity. Otherwise,
it could be yet another tricky attempt to subjugate the wisdom of
Asian religions as part of a delicious, new religious menu at their
academic or ecclesiastical dining table where Christianity is the
ultimate host. Repentance, *hospital*-ity (not *host*-ility), and fully
equal partnership (without "asymmetrical" or "primary" distinction) should be essential prerequisites to making discourse on multiple religious belonging worthwhile and valuable. In addition to
religious imperialism, we also need to guard against a wily deploy-
ment of cultural and philosophical imperialism. We Asians have
an authentic freedom and right, in front of God, to belong to both
Christianity and our native Asian traditions, as fully as Western
Christians belong to both Christianity and their own Western
traditions. Furthermore, with insights of the East Asian holistic and relational "both-and" mode of thinking, we can develop
more advanced Christian bases for a theology of multiple religious
belonging.

Finally, I would like to suggest that a positive discussion of multiple religious belonging (along with Christ's incarnation and trinitarian belonging of divine hospitality) should be combined with a
negative discussion of "none religious belonging." Martin Luther's
decree of *coram Deo* implies that there is no religious belonging
in front of God—first and foremost, no absolute belonging to the
(Roman Catholic) Church, but a direct relationship with God
only through faith in Jesus Christ. In the Protestant faith, hence,
religious belonging is finally not an ultimate but a penultimate
matter. What Christians need in front of God ultimately is total
self-denial and repentance. Between God and my existence, there
should be nothing such as religion (including Christianity), institution (church), ideas (philosophy and theology), people, or any
other form. Christians' real belonging is only to God, not to anything else, that is, "none religious belonging." If there is anything
else, it is dangerous, because it can be an idol, which violates the
first commandment.

A theology of multiple religious belonging, I believe, will
become profoundly deepened and even culminated, if it is properly

based on the paradox of none belonging and multiple belonging, analogous to the paradox of the theology of the cross (crucifixion) and the theology of glory (resurrection), held with the paradox of the Triune God with the One and Three Godhead, and furthermore, the paradox of the None Ultimate (*Mugŭk*) and the Great Ultimate (*T'aegŭk*). Indeed, this will be a fascinating topic for further discussion.

PART III

Theodao in Action:
An Ecological and Scientific Age

CHAPTER NINE

Trialogue: Christian Theologies, Asian Religions, and Natural Sciences

1. The Context: Asian Christianity

Asian Christianity is an intricate term. Geographically, Asia refers to a vast land, the largest continent on this planet. Culturally and religiously, Asia is enormously diverse and rich, as Asia is the home of world religions. Not only Siddhartha, Confucius, Laozi, and Ch'oe che-u, but also Abraham, Moses, Jesus, Paul, and Muhammad were Asians, not Euro-Americans. It is ironic that Christianity is understood as a Western religion and that Christianity in Asia is rather called "Asian" Christianity.

Philip Jenkins said that "the whole idea of 'Western Christianity' distorts the true pattern of the religion's development over time."[1] Western missionary activities under the assumption of Christianity as "the faith of Europe" and "Europeandom" have made historically massive mistakes. An African Christian leader

---

Adapted from Heup Young Kim, "Asian Christianity: Toward a Trilogue of Humility: Sciences, Theologies, and Asian Religions," originally published in *Why the Science and Religion Dialogue Matters: Voices from the International Society for Science and Religion*, ed. Fraser Watts and Kevin Dutton (Philadelphia: Templeton Foundation, 2006), 121-33.

1. Philip Jenkins, *The Next Christendom: The Coming of Global Christianity* (Oxford: Oxford University Press, 2002), 16, 39-42.

stated metaphorically, "When the [European] missionaries came to Africa they had the Bible and we had the land. They said 'Let us pray.' We closed our eyes. When we opened them we had the Bible and they had the land."[2] In the last century, nonetheless, the religious map of Christianity has been dramatically changed. Euro-American Christianity no longer occupies the majority but only a minority of global Christianity. The Christian center of gravity has shifted from Europe toward Africa, Latin America, and Asia. With "the rise of new Christianity," "the myth of Western Christianity" has been completely ruined.[3]

Nevertheless, the dialogue between religion and science remains as a Western phenomenon, a preoccupation of Western Christian theology. In this chapter, I will explore some different views from the perspective of Asian Christianity. This is not a historical survey, however, or a study covering all the complexities of Asian Christianity. Rather, I will elaborate some of my reflections based on my limited experiences as a Korean or East Asian Christian.

The Myth of Bridge-building

Western theologians patronizingly use the metaphor of bridge-building to illustrate the relation between religion and science.[4] This metaphor, however, is too romantic and misleading to the eyes of Asian Christians. First of all, theology and science are not two different worlds radically separated by a gulf to be bridged. It is undeniable that Christianity played at least a crucial role in, if not being the religious origin of, the rise of modern science.[5] John Hedley Brooke argued that terms such as "conflict" and "separation" conventionally used for the relation between science and religion

---

2. Adrian Hastings, *The Church in Africa, 1450-1950* (Oxford: Clarendon, 1996), 485.

3. Jenkins, *Next Christendom,* 79-105.

4. See W. Mark Richardson and Wesley J. Wildman, eds. *Religion and Science: History, Method, Dialogue* (New York: Routledge, 1996), xi-xiii.

5. Eugene M. Klaaren, *Religious Origin of Modern Science: Belief in Creation in Seventeenth-Century Thought* (Grand Rapids: Erdmanns, 1977).

are historically inadequate but of partisan interest.[6] Even Darwinism, Michael Ruse insisted, can be properly understood in relation to the Judeo-Christian tradition.[7]

Further, the bridge metaphor betrays a Eurocentric myopia that does not acknowledge the profound reality of other religions, which had John Polkinghorne feel pale "perplexities."[8] As the perplexities indicate, the *real* gulf exists between science and non-Christian religions. Wilfred C. Smith predicted that "the impact of agnostic science will turn out to have been as child's play compared to the challenge to Christian theology of the faith of other men."[9]

Furthermore, the bridge-building metaphor is awkward and mystifying to the people in Asia. For it was the natural sciences that attracted them when Western missionaries came to this strange world. Christianity was first welcomed because of the impressive power and advantages of the modern science that those missionaries brought with them. In this non-Christian world, therefore, science has been viewed as an inseparable part of Christianity. Missionaries explicitly used science as a means for their Oriental mission and evangelism. Matteo Ricci (1552–1610), the most famous example, introduced "the emerging physical sciences" as "the foundation for the Christian faith and the revelation of Jesus Christ."[10] The translation of science classics such as Euclid's *Elements of Geometry* was performed as a program of the Catholic mission in the Chinese world.

---

6. John Hedley Brooke, *Science and Religion: Some Historical Perspectives,* Cambridge History of Science (Cambridge: Cambridge University Press, 1991), 52-81.

7. See Michael Ruse, *A Darwinian Evolutionist's Philosophy* (Seoul: Acanet, 2004).

8. John Polkinghorne, *Belief in God in an Age of Science,* Terry Lectures (New Haven: Yale University Press, 1998), 112-13.

9. Wilfred Cantwell Smith, "The Christian in a Religiously Plural World," in *Christianity and Other Religions: Selected Readings,* ed. John Hick and Brian Hebblethwaite (Philadelphia: Fortress, 1980), 91.

10. Scott W. Sunquist, ed., *A Dictionary of Asian Christianity* (Grand Rapids: Eerdmans, 2001), 703, 703-5. See also Jacques Gernet, *China and the Christian Impact: A Conflict of Cultures,* trans. Janet Lloyd (Cambridge: Cambridge University Press, 1985), 20-22, 57-63.

Undoubtedly, natural science is not innocent but is utilized by the Christian West to perpetuate and justify colonialism, orientalism, and cultural imperialism. It is also evident that natural science itself is not neutral but is culturally dependent. The metaphor of bridge-building is not only incorrect but also misleading, because it is vulnerable to embellishing Western hegemony with the advantage of natural sciences. From the vantage point of Asian Christianity, therefore, the Western dialogue between religion and science should be subject to a *hermeneutics of suspicion*.

The Third Epoch of Christianity

Ecumenically, in 1997 Christian theologians throughout Asia assembled the Congress of Asian Theologians (CATS). In its inaugural meeting, declaring the advance of the third epoch of world Christianity, CATS called for "a third generation of missiology that goes beyond the paradigms of mission bequeathed to us by the ecumenical movement and Vatican II."[11] In the third assembly (2002), CATS further announced the following in the concluding statement:

> This Congress aimed at consolidating and advancing the new paradigm of Christian life among the rich variety of religious traditions of Asia. We acknowledge that Christian mission in Asia has been to a great extent a failure if measured by its own aims. The failure emerged from its unhelpful theology of religions and its missiology. . . . However, the experience of God does not need to be imported, for it is already here. God lives and works in the great religions of Asia and also in the folk religions, which often pose a direct challenge to institutional Christianity. Christians now must humbly acknowledge that in these many ways God has always been savingly present in the continent. In its failure to acknowledge these

---

11. See *Proceedings of the Congress of Asian Theologians (CATS), 25 May–1 June 1997, Suwon, Korea*, ed. Dhyanchand Carr and Philip Wickeri (Hong Kong: Continuation Committee of the Congress of Asian Theologians, 1997–98).

facts, Christian mission in Asia was arrogant and colonialist. It denied the possibility of pluralism.[12]

Asian theologians called for a new paradigm of theology. In the third epoch of Christianity, apologetic and dogmatic (missiological) models of theism are inappropriate, anachronistic, and backward. Unfortunately, however, these models seem to be still prevailing in the dialogue between religion and science, as they appear in the theologies of leading figures such as Ian Barbour (1923–2013) and John Polkinghorne. In Barbour's pioneering works, the apologetics of theism remain at the core of his arguments. He said, "Theism, in short, is not inherently in conflict with science, but it does conflict with a metaphysics of materialism."[13] Polkinghorne's daring reformulation of orthodox Christian faith (e.g., the Nicene Creed) in the era of science from the perspective of a theoretical physicist has a certain legitimacy in the secularized European context, but it is problematic in the Asian context, where colonialist missionaries superimposed orthodox Christianity with the threatening company of gunboats with terrifying firepower.[14] The CATS stated:

> The modern missionary era in Asia . . . was to a great extent, a dismal phase with hostile, aggressive, and even arrogant attitude to the other faiths. The local cultures and religious traditions of Asia were often looked upon as inferior that have to be replaced by Christianity and western cultural traditions. The missionary praxis, in general, was one of convert-

---

12. Danile S. Thiagarajah and A. Wati Longchar, eds., *Visioning New Life Together among Asian Resources: The Third Congress of Asian Theologians* (Hong Kong: Christian Conference of Asia, 2002), 294-95.

13. Ian G. Barbour, *Religion and Science: Historical and Contemporary Issues* (San Francisco: HarperSanFrancisco, 1997), 80. For a critical review of Ian Barbour's theology of nature, see Heup Young Kim, "The Sciences and the Religions: Some Preliminary East Asian Reflections on Christian Theology of Nature," in *God's Action in Nature's World: Essays in Honor of Robert John Russell*, ed. Ted Peters and Nathan Hallanger (Aldershot: Ashgate, 2006), 77-90.

14. See John Polkinghorne, *The Faith of a Physicist: Reflections of a Bottom-Up Thinker,* Theology and the Sciences (Minneapolis: Fortress, 1996).

ing and baptizing people of other religions and extending the churches at the cost of the social, cultural and religious values that constituted their inherent sense of dignity and identity.[15]

For the eyes of Asian Christians, it looks suspicious that such apologetic and dogmatic paradigms are still dominating the dialogue, for they can be used again as disguised, high-tech, missiological, and political plots for evangelism and cultural imperialism to perpetuate Western Christian hegemony. Such missiological fallacies should not be repeated again in the name of "the dialogue between religion and science." Asian Christians call forth an alternative paradigm of dialogue.

The Interreligious Imperative

The most distinctive religious feature of Asia lies in its "plurireligious" situation where interreligious dialogue and practice are matters of everyday life. For Asian Christians, interreligious relation is not merely a hypothetical matter with freedom of choice but precisely a living reality. Aloysius Pieris said:

> It is common knowledge that the West studies all the world religions, whereas the East simply practices them. Religion is a department in many a Western university, just as it has been a "department" in life. Among us in the East, however, religion is life. The same is true of interreligious dialogue: an academic luxury in the West, and a *modus vivendi* in the East. The interfaith encounter with all its psycho-sociological tensions constitutes a day-to-day experience in plurireligious societies of the Orient.[16]

Furthermore, religious pluralism is no longer a regional thing in Asia but a global phenomenon. In traditionally Christian cities such as London, Paris, Amsterdam, New York, Los Angeles,

---

15. Thiagarajah and Longchar, *Visioning New Life Together*, 294.

16. Aloysius Pieris, *Love Meets Wisdom: A Christian Experience of Buddhism*, Faith Meets Faith (Maryknoll, NY: Orbis Books, 1988), 3.

Chicago, and San Francisco, it is not so difficult to find Buddhist Zen centers and people practicing *Tài jí*, Daoism, and Confucianism.[17] Interreligious dialogue constitutes a significant part of contemporary theology. David Tracy affirmed, "Dialogue among religions is no longer a luxury but a theological necessity."[18] More directly, "it is dialogue or die."[19]

2. The Method: A Trialogue of Humility

A Humble Approach

Interreligious dialogue can offer useful insights in developing more appropriate paradigms of dialogue between religions and sciences. As I suggested elsewhere, for example, a fruitful dialogue can be construed in two methodological stages, namely, "a descriptive-comparative stage" (dialogue) and "a normative-constructive stage" (theology of religion). While comparable to "dialogue" and "integration" (theology of nature) models in the fourfold typology of Barbour, these two stages refer to two different moments of hermeneutics (descriptive vs. normative).

The first, the descriptive-comparative stage requires "an attitude of *reverence*" or epistemological modesty to *respect* the views and presuppositions of the other partners.[20] One should be cautious not to superimpose one's categorical schema on others so as

---

17. See Robert Cummings Neville, *Boston Confucianism: Portable Tradition in the Late-Modern World,* SUNY Series in Chinese Philosophy and Culture (Albany: State University of New York Press, 2000); and Diana L. Eck, *A New Religious America: How a "Christian Country" Has Now Become the World's Most Religiously Diverse Nation* (San Francisco: HarperSanFrancisco, 2001).

18. David Tracy, *Dialogue with the Other: The Inter-religious Dialogue,* Louvain Theological and Pastoral Monographs 1 (Louvain: Peeters, 1990), 95; also 58.

19. Diana L. Eck, *Encountering God: A Spiritual Journey from Bozeman to Banaras* (Boston: Beacon Press, 1993), x.

20. See Heup Young Kim, *Wang Yang-ming and Karl Barth: A Confucian–Christian Dialogue* (Lanham, MD: University Press of America, 1996), esp. 139-41.

not to commit a "fallacy of misplaced concreteness" (Be descriptive, not prescriptive!).[21] To make a dialogue fruitful, one may even need courage to compel an *epochē*, "faithful agnosticism," or a bracketing off of one's own *a priori* axioms.[22] In this stage, an apologetics for theistic persuasion (Barbour) or a dogmatic proclamation (Polkinghorne) is an inappropriate and risky option. In this descriptive moment, theologians rather need to be careful in order not to fall into a missiological habit of epistemological immodesty or ethical hubris. In deep humility and even with courage to bracket off their theological agenda if necessary, as in inter-religious dialogue, they should open their heart to listen to the narratives of others.

In the second, normative-constructive stage, however, theologians could have complete freedom to do constructive theology for their faith and their own Christian communities. In this theological moment, a theology of nature or science becomes appropriate and much more sensible. It should be affirmed, however, that no theology is absolute and *creatio ex nihilo*. Theologies are inevitably constructed on the basis of theologians' limited religio-cultural experiences in their particular social locations, so that theologies so conceived inexorably carry over the prejudices and limitations of the theologians who construct them. In this regard, John Templeton appropriately proposed a "humble approach":

> The Theology of Humility encourages thinking which is open minded and conclusions which are qualified with the tentative word "maybe." It encourages change and progress and does not resist any advance in the knowledge of God or of nature, but is always ready to rethink what is known and to revise the assumptions and preconditions behind our knowledge.[23]

---

21. Alfred N. Whitehead, *Science and the Modern World,* Lowell Institute Lectures 1925 (1926; repr., New York: Macmillan, 1967), esp. chapter 2.

22. See David Lochhead, *The Dialogical Imperative: A Christian Reflection on Interfaith Encounter,* Faith Meets Faith (Maryknoll, NY: Orbis Books, 1988), 40-45.

23. John Mark Templeton, *The Humble Approach: Scientists Discover God* (Philadelphia: Templeton Foundation, 1981), 167.

In the plurireligious Asian context, furthermore, the dialogue between religion and science involves double or multiple interreligious exchanges, that is to say, a *trialogue* among Christian theologies, Asian religions, and natural sciences. In this enterprise of trialogue, Asian Christianity has the greatest potentiality to enhance and globalize the dialogue between religions and sciences, namely, in and through dialogue with diverse Asian religions such as Hindu–Christian, Buddhist–Christian, Confucian–Christian, or Daoist–Christian. This *trialogue of humility*, a trialogue in and through a humble approach, would be a viable future paradigm of dialogue between religions and sciences.

Locus of Trialogue: The Wisdom (Dao) of Humanization

Often, a comparison between different traditions in terms of concept, methodology, or metaphysics does not progress beyond a scholar's mind game to searching for phenomenological parallels of one's dogma and agenda in the other tradition or prooftexts for one's cultural strength and hegemony over the other culture. Orientalism and postcolonial criticisms have exposed pungent historical errors of the Christian West by means of crusadic triumphalism.[24] For this reason, dialogue between religions and sciences needs to look for an alternative locus elsewhere than a suspicious metaphysical conceptuality.

It is more appropriate to regard an encounter between sciences and religions as a "fusion of hermeneutical horizons."[25] The goal of both religions and sciences is, after all, in the search for the way of human life to realize full humanity. Therefore, the real meeting point between sciences and religions is not so much in an abstract metaphysics, a methodology of parallelism, or an epistemology of knowledge as in a hermeneutics of the human person, the way of life—or, more concretely, the orthopraxis of humanization, that

---

24. See Edward W. Said, *Orientalism* (New York: Vintage Books, 1979); Bill Aschcroft, Gareth Griffiths, and Helen Tiffin, eds., *The Post-Colonial Studies Reader* (New York: Routledge, 1995).

25. See Hans-Georg Gadamer, *Truth and Method*, 2nd ed., trans. Joel Weinsheimer and Donald G. Marshall (New York: Crossroad, 1989).

is, the *dao* of how to be fully human.[26] Here is the significance of East Asian wisdom, whose main focus of attention is a concrete embodiment of practical wisdom for common humanity rather than a speculative postulation for unverifiable supernatural knowledge.

In this regard, Hans Küng made an important correction. Instead of the generally accepted but defective dipolar view of world religions (Middle East and India), he correctly advocated a tripolar view. Judaism, Christianity, and Islam are "the first great river system, of Semitic origin and prophetic character."[27] Hinduism, Buddhism, and other Indian religions are "the second great river system, of Indian origin and mystical character." Although neglected for a long time, Confucianism and Daoism of East Asian origin are the "third independent religious river system" of sapiential character, "equal in value" and in contrast to the first and the second.

More precisely, Neo-Confucianism is the most distinctive and common attribute of the religio-cultural matrix of East Asia since its appearance in the eleventh century as a Confucian response to Daoism and Buddhism. It emphasizes the learning of the *dao* (wisdom in the unity of theory and praxis) to attain full humanity in harmony with Heaven and the Earth (anthropocosmic vision). The primary objective of Neo-Confucian investigation is not so much the formulation of metaphysics or speculative theory as the enlightenment and embodiment of the dao, the orthopraxis of human life. Neo-Confucianism affirms that one can attain the embodiment of the dao through individually and collectively rigorous practices of

---

26. *Dao* is an inclusive term, widely used in East Asian religions, with various connotations. For example, "Tao is a Way, a path, a road, and by common metaphorical extension it becomes in ancient China the right Way of life, the Way of governing, the ideal Way of human existence, the Way of the Cosmos, the generative-normative Way (Pattern, path, course) of existence as such" (Herbert Fingarette, *Confucius—The Secular as Sacred* [New York: Harper & Row, 1972], 19).

27. Hans Küng and Julia Ching, *Christianity and Chinese Religions*, trans. Peter Beyer (New York: Doubleday, 1989), xii-xiii. Just as Christianity is not only a Palestinian religion, Confucianism and Daoism are not merely Chinese religions but East Asian religions.

self-cultivation in the "concrete-universal" network of relation-ships.[28]

Sanctification is a doctrine of Christian theology homologi-cally equivalent to this Neo-Confucian notion of self-cultivation. An ideal locus for Christian interreligious dialogue in East Asia, hence, is a faith in radical humanization (orthopraxis)— namely, self-cultivation and sanctification—rather than a metaphysics, a psychology, or the philosophy of religion. In a similar manner, an ideal locus for the dialogue between science and religion would be in the common human quest for the dao—cultivating and sanctifying our scientific and religious knowledge to be *practical* wisdom in and through mutual self-criticism and self-transfor-mation—rather than a metaphysical theory, a phenomenological parallelism, or technical knowledge.[29] The issue of how to trans-form new scientific knowledge and technologies into the wisdom of life in the "sociocosmic" network of relationships in the unity of social and ecological concerns becomes the problematique for interreligious and interdisciplinary dialogue between sciences and religions, that is, trialogue among sciences, theologies, and Asian religions.[30] That is to say, a *koan* (an evocative question) for the trialogue is how to cultivate newly acquired knowledge of natural sciences into useful wisdom to attain *new cosmic humanity* so as to embody the dao of life fully into the sociocosmic web of the universe, transcending the uncontrollable greed of commercialism and unlimited selfish desires for convenience. Without doubt, this *koan* refers to spirituality.

---

28. See Kim, *Wang Yang-ming and Karl Barth*, 33-36, 171-74.

29. The Neo-Confucian doctrine of the unity of knowledge and action refutes the dualism of knowledge and practice but insists on their ontological unity (see ibid., 29-32). Cf. Daniel Hardy, "The God Who Is with the World," in *Science Meets Faith*, ed. Fraser Watts (London: SPCK, 1998), 136-37.

30. I proposed the Dao paradigm of theology (*theo-dao*) to overcome the dualism in contemporary Christian theology between the logos paradigm (*theo-logos*; in the religion-and-science dialogue, a metaphysical theology) and the praxis paradigm (*theo-praxis*; an ecological ethics); see chapter 1, above.

3. The Content: Some Preliminary Suggestions

By adding the insights of interreligious dialogue and Asian religions, a trialogue of humility can make the dialogue between sciences and religions progress beyond its current confinement on the isolated Christian temporality toward the real, religiously plural globe.[31] Here are some of my preliminary suggestions for future studies:

1. The primary locus for the dialogue between sciences and religions is not theoretical metaphysics (knowledge) but the dao (way) of life (*wisdom*) in the common quest for a new cosmic humanity through mutual self-transformation, that is, self-cultivation and sanctification. The distinction between *inter*-religious dialogue and *intra*-religious dialogue is also helpful for the science-and-religion dialogue (R. Panikkar).[32] The prime purpose of dialogue is neither to do apologetics for one's hypothesis, theory, or system of thought nor to proselytize dialogue partners, but rather for mutual learning and growth through self-criticism, cross-examination, and self-transformation ("a humble approach").

2. The East Asian notions of *nothingness, vacuity,* and *emptiness* are worth serious consideration for the dialogue, as the reality of Non-Being becomes plausible in both the new physics and Christian theology.[33] The conception of God as the "Absolute Nothingness" might be a theological strategy better and more profound than the notion of *kenōsis*, an inevitable logical consequence of the conservative doctrines of a personal God and divine omnipotence to solve the problem of theodicy (i.e., from Non-Being to Being vs. from Being to Non-Being). When criticizing scientific materialism, theologians in the dialogue do not seem to be free of the deep-seated habits of essentialism and substantialism, a plausible cause

---

31. Christopher Southgate et al., *God, Humanity and the Cosmos: A Textbook in Science and Religion* (Edinburgh: T&T Clark, 1999), 230-31.

32. See R. Panikkar, *The Intrareligious Dialogue* (New York: Paulist Press, 1978).

33. See Fritjof Capra, *The Tao of Physics: An Exploration of the Parallels between Modern Physics and Eastern Mysticism*, 2nd ed. (Boulder, CO: Shambhala, 1983), esp. 208-23.

for materialism. Process theology's alternative strategy of "becoming" seems to be not a sufficient option either because its basis is unavoidably associated with a metaphysical dualism ("the dipolar God") of being ("entity"). A contemplation of nothingness would yield a better alternative to overcome this fundamental dilemma of the modern Western mode of theological thinking (cf. the apophatic tradition of Christian spirituality and the negative theology of *via negativa*).[34]

3. The traditional Christian notion of linear time and the supremacy of time, still operative in the dialogue between theology and science (i.e., "*when* science meets religion"), should be scrutinized in the light of the new physics and East Asian religious thoughts that underscore *the significance of space*. The logic of causality in Western thought, still prevailing in the dialogue, should be reevaluated in terms of the possibility of "*synchronicity*," a conceptual foundation of East Asian thought, *Yijīng*.[35]

4. The traditional Christian (or Greek) understanding of "nature," customary in the dialogue, is problematic, because it cannot avoid the pejorative connotation inherited by the hierarchical dualism between the supernatural and the natural. The notion of *kenōsis* (self-emptying) is a helpful but not sufficient alternative, because it still holds the vestiges of dualism and definitional ambiguity. Hence, it is worth considering the profound Daoist insights of nature and *wú wéi*(無爲; cf. "let it be itself").[36] In Chinese

---

34. See chapters 4 and 7 above.

35. C. G. Jung, "Synchronicity takes the coincidence of events in space and time as meaning something more than mere chance, namely, a peculiar interdependence of objective events among themselves as well as the subjective (psychic) states of the observer or observers" (Richard Wilhelm, trans., *The I Ching or Book of Changes*, 3rd ed. [Princeton, NJ: Princeton University Press, 1967], xxiv; also xxi-xxix).

36. Ian Barbour, *When Science Meets Religion: Enemies, Strangers, or Partners?* (San Francisco: HarperSanFrancisco, 2002), 113. Cf. Southgate et al., *God, Humanity and the Cosmos*, 233-35; Jürgen Moltmann, *God in Creation: An Ecological Doctrine of Creation*, Gifford Lectures 1984–1985, trans. Margaret Kohl (London: SCM, 1985), 87-88; also idem, *Science and Wisdom*, trans. Margaret Kohl (London: SCM, 2003), chapter 12.

characters, nature (自然) means "*self-so*," "spontaneity" or "naturalness," that is, "the effective modality of the system that informs the actions of the agents that compose it."[37] In other words, *nature* in East Asian thought is the primary "self-so" (natural) manifestation of the Dao. Natural science in Chinese denotes "self-so" science so that it does not refer to mere knowledge but wisdom. In the Bible, nature as God's creation is "good," and the denial of its goodness as "self-so" was in fact a fallacy of Gnosticism. With such an enhanced clarification of the ambiguous English term *nature*, the "theology of *nature*" would make more sense.

5. This "self-so" perspective calls for a change of the fundamental attitude toward nature, from the paradigm of domination and control to that of participation and appropriateness. The East Asian paradigm of participation and appropriateness envisions an organismic (organic + cosmic) wholeness in which everything is interconnected in the web of life. In this organismic universe, human beings are not conceived of as autonomous egos capable of transcendent self-determination to dominate, manipulate, and control nature but rather as responsible participants, appropriately responding to the interconnected whole in harmony with the "theanthropocosmic" (*theos* + *anthrōpos* + *cosmos*) trajectory (the Dao).[38] In this vision, the issue is not how to control and engineer nature for maximum human benefits but a right discernment, respect, appropriateness, and fitness to the dynamic wholeness of Nature.[39] The "trialogue of humility" (sciences, theologies, and Asian religions) so conceived, therefore, is not so much based on the Western (strife) model of dialectical dualism as on the East Asian (harmony) model of dialogical holism, whose vision appears metaphorically in the

---

37. Michael C. Kalton, "Asian Religious Tradition and Natural Science: Potentials, Present and Future," unpublished paper, the CTNS Korea Religion & Science Workshop, Seoul, January 18-22, 2002.

38. See chapters 3 and 5 above.

39. See Heup Young Kim, "A Tao of Interreligious Dialogue in an Age of Globalization: An East Asian Christian Perspective," *Political Theology* 6, no. 4 (2005): 503-16.

symbol of the "Triune Great Ultimate" (三太極).[40] The organismic holism that envisions an organic unity as the foundation of cosmic diversity is ecologically more fitting. Furthermore, arguably, it is more congruent with the findings of contemporary sciences such as quantum physics, chaos theory, complex systems, self-organization, information systems, and so forth.[41]

40. See chapter 10 below.

41. See Capra, *Tao of Physics*; idem, *The Web of Life: A New Synthesis of Mind and Matter* (New York: Doubleday, 1997).

CHAPTER TEN

Eco-Dao: Life, Ecology, and Theodao

The ecological crisis presented a great *koan* (an evocative question) for contemporary Christian theology. One scholar has worried, "If current trends continue, we will not."[1] Thomas Berry raised a serious question, "Is the human a viable species on an endangered planet?" Furthermore, Lynn White argued that, by emphasizing divine transcendence and endorsing human "domination" over nature, Christianity has offered the "historical root" of the ecological crisis. Despite his defective knowledge of Christian theology, White made an important observation: "What people do about their ecology depends on what they think about themselves in relation to things around them. Human ecology is deeply conditioned by beliefs about our nature and destiny—that is, by religion."[2] In fact, this statement of a scientist prompted scholars and theologians to reexamine Christian traditions and to seek alternative resources in other religions.

Liberation (social justice), dialogue (world religions), and ecology (life) are regarded as the three most significant themes for Chris-

---

Adapted from Heup Young Kim, "Life, Ecology, and Theo-tao: Towards an Ecumenism of the Theanthropocosmic Tao," in *Windows into Ecumenism: Essays in Honor of Ahn Jae Woong* (Hong Kong: Christian Conference of Asia, 2005), 140-56. Reprinted with permission.

1. Daniel C. Maguire, *The Moral Core of Judaism and Christianity: Reclaiming the Revolution* (Minneapolis: Fortress, 1993), 13.

2. Lynn White Jr., "The Historical Roots of Our Ecological Crisis," *Science* 155 (1967): 1203-7, esp. 1204.

tian theology in the twentieth century.[3] Various liberation, political, feminist and womanist, black, third-world, minjung theologies have argued that liberation and orthopraxis are primary but neglected motives for Christian theology owing to the white, male, middle-class privatization of Christianity on the pretext of orthodoxy. Having realized the values of world religions, Western theologians began to appreciate the wisdom of "other" religions by means of interreligious dialogue, theology of religions, comparative theology, or religious pluralism. Nonetheless, late-twentieth-century contextual and constructive theologies lingered on in the division of these two major camps, the theology of religions (inculturationist) and liberation theology (liberationist), failing to surmount the inherited Greek dualism between logos (theory) and praxis (practice).[4]

The ecological crisis offered a common *koan* for theologians in this division. Western religious scholars and theologians have strived to find alternative means to overcome the "autism" of Western religions in the interaction with the natural world. In the series foreword of *Religions of the World and Ecology*, Mary Evelyn Tucker and John Grim wrote:

> [W]e are currently making macrophase change of the life systems of the planet with microphase wisdom. Clearly, we need to expand and deepen the wisdom base for human intervention with nature and other humans. This is particularly true as issues of genetic alternation of natural processes are already available and in use. If religions have traditionally concentrated on divine–human and human–human relations, the challenge is that they now explore more fully divine–human–earth relations.[5]

---

3. See Peter Hodgson, *Winds of the Spirit: A Constructive Christian Theology* (Louisville: Westminster John Knox, 1994), esp. part 2.

4. See chapters 2 and 3 above.

5. Mary Evelyn Tucker and John Grim, "Series Foreword," in *Christianity and Ecology: Seeking the Well-Being of Earth and Humans*, ed. Dieter T. Hessel and Rosemary Radford Ruether, Religions of the World and Ecology (Cambridge, MA: Harvard University Press, 2000), xxiv.

Having realized the problems of anthropocentric ethics and world-views in Abrahamic religions (Judaism, Christianity, and Islam), Western scholars begin to pay attention to eco-friendly and life-affirming East Asian religions.

Harvard University's Center for the Study of World Religions organized an important conference entitled "Christianity and Ecology."[6] Most of the Western theologians at the conference agreed that three theological revisions are necessary to construct proper Christian ecotheology (e.g., Elizabeth A. Johnson, Sallie McFague, Mark Wallace): (a) a shift of the fundamental vision from anthropocentrism to cosmo- or earth-centrism, (b) a revision of theological metaphors and symbols, and (c) a shift of focus from orthodoxy and Christology to orthopraxis and pneumatology. Yet, in spite of these valid revisions, Western ecotheologies so conceived seem to have not suitably overcome the inherited habit of Greek anthropomorphism.[7] It might be too much to expect Westerners accustomed to personifying God in human form to fully transcend this deeply embedded inclination.

Therefore, to construct ecotheology or the theology of life would be rather a mission bestowed on East Asians who are not so much addicted to a narcissistic attachment to the human body but instead are more interested in keeping harmony with nature such as mountains, waters, and trees (compare Greek sculptures and East Asian landscapes). Grounded in "the harmony and symbiosis of humanity and things," Korean thought is particularly ecological and life affirming.[8] Korean and East Asian religious thoughts can be profound resources for Christian ecotheology, but Christian theology needs an East Asian enlightenment to utilize them. Furthermore, *Yang* Christianity developed in the soil of the anthropo-

---

6. The conference was held in Cambridge, Massachusetts, USA, April 16–19, 1998. Proceedings were published in Hessel and Ruether, *Christianity and Ecology.*

7. See Gordon D. Kaufman, "Response to Elizabeth A. Johnson," in Hessel and Ruether, *Christianity and Ecology,* 23-27.

8. Hee-byung Park, *Hankook ŭi Sangtae Sasang* [The Ecological Thought of Korea] (Seoul: Dolbaegye, 1999), 35.

morphic Greek culture that flourished for two millennia seems to have arrived at its limit, and a paradigm shift toward *Yin* Christianity is in progress. The late Bede Griffiths said well:

> This may sound very paradoxical and unreal, but for centuries now the western world has been following the path of *Yang* of the masculine, active, aggressive, rational, scientific mind and has brought the world near destruction. It is time now to recover the path of *Yin*, of the feminine, passive, patient, intuitive and poetic mind. This is the path which the *Tao Te Ching* sets before us.[9]

In this chapter, I will propose three East Asian alternatives with reference to the revisions of Western ecotheology (vision, metaphor, and focus): a theanthropocosmic vision, a theodao (dao), and a pneumatosociocomsic biography of the exploited life. In sum, (1) I advocate adapting a theanthropocosmic vision, an East Asian triadic worldview in organismic unity of Heaven, Earth, and humanity, as the foundation of ecotheology. (2) I propose constructing a new paradigm of theology, theodao, by changing the theological root-metaphor from two Western metaphors—the logos and the praxis—to the life-affirming East Asian metaphor, the dao. And (3) I suggest focusing on a pneumatosociocosmic biography of the exploited life in the planet, pneumatologically and ecologically expanding the notion of the sociobiography of minjung.

1. Theanthropocosmic Vision

First of all, I advocate that a theanthropocosmic vision be adopted as the foundation of Christian theology in the ecological age. Heavily influenced by the tradition of salvation history and modern historical consciousness, theology became anthropocentric and history centered. For the last five hundred years, the Earth, nature, and the cosmos "got lost" in Christian theology with an exclusive focus on God and the human self. In this situation, the ecologi-

---

9. Bede Griffiths, *Universal Wisdom: A Journey through the Sacred Wisdom of the World* (San Francisco: HarperSanFrancisco, 1994), 27-28.

cal disaster in fact has awakened Western theologians to realize the devastating results of "such amnesia about the cosmic world" and to become eager to find creation in the Christian tradition.[10] Nevertheless, the inherited Western habit of dividing ("either-or") seems to be problematic again, selecting either God or Earth, and either humans or nature. God, Earth (the cosmos), and humanity, however, compose a triad, an ontologically indivisible reality. True humanity can be realized only through the right relationship with God and the Earth. A theanthropocosmic vision refers to this triadic communion of God, the cosmos, and humans. As North American ecofeminist theologian Elizabeth A. Johnson has elaborated, the loss of the creation or the amnesia of the Earth is a modern phenomenon that did not occur for the first fifteen hundred years of Christianity. First of all, both "the Jewish and Christian scriptures honor the religious value of the earth." The Jewish scriptures speak of the Earth filled with the glory of God. The Christian scriptures are obviously "Earth-affirming," as it is expressed in the notions of incarnation, resurrection of the body, eucharistic sharing, and eschatological hope. Early and medieval theologies dealt with humanity in association with the natural world as the common creation of God. "God–world–humanity: these form a metaphysical trinity." "[C]osmology, anthropology, and theology of God formed a harmonious unity" (e.g., Hildegard of Bingen, Bonaventure, and Aquinas).[11] Hence, the theanthropocosmic vision is nothing new but an original vision of Christian theology.

Nevertheless, both Catholic and Protestant theologies "focused on God and human self, leaving the natural world to the side." The Reformation's doctrines of Christ alone, faith alone, grace alone, and scripture alone brought about, in Protestant theology and subsequently in Catholic theology, "an intensely anthropocentric turn." "The center of gravity shifts to the human subject."[12] However, the thoughts of reformers like John Calvin were in fact

---

10. Elizabeth A. Johnson, "Losing and Finding Creation in the Christian Tradition," in Hessel and Ruether, *Christianity and Ecology*, 4.

11. Johnson, "Losing and Finding Creation," 5-6; see also 6-8.

12. Ibid., 8-9.

affirmative toward nature, endorsing it as the inscribed locus of the divine glory. The antinatural views of modern science, philosophy, and history accelerated this shift. Francis Bacon proudly declared, "[use] nature with all of her children to bind her to your service and make her your slave."[13] The Cartesian idea of the self and the Kantian turn to the subject "divorced" the human person (the internal, active subject) from nature (the external, passive object). The modern emphasis on history reinforced this division. History (actual events in linear time) was regarded as the locus of God's salvific work, whereas nature (cyclical time) was seen as the realm of paganism. Most of the twentieth-century theologies, such as existentialist theology, neo-orthodoxy, political theology, and early liberation theologies, did not take creation seriously. At last, the ecological crisis has awakened Western theologians "to incorporate the natural world as part or even the center of their work." Geocentric, unchanging, hierarchical medieval cosmology and the deterministic, mechanistic modern worldview are inaccurate views. Rather, the natural world discovered by contemporary science is "surprisingly dynamic, organic, self-organizing, indeterminate, chancy, boundless, and open to the unknown." Furthermore, the "rape of the earth" has a close link with "male hierarchy over women and nature," that is, "violent sexual conquest of women, and of virgin forest." Accordingly, Johnson argued for an ecofeminist approach: "To be truly effective, therefore, conversion to the earth needs to cut through the knot of misogynist prejudice and shift from the worldview of patriarchal hierarchy to a holistic worldview of relationships and mutual community."[14]

Ecofeminist theology is without doubt an important contemporary theological movement with rightful correctives to Western theologies. From an East Asian perspective, however, it is still questionable whether ecofeminist theology can fully transcend the inherited habit of an "either-or" way of thinking (either anthropocentrism or cosmocentrism) or monistic dualism (not unrelated

---

13. Francis Bacon, *The Masculine Birth of Time*, cited in Johnson, "Losing and Finding Creation," 10.

14. Ibid., 11, 13, 17.

to essentialism, substantialism, and reductionism, though eco-feminist theology tries to avoid them). By monistic dualism, one cannot achieve a genuine holistic, mutual, and reciprocal mode of relationship (cf. Tillich's analysis of monism and dualism). A the-anthropocosmic vision presupposes an entirely different paradigm that is "both-and," pluralistic (triadic) and concentric. The history of world religions presents three great religious visions, namely, ancient cosmocentrism, medieval theocentrism, and modern his-torico-anthropocentrism (R. Panikkar).[15] However, all of these are inaccurate, one-sided, reductionistic views (monocentrism) of real-ity. On the contrary, God, humans, and the cosmos constitute three inseparable and concentric axes of one reality. Early and medieval theologies presupposed this theanthropocosmic (or cosmothean-dric) vision. Moreover, the genius of the doctrine of the Trinity lies in its capacity to articulate the pluralistic and concentric reality of the Triune Godhead beyond Greek monistic dualism.[16]

Since the beginning of their history, Korean people have believed in the triadic reality of Heaven, Earth, and humanity, by calling it the Trinity (三才) or the Triune Ultimate (三極). The ideographic structure of the Korean language prominently embodies this triadic vision. It also appears saliently in the trigrams and the hexagrams of *Yijing*, a foundation of East Asian thought.[17] In this regard, Con-fucian scholar Cheng Chung-ying made an illuminating suggestion:

> The concept of the trinity is derived from Christian theology, in which God the Father, God the Son, and God the Holy Spirit form a triad and yet are considered one, though as three positions within one. As this trinity is historically soteriologi-cal, the question of how a trinity may be applied to cosmol-ogy, ecology, and ethics is a subtle and challenging question. . . . [W]e might see God the Son as the ideal human, God

---

15. See Raimon Panikkar, *The Cosmotheandric Experience: Emerging Religion Consciousness* (Maryknoll, NY: Orbis Books, 1993).

16. See Hodgson, *Winds of the Spirit*, esp., 45-50, 109-10.

17. See Hellmut Wilhelm, *Heaven, Earth, and Man in the Book of Changes: Seven Eranos Lectures* (Seattle: University of Washington Press, 1977).

the Father would be Heaven (the creative spirit), and God the Holy Spirit the earth (the receptive co-spirit), or agent of the world which testifies to the accomplishment of the divinity.[18]

Furthermore, in Korean Christianity, the theohistorical vision (salvation history) of Christianity encounters the anthropocosmic vision of East Asian religions (especially Neo-Confucianism). This encounter leads to a fusion of hermeneutical horizons that entails a theanthropocosmic vision.[19] In Korean Christianity, Christian theology, East Asian religions, and ecology meet together. It is an ideal locus in which to construct a viable paradigm of the theology of life for the third millennium. Christian theology presents a thoughtful view of God (Heaven); East Asian religions (Neo-Confucianism) offer profound wisdom regarding humanity and life (the Son); and ecology (natural sciences) submits the most updated knowledge concerning the Earth (the Holy Spirit). Therefore, Christian theology, East Asian religions, and ecology constitute the triadic polarities that entail a Triune Great Ultimate (三太極). A theanthropocosmic paradigm of Christian theology can be constructed with these three great resources in a Triune Great Ultimate. These relations may be illustrated as follows:

---

18. Cheng Chung-ying, "The Trinity of Cosmology, Ecology, and Ethics in the Confucian Personhood," in *Confucianism and Ecology: The Interrelation of Heaven, Earth, and Humans*, ed. Mary Evelyn Tucker and John H. Berthrong, Religions of the World and Ecology (Cambridge, MA: Harvard University Press, 1998), 225.

19. Simply, the anthropocosmic vision refers to the Confucian idea of the unity of Heaven and humanity, whereas the theohistorical vision means the Protestant view of salvation history. For the anthropocosmic vision, see Tu Wei-ming, *Centrality and Commonality: An Essay on Confucian Religiousness*, rev. ed., SUNT Series in Chinese Philosophy and Culture (Albany: State University of New York Press, 1989). For the fusion of these two hermeneutical horizons, see Heup Young Kim, *Wang Yang-ming and Karl Barth: A Confucian–Christian Dialogue* (Lanham, MD: University Press of America, 1996), esp. 175-80.

Triune Great Ultimate of Theodao

Christian Theology	*Theos*	Heaven	*Ki (Qi, Pneuma)*	Father	Emancipation
East Asian Religions	*Anthrōpos*	Human (Life)	*Society*	Son	Dialogue
Ecology (Natural Sciences)	*Cosmos*	Earth	*Cosmos*	Holy Spirit	Ecology
Theanthropocosmic Vision			*Pneumatosociocosmic Biography*		

2. The Dao Paradigm of Theology: Theodao

Second, I argue that theodao should be a paradigm of Christian theology for the third millennium. Theodao searches for the theanthropocosmic Dao, the Way of the Triune Great Ultimate where the Heavenly way (天道), the human way (人道), and the earthly way (地道) are united as one. It seeks the way to embody the trinity of theology, life, and ecology through the profound insights of Christianity, East Asian religions, and the natural sciences. Therefore, theodao is a theology of learning how to participate in this holistic trajectory, that is, the theanthropocosmic Dao.

The dominant root-metaphor of Christian theology for the last two millennia, logos, seems to have reached a limit. Rooted in Greek hierarchical dualism, it was reduced to technical reason by the influence of modernism. Logos has become an inappropriate root-metaphor for ecotheology. Thus, I argue instead that dao should be the new root-metaphor of the Christian theology of life. First of all, dao is "the most life-affirming" root-metaphor.[20] Further, dao is more biblical than logos. For Jesus said, "I am the way, the truth, and the life" (John 14:6a), that is to say, the ultimate way (dao) of life. Jesus did not identify himself as the incarnate logos but as the dao toward God (John 14:6b). Furthermore, the original title for Christianity in Greek was *hodos* (way), which was translated as dao in the Korean Bible (Acts 9:2; 19:9; 22:4; 24:14, 22).

---

20. Tucker and Grim stated, "The East Asian traditions of Confucianism and Taoism remain, in certain ways, some of the most life-affirming in the spectrum of world religions" ("Series Foreword," in Hessel and Ruether, *Christianity and Ecology*, xxvi).

I coined the term *theo-dao* (*dao*) to contrast with the traditional *theo-logy* (*logos*) and its modern alternative, *theo-praxis* (*praxis*).[21] As its Chinese character consists of two ideographs, meaning "head" (being) and "vehicle" (becoming), dao means both the source of being (logos) and the way of becoming (praxis). It denotes the being in becoming or the logos in transformative praxis. Dao does not refer to an option of "either-or" but embraces the whole of "both-and." It does not force one to stay at the crossroad of logos (being) and praxis (becoming), but actualizes one to participate in a dynamic movement to be united in the cosmic track. The dao as the ultimate way and reality embodies the transformative praxis of the sociocosmic trajectory of life in the unity of knowing and acting.

If *theo-logy* is a perspective from above and if *theo-praxis* is that from below, then *theo-dao* is a perspective from an entirely different dimension, theanthropocosmic intersubjectivity. Theodao as a theology of life is neither logos-centric (knowledge) nor praxis-centric (action) but dao-centric (so to speak, *sophia* in action). Theodao can be reduced neither to an orthodoxy (a right doctrine of the church) nor to an orthopraxis (a right practice in history) but should embrace holistically the right way of life (ortho-dao), the transformative wisdom of living in a theanthropocosmic trajectory. What theodao pursues is neither only a metaphysical debate for church doctrines nor exclusively an ideological conscientization for social action but a holistic way of life. The key issue is whether we are in proper communication with the Spirit to participate in the loving process of theanthropocosmic reconciliation and sanctification.

While orthodoxy emphasizes faith and while orthopraxis underscores hope, orthodao focuses on love (1 Cor. 13:13). Whereas the primary theme of traditional theology is the epistemology of faith and whereas that of modern theopraxis is the eschatology of hope, the cardinal theme of theodao is the pneumatology of love. If the classical definition of theology is *faith-seeking-understanding* (*fides quaerens intellectum*) and if that of theopraxis is *hope-seek-*

---

21. See chapter 2 above.

ing-practice, then theodao takes the definition of *love-seeking-dao*. Whereas theology (God-talk) focuses on the right understanding of Christian doctrines and whereas theopraxis (God-walk) concentrates on the right practice of Christian ideologies, theodao (God-live) searches for the way and wisdom of Christian life.

In fact, the actual teachings of Jesus were not so much an orthodox doctrine, a philosophical theology, a manual of orthopraxis, or an ideology of social revolution, but the dao of life and living. Jesus Christ cannot be divided between the historical Jesus (theopraxis) and the kerygmatic Christ (theology). Following the first Korean Catholic theologian Yi Pyŏk (1754–1786), theodao conceives of Christ as the crossroad of the Heavenly Dao and the human dao; that is to say, the theanthropocosmic Dao (neither Christo-logy nor Christo-praxis, but *Christo-dao*).[22] Christodao comprehends Jesus Christ as both the Dao of crucifixion, the way of theanthropocosmic reconciliation, and the Dao of resurrection, the way of theanthropocosmic sanctification, which teaches us how we, cosmic sojourners, can live fully human in solidarity with other cosmic co-sojourners, particularly with the fullness of other exploited lives.

Ryu Yŏng-mo (1890–1981), a seminal Korean Christian thinker, conceived of the cosmogonic Christ from the deepest heart of the East Asian hermeneutical universe of dao. He believed that, in Christ, the Non-Ultimate (or the Ultimate of Non-Being; 無極) and the Great Ultimate (太極) become one. In Neo-Confucianism, this unity denotes the ultimate complementary and paradoxical opposites of the ineffable Vacuity (the Non-Ultimate) and the Cosmogony (the Great Ultimate).[23] From the vantage point of this supreme cosmogonic paradox, Ryu understood "the cross as both the Non-Ultimate and the Great Ultimate. . . . Jesus is the one who

---

22. For Yi Pyŏk, see Jean Sangbae Ri, *Confucius et Jésus Christ: La première théologie chrétienne en Corée d'après l'oeuvre de Yi Piek lettré Confucéen, 1754–1786*, Beauchesne Religions 10 (Paris: Beauchesne, 1979). For *christodao*, see chapter 3 above.

23. See Chan Wing-tsit, *A Source Book in Chinese Philosophy* (Princeton, NJ: Princeton University Press, 1963), 463-65; also *To Become a Sage: The Ten Diagrams on Sage Learning by Yi T'oegye*, ed. and trans. Michael Kalton (New York: Columbia University Press, 1988), 37-50.

manifested the ultimate in Asian cosmology. Through the sacrifice of himself, he achieved genuine humanity [rén]. That is to say, by offering himself as a sacrifice, he saved the human race and opened the kingdom of God for humanity."[24]

Further, Ryu articulated the cross as "the blood of the flower" (kkot-pi) through which the Son reveals the glory of the Father and the Father, the glory of the Son.[25] Seeing the blossom of this flower of Jesus (at the cross), he envisioned the glorious blossom of the cosmos (cosmogony). For Ryu, "the cross is a rush into the cosmic trajectory, resurrection is a participation in the revolution of the cosmic trajectory, and lighting up the world is the judgment sitting in the right-hand side of God."[26] Hence, according to him, the crucifixion and the resurrection of Jesus Christ do not refer to a narrow story about God's saving work exclusively for a species of homosapiens in the linear history in a tiny planet of the solar system, the Earth. On the contrary, these events signify a grand narrative of theanthropocosmic drama that Jesus, true humanity, has successfully penetrated into the cosmic trajectory to achieve the cosmotheandric union, lightening up the entire universe, and thus becoming the christic dao of true life (cf. Col. 1:16-17; John 1:3).

Furthermore, according to Ryu, the crucifixion and the resurrection are events that make the Being in Non-Being. Western Christologies, preoccupied by being (substantialism), neglect this dimension of non-being. In fact, the core of Christology is in this paradoxical mystery of creating being (resurrection) from non-being (crucifixion), which is God's cosmogonic principle (creatio ex nihilo). From this vantage point, Ryu formulated a fascinating Korean apophatic Christodao. Jesus is the One who "Is" in spite of "Is-Not," that is to say, "Being-in-Non-Being" (Ŏpshi-gyeshin

---

24. Kim Heung-ho, "Ryu Yŏng-mo's View of Christianity from the Asian Perspective," in Dasŏk Ryu Yŏng-mo, ed. Park Young-ho (Seoul: Muae, 1993), 299.

25. By this Korean word, Ryu expressed two metaphorical meanings of the cross simultaneously. On the cross, Jesus spilled blood like the blood of flower, which is also like the blossoming of the flower (of life).

26. Kim Heung-ho, "Yu Yŏng-mo's View," 301.

nim). Whereas we are those of non-being-in-being, he is the One of Being-in-Non-Being. Whereas we are the "forms" that are "none other than emptiness" (*Heart Sutra*), he is the "emptiness" that is "none other than form."[27] Christian theology needs to embody this cosmogonic principle of Being-in-Non-Being in order to be ecological and life affirming. Here is the significance of the medieval traditions of negative theology (*via negativa*) and *kenōsis* (emptiness).

Dàodéjīng describes dao with basically feminine metaphors: "mother of all things," "the root," "the ground" (of Being), or "the uncarved block" (the original nature). Dao is called "the mystical female": "The spirit of the valley never dies. It is called the mystical female. The gateway of the mystical female is called the root of Heaven and Earth" (*Dàodéjīng:* 6). "Can you play the role of the female in the opening and closing the gates of the Heaven?" (10).[28] This feminine vision is based on Laozi's principle of "reversal." Laozi always put the preferential option to the strategy of *yin* rather than that of *yang*.[29] This *yin* principle of reversal is closely connected with the principle of return. "Attain complete vacuity, maintain steadfast quietude. All things come into being, and I see thereby their return. All things flourish, but each one returns to its destiny. To return to destiny is called the eternal (Dao). To know the eternal is called enlightenment" (16).[30] The principles of reversal and radical return entail the spirituality of dao with the paradoxical power of weakness and emptiness.

---

27. Kim Heung-ho, *Jesori* [The Genuine Voice: The Words of Ryu Yŏng-mo] (Seoul: Pungman, 1985), 68.

28. Chan, *Source Book*, 144.

29. A. C. Graham, *Disputers of the Tao: Philosophical Argument in Ancient China* (La Salle, IL: Open Court, 1989), 223. Graham contrasted the strategies of *yin* and *yang* in the following chain of oppositions:

Yang	Yin	Yang	Yin
Something	Nothing	Before	Behind
Doing Something	Doing Nothing	Moving	Still
Knowledge	Ignorance	Big	Small
Male	Female	Strong	Weak
Full	Empty	Hard	Soft
Above	Below	Straight	Bent

30. Chan, *Source Book*, 147.

3. *Pneumatosociocosmic Biography of the Exploited Life*

Third, I suggest that theodao, as a theology of life in this age of ecological crisis, should take this spirituality of dao seriously. In order to resist merciless processes of genocide, biocide, and ecocide, theodao needs to be equipped with a strong Christian spirituality that embodies the principle of radical return and reversal with the paradoxical power of weakness and emptiness. Through his life-act, Jesus Christ taught us this spirituality of dao. The life-saving mystery of his resurrection entails a Christian principle of radical return (the victory of life over the power of death). At the same time, Jesus's crucifixion on the cross denotes a Christian principle of reversal with the paradoxical power of weakness and emptiness (cf. Isa. 53:5; Luke 6:20-21; 1 Cor. 1:18). The preferential option (the *yin* strategy) should be not only for the poor, minjung, and women but also for the wounded ecosystem as a whole including endangered species. In this regard, theodao should focus on sociocosmic biographies of the exploited life, that is, underside histories of ecological suffering, oppression, and exploitation. With these narratives as a point of departure, theodao can embody the Christian spirituality of reversal and return to execute sociocosmic transfromative praxis, the dao, healing the wounded mother Earth. In Christian faith, this spirituality implies nothing other than the eschatological hope of resurrection.

Kim Yong-bock, a Korean minjung theologian, argued that the social biography (the underside history) of minjung is a more authentic historical point of reference for theological reflection than doctrinal discourses (the official history) superimposed by the church and in the orientation of Western rationality.[31] It was an important proposal for Asian theology to realize minjung as the subject of history and a legitimate correction to traditional theology, primarily based on autobiographical (psychological) or church (official) narratives. Nevertheless, its focus on the political history of God and subsequently on anthropocentric history hinders Asian

---

31. Kim Yong-bock, "Theology and the Social Biography of Minjung," *CTC Bulletin* 5.3–6.1 (1984–85): 66-78.

theology from embracing the profundities of Asian religious and ecological thoughts. Theodao as an Asian theology includes underside histories of whole life systems on the Earth. It needs to thematize a sociocosmic (not only social but also cosmic) narrative of the exploited life, creatively crossing over both the social biography of minjung and the East Asian anthropocosmic vision. It is impelled to tell the story of the sociocosmic network of the exploited life in the light of the spiritual communion of outpouring *sin-ki* [*shén qì*; *pneuma*], a primordial *ki* or vital energy that is salvific, emancipatory, and reconciliatory.[32] Hence, theodao should focus on the pneumatosociocosmic biography of the exploited life.

Kim Chi Ha, a famous Korean poet, wrote an insightful essay, "The Ugŭmch'i Phenomenon," that illuminates the deeper meanings of *sin-ki* and the pneumatosociocosmic biography of the exploited life.[33] To heal his sickness from the long period of imprisonment by the military dictatorship, Kim Chi Ha retired to a small city in the southwestern part of Korea. In front of his house there was a little stream. The once pristine stream was now hopelessly polluted by industrial waste. When it rained, however, the situation changed. The rain not only swept out the wastes but also made the water clean again. Moreover, he was surprised to see many small fish swimming upstream against the flood of water! How could

---

32. This term *sin-ki* (Korean romanization) is composed of two Chinese characters 神氣. The first character *sin* [*shén*] has various translations such as ghost, spirit, soul, vitality, and sacred. The second character *ki* [*qì*] well known in the Chinese term *ch'i*, similar to the Greek word *pneuma*, has also various translations such as energy, vital force, material force, and breath. For the following Chinese terms, in this paper, I use their Korean transliterations to preserve peculiar nuances in their Korean usage:

	氣	神氣	太極	無極
Chinese	*qì* [*ch'i*]	*shén qì* [*shen-ch'i*]	*Tài jí* [*T'ai-chi*]	*Wú jí* [*Wu-chi*]
Korean	*ki*	*sin-ki*	*T'aegŭk*	*Mugŭk*
Translation	energy	vital energy	Great Ultimate	Non-Ultimate

33. Kim Chi Ha, *Saengmyŏng* (Seoul: Sol, 1992), 188-92. For a full English translation, see chapter 2 above.

such feeble fish swim upward against such a turbulent flow? This act puzzled him.

Through meditation, he realized that such a thing could happen by the work of *sin-ki*. The movement of one's *sin-ki* enables one to be aware of the *sin-ki* of others. When the *sin-ki* of a feeble fish becomes united with that of water, it can swim against even a mighty turbulent flood. Furthermore, as *ki*, "energy," always consists of *yin* and *yang*, the *ki* of water also moves in both directions of *yin* and *yang*. From the exuberant palpitation of the *sin-ki* of many fish in union with the *yin* movement of the water, Chi Ha discovered the key to understanding the mystery of the Ugǔmch'i War[34] in which the feeble minjung—literally a multitude of people (in this case several hundred thousands)—fought vigorously against Japanese troops armed with powerful mechanized weapons. Their collective *sin-ki* inspired and empowered the minjung to participate courageously in the movement and to be united with the primordial *ki*, in the same manner as the feeble fish that swim vigorously upstream against the formidable flood to be in union with the *yin* movement of the water. The fierce palpitation of the minjung against the turbulent flood of historical demons is in fact a great cosmic movement united with the *yin-yang* movement of *ki*. Chi Ha called this the ugǔmch'i phenomenon.

The first realization of Chi Ha in this parable was an ecological insight that nature ("rain") has a self-saving power to bring forth life in a fateful environment ("the polluted water") seemingly beyond remedy. He saw a hope for life in this spiritually fragmented and ecologically destructive world spawned by the developmental ideology of modern technological, commercialized, and cemented culture. A more important realization, however, is that from the *dao* world he found the clue to transcending historical dualism and the real source of the life energy that pours out such a vigorous vitality to the feeble fish and the minjung in Ugǔmch'i.

---

34. The last and fiercest battle during the second uprising of the Tonghak peasant revolution that broke out on the Ugǔmch'i Hill of Gongju, Korea, in December 1894.

This marked a radical turning point for his thought. Chi Ha was the one who had formulated a creative Korean hermeneutics of suspicion from the perspective of *han*, "the suppressed, amassed and condensed experience of oppression caused by mischief or misfortune so that it forms a kind of 'lump' in one's spirit."[35] He argued that minjung must be free from the vicious cycle of *han*-riddenness to resolve their *han*. This inspired Korean theologians to formulate minjung theology, and *han* has become a famous idiom of minjung theology. Some minjung theologians went forward to argue that a main task of theologians is to become priests of *han* to motivate and participate in the movement of *hanpuri* (a collective action to release *han*) of minjung and women.[36]

Chi Ha finally returned to the old dao world. This tells of a paradigm shift in his thought from a Korean version of the dualistic mode of contradiction (*han*) to the East Asian correlative mode of complementary opposites (*yin-yang*). The shift involves his enlightenment to the true source of the tremendously life-empowering force manifested by the feeble fish in the turbulent flood and the multitude of minjung in the Ugŭmch'i War. The key to revealing the mystery of the ugŭmch'i phenomenon is the notion of *ki*, a very East Asian term. Just like *pneuma*, *ki* is not so much dualistic and analytic as holistic and embracing; at the same time, it is both the source and the medium of empowerment. In this phenomenology of *ki*, the East Asian anthropocosmic vision can be expanded to the new horizon in the unity of Heaven (God), Earth (the cosmos), and humanity through the spirit (*ki, pneuma*), namely, "a pneumatoanthropocosmic vision."[37] This pneumatoanthropocosmic vision can cultivate a symbiosis of the life network through the communica-

---

35. The definition of Suh Nam-dong, a founder of minjung theology, in *Minjung Theology: People as the Subjects of History*, ed. Kim Yong Bock (Singapore: Commission on Theological Concern, Christian Conference of Asia, 1981), 65. Suh's theology of *han* was heavily influenced by Chi Ha's philosophy of *han*.

36. See Chung Hyun Kyung, "*Han-pu-ri*: Doing Theology from Korean Women's Perspective," *Ecumenical Reviews* 40, no. 1 (1988): 27-36.

37. For the pneumatoanthropocosmic vision, see chapter 2 above.

tion of *ki,* which fosters the human race's relationship with other lives more holistically and profoundly.

Neither the logos paradigm nor the praxis paradigm fits with this phenomenology of *sin-ki,* and both fall short of the analogical imagination that it presents. If the polluted flood metaphorically refers to the force of destruction, the feeble fish represent the force of life. Deconstuctionism has revealed that the logosphonocentric paradigm has had more affinity with the force of destruction than with the force of life. Rather, it has helped the demonic movement of the historical flood, by its involvement with sociological plots such as androcentrism and ethnocentrism and endangering global life by its dualistic fragmentation.

Although the praxis paradigm aggressively resists the force of destruction, it also remains within the limit of narrowly defined historical, social, and economic concerns that do not proceed beyond the logic that the force of destruction constitutes. It does not set out a self-sufficient description for the force of life but ends with a reactionary articulation against the force of destruction. Nor does it retain a deep understanding of the complex relation among God, humanity, and the cosmos such as those expressed in the Asian theanthropocosmic vision and the phenomenology of *sin-ki.*

Therefore, theodao needs to thematize a *sociocosmic biography of the exploited life,* creatively pushing beyond a dialectical sociobiography of minjung and an innocent anthropocosmic vision.[38] The ugŭmch'i phenomenon is an example of the sociocosmic biography of the exploited life, metaphorically telling the story of the two exploited lives, the feeble fish in the turbulent stream and the multitude of minjung in the Ugŭmch'i War. In addition, *ki* as both spirit and matter offers a clue to the mystery of the incarnation. While the birth story of Jesus refers to the pneumatoanthropocosmic vision par excellence, the passion narratives of Christ tell the

---

38. For the sociocosmic narrative of the exploited life, see chapter 2 (especially the discussion of the pneumato-anthropocosmic vision in section 3) and chapter 3, especially the section on Christ as the serendipitous pneumatosociocosmic trajectory in section 4).

sociocosmic biography of the exploited life par excellence. Jesus Christ as the theanthropocosmic Dao entails the life-breathing *pneumatosociocosmic trajectory* of the *sin-ki*.

Finally, theodao as a new paradigm of theology for the third millennium invites us to participate in rehabilitating the exploited life, including not only minjung and women but also endangered life systems and polluted nature, by the outpouring power of *sin-ki*. As the ugŭmch'i phenomenon illuminates, it requires the spirituality of dao, which empowers the principle of radical return and reversal with the paradoxical power of weakness and emptiness. A primary task of theodao as a Christian theology in the third millennium is to rehabilitate our planetary and cosmic habitats, that is, "our" home (*oikos*) in the universe, with the re-visioning of the true communion among God, humanity (the life), and Earth (the cosmos) and by the outpouring power of the cosmic Spirit, *sin-ki*. Therefore, a proper ecumenism for the third millennium demands not just an inter-Christian or an interreligious dialogue but a theanthropocosmic com-union to embody the transformative praxis in the pneumatosociocosmic trajectory, the Dao.

CHAPTER ELEVEN

Bio-Dao: Human Embryonic Stem-Cell Debates

1. The Political Hermeneutics of Life: A Contemporary Koan[1]

Human survival requires both the act of defining and the responsible action that flows from definition. That is what it means to be created co-creator. This self-definition, itself both reflective and political in character, configures the encounter with transcendence in our lives.[2]

This provocative statement by Philip Hefner has become a fulfilled prophecy in the arena of international politics. On March 8, 2005, the General Assembly of the United Nations (UN) adopted the Declaration on Human Cloning, "by which Member States were called on to adopt all measures necessary to prohibit all forms of human cloning inasmuch as they are incompatible with human dignity and the protection of human life."[3] This controversial dec-

---

Adapted from Heup Young Kim, "Sanctity of Life from a Confucian-Christian Perspective: A Preliminary Reflection on Stem Cell Debates," originally published in *Omega: Indian Journal of Science and Religion* 4, no. 2 (2005): 28-42. It was reprinted in *Global Perspectives on Science and Spirituality*, ed. Pranab Das (West Conshohocken, PA: Templeton, 2009), 107-24.

1. A Japanese word that means "evocative question."
2. Philip Hefner, "Biocultural Evolution and the Created Co-Creator," in *Science and Theology: The New Consonance*, ed. Ted Peters (Boulder, CO: Westview, 1998), 180.
3. United Nations, "United Nations Declaration on Human Cloning," March 8, 2005.

laration brings about a new battle of definition pertaining to life; in other words, it places the political hermeneutics of life at the center of international geopolitics. After voting against it, the representative from Korea stated, "The term 'human life' meant different things in different countries, cultures and religions. [Thus,] it was inevitable that the meaning of that ambiguous term was subject to interpretation."[4] The representatives from China, Japan, and Singapore gave similar responses. This dialogue is reminiscent of the case when Asian, traditionally Confucian, countries advocated Asian values vis-à-vis the human rights issues initiated by the United States. Whereas the latter case is related to social ethics (macro), the former case is related to bioethics (micro).

At any rate, life is not only an academic, metaphysical subject but a concrete concept related to geopolitical power. The dignity or sanctity of life has become a great *koan* for this century, a "biotech century." The central issue at this moment is human embryonic stem (hES) cell research. As in the UN Declaration, contemporary hES cell debates include four key words, namely (the sanctity and protection of human) life, (the compatibility with human) dignity, respect, and (the prevention of the exploitation of) women.

The hES cell debate since the beginning, particularly in the case of the United States, has been heavily rhetorical, for it is directly related to government funding and public policy for human health. It is said that the rhetoric for the research is characterized by exaggeration and inflation of promises, and some called it "gene-hype."[5] In fact, there is "the immense and substantive gap between discovery and cure." This high-tech, time-consuming, labor-intensive, and extremely expensive research is much more relevant to "the wealthier areas of the society, where the money is to be made."[6] It holds the position that disease is an individual problem (of the genetic code), neglecting its social and environmental causes. The

---

4. United Nations, Press Release GA/L/3271, February 18, 2005.

5. Thomas A. Shannon, "From the Micro to the Macro," in *The Human Embryonic Stem Cell Debate: Science, Ethics, and Public Policy*, ed. Suzanne Holland et al., Basic Bioethics (Cambridge, MA: MIT Press, 2001), 181.

6. Ibid.

question of who will benefit from stem-cell research is crucial and is not adequately addressed. "The rhetoric is that all will benefit. . . . [However,] even should stem cell–based therapy prove successful, the number of people who stand to benefit from it are a small subset of the whole population and perhaps even a small subset of all those with genetic diseases."[7] In fact, the macro issue is more important than the narrow micro issue. Thomas Shannon argued,

> [T]he micro ethical debate over the use of early human embryos is not the key factor in resolving the larger stem cell debate. Although a case can be made for the use of such stem cells, another more critical variable is the consequence of objectification of human nature in this way. In principle an argument for the use of such cells exists, the consequences of such use might be more problematic than we realize. However, I think the more important point is the macro issue, the social context in which such cells would be used.[8]

Furthermore, stem cells have been regarded as a subject of "expert bioethics" that necessitates "professional discourse."[9] "Public debate has been minimal," and the rhetoric has been dominated by elites and experts in the biomedical industrial complex. In this politics of rhetoric, "whoever captured the definition of hES cell research had won half the battle."[10] Also, scientific expertise has been used "as a weapon to control definitions."[11] Moreover, differentiating hES cell research from human cloning is a rhetorical strategy to avoid the emotionally charged cloning issue. The experts seem to have learned the following lesson from the cloning controversy: "*in modern bio-technological controversies, public debate must be shepherded and fostered by an elite that is prepared to seize rhetorical primacy, and*

---

7. Ibid., 182.
8. Ibid., 183
9. Paul R. Wolpe and Glenn McGee, "'Expert Bioethics' as Professional Discourse: The Case of Stem Cells," in Holland et al., *Human Embryonic Stem Cell Debate*, 185.
10. Ibid., 182.
11. Ibid., 183.

to mold existing institutions or create new ones for that purpose."[12] Paul R. Wolpe and Glenn McGee attempted to liberate the stem-cell discourse from the rhetoric of expert domination. "The process of deciding who will refine, reform, or reify definitions of these cells is a sociomoral exercise that has implications for the broader battle for or against hES cell research."[13]

2. Is the Embryo Life?

The initial, obvious but blunt debate in the United States is about whether the embryo is a person or property. On the one hand, most scientists and supporters for hES cell research claim that an embryo cannot be regarded as a person but rather can be regarded as a property (or a cell mass), because it has not yet attached to the uterine wall and gastrulation has not yet occurred (the "fourteen-day rule"). On the other hand, strong oppositions come from Roman Catholic and conservative Protestant churches. The Vatican's position is most resolute and clear-cut. The embryo possesses full human personhood, dignity, and moral status from the moment of fertilization. Therefore, it is not permissible to harm and destroy the blastocyst (trophectoderm) to derive stem cells from the inner cell mass.

Both positions are problematic. More careful and sophisticated but still ambiguous discussions have been generated by the National Bioethics Advisory Commission (NBAC) that the US government established at the request of President Bill Clinton in 1998. The NBAC proposed the more moderate position that the embryo is a form of human life but not a person (a human subject) yet. So is it not a property and must be treated with respect, though not at the same level as for a person. This position further makes a delicate distinction between totipotency and pluripotency. Simply, embryos are totipotent, while stem cells are pluripotent. A totipotent embryo (a potential human person) cannot be subject to research, because it requires harm and destruction. But a pluripotent hES cell can be subject to research, because it is not an embryo, so not a potential

---

12. Ibid., 195. Italics are original.
13. Ibid., 189.

person. This rhetoric of stem-cell research is ambivalent, because the nonindividuated embryo *ipso facto* cannot be an individual person.

Another issue in the debate involves a distinction between the principles of "beneficence" and "nonmalificence." It resembles the controversy between the utilitarian ethos and the principle of equality of protection on the issue of abortion. On the one hand, the beneficence position argues for hES cell research for the sake of utilitarian benefits for human health and well-being. On the other hand, the nonmalificence (or embryo protection) position opposes hES to protect the dignity of the embryo, the most vulnerable form of human life. It argues that the destruction of blastocysts is a devaluation of human life and is, so to speak, a kind of infanticide or even a new eugenics of euthanasia. This position presupposes that the human embryo is a human being and so has dignity, which raises the issues of defining and understanding human dignity and personhood.

3. What Is Human Dignity?

The definition of dignity frequently used in stem-cell debates in the United States derives from the philosophy of Immanuel Kant. Treat "each human being as an end, not merely as some further end."[14] This position is also the dominant view of Christian churches. The United Church of Canada has elaborated: "In non-theological terms it means that every human being is a person of ultimate worth, to be treated always as an end and not as a means to someone else's ends."[15] The conservative Southern Baptist Convention explicitly identifies human embryos as "the most vulnerable members of the human community."[16] Even the liberal United Methodist Church takes a similar position against

---

14. Ted Peters, ed., *Genetics: Issues of Social Justice* (Cleveland, OH: Pilgrim, 1998), 33.

15. The Division of Mission in Canada, "A Brief to the Royal Commission on New Reproductive Technologies on Behalf of the United Church of Canada, January 17, 1991," 14, cited from Peters, *Genetics*, 33.

16. Southern Baptist Convention, "On Human Embryonic and Stem Cell Research," cited in Ted Peters, "Embryonic Persons in the Cloning and Stem Cell Debates," *Theology and Science* 1, no. 1 (2003): 58.

hES cell research: "such practices seem to be destructive of human dignity, and speed us further down the path that ignores the sacred dimensions of life and personhood and turns life into a commodity to be manipulated, controlled, patented, and sold."[17] The Vatican's position is also clear: "the ablation of the inner cell mass of the blastocyst, which critically and irremediably damages the human embryo, curtailing its development, is gravely immoral and consequently gravely illicit."[18]

The underlying logic behind the Vatican's argument is "a tacit association" between "ensoulment" (the infusion of the spiritual soul into the physical body) and "genetic uniqueness" (a new genome) established at conception.[19] Following Pius XII, Pope John Paul II affirmed, "If the human body takes its origin from pre-existent living matter [evolution], the spiritual soul is immediately created by God."[20] In *Evangelium Vitae* (1995), he stipulated:

> The Church has always taught and continues to teach that the result of human procreation, from the first moment of its existence, must be guaranteed that unconditional respect which is morally due to the human being in his or her totality and unity in body and spirit: The human being is to be respected and treated as a person from the moment of conception; and therefore from that same moment his rights as a person must be recognized, among which in the first place is the inviolable right of every innocent human being to life.[21]

Hence, the door for hES cell research in the Roman Catholic Church is completely closed: "intentional destruction of innocent

---

17. The General Board of Church and Society, "Letter to Extend Moratorium on Human Embryonic Stem Cell Research," from Jom Winker to President George W. Bush, July 17, 2001.

18. Pontifical Academy for Life, "Declaration on the Production and the Scientific and Therapeutic Use of Human Embryonic Stem Cells" (Vatican City, August 2000), cited in Peters, "Embryonic Persons," 59.

19. Ibid., 60.

20. Pope John Paul II, "Evolution and the Living God," in Peters, *Science and Theology*, 151.

21. Pope John Paul II, *Evangelium Vitae* (March 25, 1995), *Acta Apostolicae Sedis* 87 (1995): 401–522, cited in Peters, "Embryonic Persons," 59.

human life at any stage is inherently evil, and no good consequence can mitigate that evil."[22]

The tacit association, however, between ensoulment and genetic uniqueness has been seriously challenged. First of all, embryology denies the actuality of "a moment of conception" but proves that "conception is a process" for nearly two weeks leading to implantation.[23] Further, "the blastocyst is not an individual person but a potential person." A potential person cannot be regarded as an actual person just as an acorn is not an actual oak tree. The Vatican's view assumes that genetic uniqueness is the basis for human dignity. But this is hardly tenable, because twinning is a natural phenomenon that occurs prior to fourteen days after fertilization. Mistakenly, it denies the human dignity of monozygotic twins by identifying their undeniable existence as a result of genetic abnormality. Furthermore, it has no room to acknowledge the dignity of cloned people who might appear in the future.

The Western notion of human dignity is primarily based on two pillars, the Christian view of the sanctity of the human person and the Enlightenment idea of the intrinsic value of a human person. Christian theology claims a human person as "an everlasting object of God's love," and Kant views self-determination or autonomy as the central value of human personhood.[24] However, both positions view dignity basically as intrinsic, still maintaining problems of Western anthropology such as substantialism, individualism, anthropocentrism, and archonic thinking (morality is grounded in a suitable interpretation of origins).

4. What Does Human Person Mean?

Ted Peters suggested three models of Christian anthropology: person as innate, person in communion, and person as proleptic.[25] The first, most prevailing but defective model discussed in the previous

---

22. Richard Doerflinger, "The Policy and Politics of Embryonic Stem Cell Research," *National Catholic Bioethics Quarterly* 1, no. 2 (Summer 2001): 143.
23. Peters, "Embryonic Persons," 64.
24. Ibid., 68.
25. Ibid., 68–72.

section assumes that dignity is intrinsic or innate. Theologically, dignity is not only intrinsic but also conferred, because human dignity is ultimately endowed by God. "Dignity is first conferred, and then claimed."[26] But Western thought since the Enlightenment has assumed that human dignity is inherent, so present at birth. In the genetic age, this archonic thinking generates such a view as the Vatican's that human dignity refers to the genetic uniqueness established at the moment of ovum fertilization and zygote creation.

The second model believes that dignity is not just inborn; rather, it—at least in the sense of self-worth—is relational, "the fruit of relationship."[27] The logic of genetic uniqueness "cannot count as a measure of personhood, dignity, or moral perfectibility," by the reality of monozygotic twins and the possible occurrence of cloned persons in the future. It certainly represents "the legacy of individualism" and "an unrealistic view of individual autonomy." "Nature is more relational. DNA does not make a person all by itself. . . . [For] once the embryo attaches to the mother's uterine wall about the fourteenth day, it receives hormonal signals from the mother that precipitates the very gene expressions necessary for growth and development into a child."[28] Ontologically, relationality precedes innateness. "Dignity is first conferred relationally, and then it is claimed independently." Theologically, dignity is ultimately a gift conferred by the grace of God.

Furthermore, Christian personhood is a communitarian concept in the context of the doctrine of the Trinity, "persons-in-communion" or "persons-in-relation." "The self-relatedness of God makes possible the self-relatedness of human beings; the other-relatedness of God makes possible the other-relatedness of human beings."[29] This relatedness denotes an "openness of being" beyond the individual and his or her biological origin. "A person is a self in the process of transcending the boundaries of the self. This self-transcendence is the root of freedom. . . . True personhood arises

---

26. Ibid., 68.
27. Ibid., 69.
28. Ibid., 70.
29. Ibid., 70-71.

through a trans-biological communion with God that transforms our relationship to the physical world."[30]

Underscoring Christian eschatology, the third model argues that the dignity of person is "proleptic," or "future oriented."[31] "Dignity derives more from destiny than from origin, more from our future than from our past." Peters said, "Persons whom we know and love today are on the way, so to speak; they anticipate their full essence as human beings by anticipating their resurrection and unity with Christ within the divine life. Our present dignity is itself part of this anticipation, a prolepsis of our eternal value conferred upon us by the eternal God. Dignity is not originally innate; it is eschatological and retroactively innate." Therefore, Peters concluded,

> Our final dignity, from the point of view of the Christian faith, is eschatological; it accompanies our fulfillment of the image of God. Rather than something imparted with our genetic code or accompanying us when we are born, dignity is the future end product of God's saving activity which we anticipate socially when we confer dignity on those who do not yet claim it. The ethics of God's kingdom in our time and in our place consists of conferring dignity and inviting persons to claim dignity as a prolepsis of its future fulfillment.[32]

As Peters elaborated, Christian theological anthropology advocates the person in relationship and persons as prolepsis of the eschatological humanity. This refers to the interpretation of the doctrine of the image of God (*imago Dei*) fully manifested in the personhood of Jesus Christ.

5. Respect for Life

Definitions of dignity so far defined are relatively anthropocentric and rather elitist by emphasizing full personhood. So another important language used in the discussion is *respect*. Ethical bod-

---

30. Ibid., 71.
31. Ibid.
32. Ibid., 72.

ies such as the US Human Embryo Research Panel (1994), the US National Bioethics Advisory Commission (1999), and the Geron Ethics Advisory Committee (1999) declared that the human embryo (and so the blastocyst) should be treated with proper and appropriate respect. Although the embryo is not regarded as fully as an individual person, it is entitled to respect. The meaning of respect, however, is "elusive." What does "respect" really mean in the context of hES cell research at the points of the creation, derivation, and manipulation of human embryos? To clarify this question, Karen Lebacqz suggested five models of respect in relation to persons, nonpersons, sentient beings, plants, and the ecosystem.[33]

Respect for person is again based on the Kantian criteria for personhood. They attribute the distinctiveness of personhood to self-determination or autonomy, that is, the ability to reason, to use the rational will, and to govern conduct by rules (*auto-nomos*). Respect in this context includes "active sympathy and readiness to hear the reasons of others and to consider that their rules might be valid."[34] However, embryos lack the ability of self-determination or autonomy, though they may have a potential to develop reason and become rule-governed beings. The Kantian personhood does not fit the nature of embryos.

The Judeo-Christian tradition endows a preferential option to the poor or to the minjung (民衆), the members of society who are most vulnerable to oppression, such as outcasts, strangers, sojourners, orphans, and widows. From this vantage point, though embryos are not a Kantian person, "the requirement for respect is not diminished."[35] This second model, however, is still anthropocentric. At this point, *respect for sentient beings* becomes relevant. Since sentience (an ability to feel pain and suffering) is distinctive of personhood, it can be the basis of respect for those who are not fully persons. However, Lebacqz does not propose a full vegetarianism. Humans are permitted to slaughter animals for the sake of

---

33. Karen Lebacqz, "On the Elusive Nature of Respect," in Holland et al., *Human Embryonic Stem Cell Debate*, 149-62.

34. Ibid., 151.

35. Ibid., 153.

nourishment. Respect in this context refers to a requirement that pain, fear, and stress be minimized. The biblical law that prohibits ingesting the blood of animals and the Native American practice of prayer to ask forgiveness of an animal to be killed for food illuminate this insight. The implication of this third model for research is that the destruction or manipulation of embryos is not necessarily disrespectful but requires great care and commitment to minimizing pain and reducing fear or stress.

Neither is the early embryo, still without the physical capability for feeling and emotion, a sentient being. The minimizing of pain and the reduction of fear are not so relevant in this context. Hence, the fourth and the fifth models concern nonsentient things such as plants and the ecosystem. Respect in these models implies attention to "the concrete reality" or "the independent value" of the other and of the ecosystem.[36] Respect requires us "to perceive the other in itself" and to see nature "as valuable *in and of itself*" rather than to see it as valuable *for us*. That necessitates decentering human perspective with deep epistemic humility and seeing other beings and things, including "not just sentient creatures, but land, rocks, trees, and rivers," "with respect and awe."[37] Lebacqz summarized the implications of this analysis with respect to the hES cell research.

> Researchers show respect toward autonomous persons by engaging in careful practices of informed consent. They show respect toward sentient beings by limiting pain and fear. They can show respect toward early embryonic tissue by engaging in careful practices of research ethics that involve weighing the necessity of using this tissue, limiting the way it is to be handled and even spoken about, and honoring its potential to become a human person by choosing life over death where possible.[38]

---

36. Ibid., 156-57.
37. Ibid., 156, 159.
38. Ibid., 160.

6. *Some Preliminary East Asian Christian Reflections*

Through the advance of embryology and genetics, the sanctity of life has become an ambiguous and elusive notion. Today, this concept is subject to reinterpretation that may necessitate a demythologization and even a scientification. This issue is one of the most significant and practical hermeneutical imperatives we are facing now. So far I have surveyed some major themes generated in North American discussions focusing on Christian theology and ethics. Overall, they do not seem to overcome fully their Western legacies of substantialism, individualism, anthropocentrism (dignity, person, and respect as individual entity). Nonetheless, there are some intriguing developments to my East Asian Christian eyes. Here are some of my preliminary reflections on those.

1. The language of respect is especially fascinating, because *kyŏng* (*jìng*, 敬) stands at the heart of Korean Neo-Confucian thought culminated by Yi T'oegye (1501–1570). For T'oegye, *kyŏng* entails not only epistemic humility but also profound ecological sensitivity (avoid treading the antmounds!). *Kyŏng* signifies the state of human mind-and-heart ready to realize its ontological psychosomatic union with nature, to fulfill the Confucian theanthropocosmic vision (the communion among the triad of Heaven, Earth, and humanity, 天地人). By attaining this state of mind, a person can possess an ability to hear the voices and feel the pain and sufferings of nature (commiseration) and can exercise beneficence (*rén*, 仁) whose attributes Confucianism calls Four Beginnings, namely, humanity, propriety, righteousness, and wisdom.[39] Western bioethicists such as Lebacqz are eagerly searching for precisely the state that Confucian sages saw as the starting point for self-cultivation in their students. In his doctrine of "the Oneness of All Things," Wang Yang-ming articulated,

> The great man regards Heaven, Earth, and the myriad things as one body. He regards the world as one family and the coun-

---

39. Michael C. Kalton, *To Become a Sage: The Ten Diagrams on Sage Learning by Yi T'oegye*, ed. and trans. Michael C. Kalton (New York: Columbia University Press, 1988), 119-41.

try as one person. As those who make a cleavage between objects and distinguish between the self and others, they are small men. That the great man can regard Heaven, Earth, and the myriad things as one body is not because he deliberately wants to do so, but because it is the natural humane nature of his mind that he does so.[40]

2. The definition of human personhood that Peters endeavored to introduce also resonates with Neo-Confucian anthropology. The human person in Confucianism does not mean "a self-fulfilled, individual ego in the modern sense, but a communal self or the togetherness of a self as 'a center of relationship.'" The second model of Peters, person-in-relation, is in fact the basic presupposition for the whole Confucian project. The crucial Confucian notion of *rén* denotes the ontology of humanity as being-in-relationship or being-in-togetherness. Again, in his famous passage of the Western Inscription, Zhāng Zài (1020–1077) wrote,

> Heaven is my father and Earth is my mother, and even such a small creature as I finds an intimate place in their midst. Therefore, that which fills the universe I regard as my body and that which directs the universe I consider as my nature. All people are my brothers and sisters, and all things are my companions.[41]

Moreover, Confucianism regards humanity as the heavenly endowment (天命; *Tiān mìng*), similar to the manner in which Christian theology understands humanity as the image of God (*imago Dei*). The dialogue I developed between Calvin and T'oegye shows clearly this characteristic of a relational and transcendental anthropology. "The Christian doctrine of *Imago Dei* and the Neo-Confucian concept of *T'ien-ming* reveal saliently this character-

---

40. Chan Wing-tsit, *Instructions for Practical Living and Other Neo-Confucian Writings* (New York: Columbia University Press, 1963), 272; also see Heup Young Kim, *Wang Yang-ming and Karl Barth: A Confucian–Christian Dialogue* (Lanham, MD: University of America Press, 1996), 43.

41. Chan Wing-tsit, *A Source Book in Chinese Philosophy* (Princeton, NJ: Princeton University Press, 1963), 497-98.

istic of a relational and transcendental anthropology. Calvin and T'oegye both define humanity as a mirror or a microcosm to image and reflect the glory and the goodness of the transcendent ground of being."

3. The final model of Peters, person as proleptic, is most intriguing. Dignity refers to *telos* (destiny) rather than origin. Peters brought the developmental and eschatological dimensions of Christian anthropology to the stem-cell debates. Dignity of life in the Christian sense ultimately (*telos*) means the eschatological personhood of Jesus Christ, just as that in the Confucian sense denotes future sagehood (聖人). In fact, this is precisely the significance of the Christian doctrine of sanctification and the Confucian teaching of self-cultivation. The sanctity of life has been ontologically and eschatologically conferred (as it is the *T'ien-ming* and the *imago Dei*) in every stage; it is primarily given (relational) rather than innate (substantial). Yet, in existence, it is ambivalent because of this transcendental potentiality (transcendent yet immanent). So it requires a rigorous process of self-realization, that is, sanctification and self-cultivation.

The human embryo should be treated with respect or reverence, but it is the sanctity of life in potential and in prolepsis that necessitate a full realization. The hES cell research can be a means to this self-realization of life (embryos) in the cosmic relationship. But life science cannot be the telos for itself in dealing with any stage or form of life system. Science is neither inevitable nor unstoppable.

4. From the East Asian Christian perspective, therefore, the sanctity of life rather implies the imperative for a life to realize itself to the fullest end of what it ought to be. This involves the diligent practice of sanctification and self-cultivation in mindfulness (or respect). A researcher in a laboratory is also a human person who needs to engage in this rigorous practice of mindfulness. This understanding may be the prerequisite to exercise one's freedom to help other forms of life accomplish their imperative for self-realization. But it denotes not so much a self-defined created co-creator self-consciously stretching to create techno-sapiens or the superhuman cyborg, as a humble cosmic co-sojourner participating in the great transformative movement of theanthropocosmic

trajectory, that is, the Dao (the Way).[42] Finally, the sanctity of life from an East Asian Christian perspective means a fulfillment and embodiment of the proleptic Dao, in its own freedom of life (*wú wéi*, 無爲). After all, both science and religion are daos for life, the great openness for cosmic vitality (*saeng-myŏng*, 生命).

---

42. Hefner has made an intriguing proposal of the created co-creator. "*Homo sapiens* is created co-creator, whose purpose is the stretching or enabling of the systems of nature so that they can participate in God's purposes in the mode of freedom. As a metaphor it describes the meaning of biocultural evolution and therefore contributes to our understanding of nature as a whole" (Hefner, "Biocultural Evolution," 174). Although sympathetic toward it, the East Asian Christian perspective does not endorse this proposal. For it still carries over the language of substantialism, individualism, and anthropocentrism as well as the modern paradigm of domination and control. In the East Asian Christian perspective, the freedom of life refers not so much to "the freedom to alter," change, or modify nature or life systems as to "the freedom not to alter" unless it is ultimately helpful for ecological and cosmic sanctification. It warns against the dangerous rise of techno eugenics under the pretext of superhuman ideology. Here, the distinction "between eugenic purposes and compassion purposes" is well taken. Genetic selection to help prevent or reduce suffering may be understandable, but genetic engineering to enhance genetic potential to produce "designer babies" (imagine their quality control!) in "the perfect child syndrome" is not permissible (see Ted Peters, *Science, Theology, and Ethics*, Ashgate Science and Religion Series [Aldershot: Ashgate, 2003], 191-99).

CHAPTER TWELVE

Techno-Dao: Transhumanism Debates (Cyborg, Sage, and Saint)

1. A Most Dangerous Idea for East Asia

My first response as an East Asian theologian to the "transhumanism" movement[1] was to regard it as one of "the most dangerous ideas" the West has ever produced.[2] This alarmed reaction to this enthralling but controversial movement was based on my experiences in the Korean and East Asian situations. A nation like Korea could once again easily turn into a laboratory and testing ground, as it did in the notorious case of the human embryonic stem-cell research performed by Dr. Hwang Woo-suk.[3] This embarrassing

---

Adapted from Heup Young Kim, "Cyborg, Sage, and Saint: Transhumanism as Seen from an East Asian Theological Setting," in *Religion and Transhumanism: The Unknown Future of Human Enhancement*, ed. Calvin Mercer and Tracy J. Trothen (Santa Barbara, CA: Praeger, 2014), 97-113. Republished by permission of ABC-CLIO, LLC, through Copyright Clearance Center, Inc.

1. According to Nick Bostrom, "Transhumanism is a loosely defined movement that has developed gradually over the past two decades, and can be viewed as an outgrowth of secular humanism and the Enlightenment. It holds that current human nature is improvable through the use of applied science and other rational methods, which may make it possible to increase human health-span, extend our intellectual and physical capacities, and give us increased control over our own mental states and moods" ("In Defense of Posthuman Dignity," *Bioethics* 19 [2005]: 202-14).

2. Francis Fukuyama, "The World's Most Dangerous Ideas: Transhumanism," *Foreign Policy* 144 (2009): 42–43.

3. See http://en.wikipedia.org/wiki/Hwang_Woo-suk.

case involved not only the conduct of a team of infamous scientists in Korea but also complex issues associated with the advancement of an East Asian country into a developed nation with respect to new technologies, potential markets, economic profits, global competition, national interests, and so on. In this context, scientists and government administrators can be tempted and pressured to promote cutting-edge science and technology by doing something sensational. In this respect, even Japan, the most developed country in Asia, has fallen prey to this temptation, as evidenced by controversies around stem-cell research; in particular, note the recent STAP (stimulus triggered acquisition of pluripotency) case related to the young rising Japanese star scientist Haruko Obokata.[4]

Amid the pressures to succeed and produce advances in science and technology, questions of ethics are not very popular. For some laboratory scientists and policy makers in government and industry, with the strong support of zealous nationalists, ethics reviews are seen as picky, uncooperative, hindering, and impractical backbiting. Further, many have become aware that dominant global standards (as influenced by the Judeo-Christian tradition) are neither neutral nor innocent but rather have significant politico-economic implications, mostly for the benefit of powerful nations in the West.[5] Furthermore, traditional, sophisticated Neo-Confucian moral systems have been compromised by the demand for national survival and development in this competitive world. For some, this has left science and technology enthroned with a pseudo-divine status in East Asia. The rivalry in the global market, particularly among neighboring countries, justifies aggressive research programs: "If we don't do this now, other countries will do it anyway!" And newly acquired luxuries and pleasures from capitalism reinforce the legitimacy of this drive.

The West has as its religio-cultural foundation the Judeo-Christian tradition, which continues to maintain its role as an ethical filter for challenges from science and technology.

---

4. See "RIKEN finds discrepancies, advises STAP retraction," *The Japan News*, March 15, 2014, http://the-japan-news.com.

5. See chapter 11.

Although its effectiveness is arguable, from the eyes of an East Asian theologian, the tradition still seems to be able to provide a framework for social discussion and ethical scrutiny of new technologies. For example, the United States President's Council on Bioethics summarized the arguments against transhumanism: "appreciation of and respect for 'the naturally given,' threatened by hubris; the dignity of human activity, threatened by 'unnatural' means; the preservation of identity, threatened by efforts at self-transformation; and full human flourishing, threatened by spurious or shallow substitute."[6] Unfortunately, however, it is hard to find even this level of discussion in East Asia. Moreover, a sturdy historical and emotional counter-orientalism within East Asian culture underlies the self-induced pressure on East Asians to advance into technological research. East Asian intellectuals resent the errors their ancestors made because of their idealistic Confucian virtue ethics. In their view, their forebears, by insisting too much on enlightened personhood with ethical systems too complicated to be practical, lost critical momentum, enabling uncivilized nomadic Europeans to overtake East Asia. They allowed the Europeans to take advantage of the very technologies they had developed but had been hesitant to use extensively. This hesitancy was due to fear of causing harm to the benevolence (*rén*) of humanity, a primal virtue of Confucianism.

2. A Naïve, Ultra-Right Ideology from the West

As I looked further into transhumanism, I came to realize that transhumanism is a naïve, ultra-right ideology arising from the Judeo-Christian and Enlightenment traditions. It is naïve, because transhumanists (with overconfidence in their techno capabilities) do not seem to recognize either the reality of the global world in which they are living, or the complexities of human history and nature itself.

---

6. The President's Council on Bioethics and Leon Kass, *Beyond Therapy: Biotechnology and the Pursuit of Happiness: A Report of the President's Council of Bioethics* (New York: HarperCollins, 2003), 155.

Like the theory of evolution, "transhumanism has emerged from a culture shaped by Christianity."[7] Transhumanism looks like a techno-secularization of the Judeo-Christian vision. For example, its idea of antiaging enhancement (radical life extension) toward immortality is reminiscent of Adam and Eve in the original creation, and the transhumanist vision of a post-singularity society sounds like a technocized Christian eschatology of the new Heaven and the new Earth, where there will be "no more death or mourning or crying or pain" (Rev. 21:4). James Hughes, a former executive director of the World Transhumanist Association, said, "Most Singularitarians are like pre-millennialist Christians. . . . The unbelievers not prepared to take advantage of the TechnoRupture and be born again into new eternal bodies are likely to suffer the Tribulations of being impoverished, wiped out or enslaved."[8] As Ronald Cole-Turner has said, there are considerable similarities between the goals of transhumanism and biblical visions.[9] Acknowledging those similarities, theologians in the West have been endeavoring to clarify the differences between Christianity and transhumanism. However, the hermeneutical horizons those theologians employ to make comparisons seem to be limited to the context of the European West.

Even in the intellectual history of the West, it would be illuminating to take a wider view, addressing, in particular, the relationship between transhumanism and communism. If Karl Marx's communism represents a social secularization of the Christian millenarian vision, then transhumanism represents a techno-scientific secularization of the Christian millenarian vision. These two movements resemble each other as secularized children of Christianity in light of Christian eschatology, the biblical vision of original human nature, the first Christian community, and the strong liberation

---

7. Ronald Cole-Turner, "Transhumanism and Christianity," in *Transhumanism and Transcendence: Christian Hope in an Age of Technological Enhancement*, ed. Ronald Cole-Turner (Washington, DC: Georgetown University Press, 2011), 193.

8. James Hughes, *Citizen Cyborg: Why Democratic Societies Must Respond to the Redesigned Human of the Future* (Boulder, CO: Westview, 2004), 173.

9. Cole-Turner, "Transhumanism and Christianity," 193-203.

motive for transformative praxis. Both argue and crusade for transformation but through different means; the former through global, social class struggle, and the latter through cosmic, technological transformation. Both prophesy a singularity (a moment of apocalyptic change in human history): the former to be realized by communist or socialist society (egalitarian utopia), and the latter by transhuman or posthuman evolution (cybernetic technopia).

There are clear distinctions between communism and transhumanism; the former aims at a change of the social superstructure in and through class struggle, whereas the latter focuses on the transformation of the fragile and inferior human body and brain (bio-fatalism) by means of radical technological enhancements. In an odd but dramatic way, however, transhumanism and communism are united in continuing the legacy of dualism in the history of Western thought, namely, nature versus nurture. While the latter focuses on the change of society (environment), the former emphasizes the transformation of human nature (substance). Each proudly proclaims itself a rightful descendant of the Enlightenment. In the West's dualistic framework, however, they represent the extreme left and extreme right wings of modern ideology.

A point already mentioned in reference to the East Asian setting needs to be repeated at this juncture. The European West, as the birthplace of both communism and transhumanism, seems to be capable of providing an ethical filter and has the societal power to put radical movements and ideologies, no matter how nominal, under social scrutiny. The East, however, has not been prepared to deal with such movements because westernization has compromised traditional moralities and value systems. A dramatic example of this dynamic is the anti-Confucius campaign in China during the Cultural Revolution. Furthermore, although the global experiment with communism is almost over, the Korean peninsula, the only remaining divided nation in the world, still suffers the tragic consequences of the Cold War. A recent example of the tensions between North and South Korea was the launching of a large number of rockets and missiles by North Korea toward the East Sea during the military drills of the allied forces of the United States and South Korea. This was a disturbing event, given that

South Korea's capital city, Seoul, which contains almost half of the population of South Korea, including my family, is within range of North Korea's firepower.

Although historically it has been the West that has developed new ideologies and initiated experiments for social transformation, it is not the West (strong nations) but the East (weak nations) where these ideological experiments have been forced into systematic practice and where people have suffered from their tragic consequences. For example, Japan was the aggressor nation that attacked Hawaii to bring the United States into World War II. Nevertheless, unlike Germany, it was not Japan (the West in the East) but Korea that was forcefully divided by the United States and the USSR after the war, without the consent of its own people, and which consequently experienced the most bloody global warfare of the Cold War. For a Korean theologian who has witnessed this historical reality and experienced the sufferings of people owing to this dehumanizing misconduct executed by the so-called superpowers in the West, suspicion of any new experimental ideology emerging from the West is inevitable. Therefore, any new experimental ideology arising from the powerful nations in the West should be subject to a serious hermeneutics of suspicion.

Although its political experiments have been not very successful, socialism supplies some helpful ethical tools. In fact, Marxist social analysis made important contributions to the rise of liberation theology in the third world (the so-called global South) which has helped to some extent to justify and purify Christianity in the twentieth century, by liberating Christian theology from the domination of the first world (the so-called North). Liberation theology has become an indispensable part of global Christianity, and even North American theologians have accepted that: "Liberation theology has become the ecumenical and global theology of our time."[10] The significance of liberation theology is not just symbolic and rhetorical but concrete. For example, the election of Pope Francis has helped to give Latin American liberation theology voice and credence.

---

10. Peter Hodgson, *Winds of the Spirit: A Constructive Christian Theology* (Louisville: Westminster John Knox, 1994), 67.

Although this divided and unjust world is still in need of an "emancipatory quest," transhumanism does not seem to be healing the division between the North and the South or providing benefits to people in developing countries in the South.[11] On the contrary, it displays a tendency to support and promote *laissez-faire* capitalism, and indications are that it will accelerate the depth of the division between these nations, adding technological and genetic aspects. As Ray Kurzweil said, "Although the argument is subtle I believe that maintaining an open free-market system for incremental scientific and technological progress, in which each step is subject to market acceptance, will provide the most constructive environment for technology to embody widespread human values."[12] While it presents rosy scenarios and science fiction fantasies, transhumanism, from the eyes of a theologian based in the realistic global situation in Asia, does not seem to go much beyond the wild dreams and armchair imaginations of futurist techno-enthusiasts in the first world.

Technology is fascinating and offers promise to humanity. However, history shows that strong, technologically advanced countries are more interested in using newly acquired advantages to maintain their hegemonies and strengthen their supremacies, rather than to help the human race as a whole. The situation of the real world we live in is and will be much more complicated than the virtual realities that techno-visionaries in the first world have imagined with their techno-hypes and digital fantasies expressed in science fiction films such as *Star Trek, Star Wars, The Matrix,* and *Avatar.*

3. The Roots of Transhumanism: Christianity and the Enlightenment

Various first world theologians have been endeavoring to formulate practical Christian theologies in realistic response to transhumanism.[13] As the Bible endorses the coming of the new Heaven,

---

11. Ibid., 64-85.

12. Ray Kurzweil, *The Singularity Is Near: When Humans Transcend Biology* (New York: Viking Penguin, 2005), 420.

13. See Cole-Turner, *Transhumanism and Christianity.*

Earth, and humanity through radical transformation, they argue, Christian theology need not block transhumanism and resist developing new enhancing technologies. While sympathetic to the movement, American Lutheran theologian Ted Peters has pointed out the naiveté of transhumanism in understanding progress and human sinfulness: "Transhumanist assumptions regarding progress are naïve, because they fail to operate with anthropology that is realistic regarding the human proclivity to turn good into evil. . . . They should maintain watchfulness for ways in which these technologies can become perverted and bent toward destructive purpose."[14] Simon Young proudly declared, "Bio-fatalism will increasingly be replaced by techno-can-do-ism—the belief in the power of the new technology to free us from the limitations of our bodies and minds. . . . In the twenty-first century, the belief in the Fall of Man will be replaced by the belief in his inevitable transcendence—through Superbiology."[15] This is naïve and overconfidently Promethean: "Let us cast aside cowardice and seize the torch of Prometheus with both hands."[16]

Transhumanists find their ideological roots in the Enlightenment and Western humanism, as Nick Bostrom explained, "Transhumanism is a loosely defined movement that has developed gradually over the past two decades, and can be viewed as an outgrowth of secular humanism and the Enlightenment."[17] Transhumanists view postmodernism as a nihilistic failure, because it critiques the Enlightenment values of reason and progress. However, the strong confidence in reason and progress of the "Enlightenment mentality" has been proven erroneous in this post-Western or post-Christian era (of "global Christianity").[18] Even in North America,

---

14. Ted Peters, "H-: Transhumanism and the Posthuman Future: Will Technological Progress Get Us There?" (September 1, 2011), http://www.metanexus.net.

15. Simon Young, *Designer Evolution: A Transhumanist Manifesto* (Amherst, NY: Prometheus Books, 2006), 20.

16. Ibid., 40.

17. Bostrom, "In Defense of Posthuman Dignity," 202.

18. See Philip Jenkins, *The Next Christendom: The Coming of Global Christianity* (Oxford: Oxford University Press, 2011).

constructive theologians such as Peter Hodgson have presented a convincing criticism of modernism.[19] From an Asian vantage point, furthermore, postmodernism is not a failure but rather is helpful in suggesting some necessary correctives to the errors of the "Enlightenment mentality" as it is embedded in a mythological belief in history and progress.[20] History has already shown that the positivistic optimism for human progress of Enlightenment thinking is naïve wishful thinking, as it was demonstrated by two dreadful world wars in the European West, not to mention Auschwitz and Hiroshima. Tu Wei-ming, a Chinese-American Neo-Confucian scholar at Harvard, evaluated the Enlightenment mentality as follows:

> A fair understanding of the Enlightenment mentality requires a frank discussion of the dark side of the modern West as well. The "unbound Prometheus," symbolizing the runaway technology of development, may have been a spectacular achievement of human ingenuity in the early phases of the industrial revolution. . . . [However,] the Enlightenment mentality, fueled by the Faustian drive to explore, to know, to conquer, and to subdue, persisted as the reigning ideology of the modern West. It is now fully embraced as the unquestioned rationale for development in East Asia.
>
> However, a realistic appraisal of the Enlightenment mentality reveals many faces of the modern West incongruent with the image of "the Age of Reason." In the context of modern Western hegemonic discourse, progress may entail inequal-

---

19. Arguing for a paradigm shift from modernism to postmodernism, Peter Hodgson elaborated seven crises of modernism: the cognitive crisis (Western logocentrism), the historical crisis (a theory of progress), the political crisis (the ending of Western hegemony), the socioeconomic crisis (the collapse of state capitalism and the increase of global economic injustice), the ecological crisis, the sexual and gender crises, and the religious crisis (the decline of Western Christianity, the spread of religious fanaticism, and interreligious dialogue). See Peter Hodgson, *Winds of Spirit*, 53-61.

20. See Tu Wei-ming, "Beyond the Enlightenment Mentality," in *Confucianism and Ecology: The Interrelation of Heaven, Earth, and Humans*, ed. Mary Evelyn Tucker and John Berthrong (Cambridge, MA: Harvard University Press, 1998), 3-22.

ity, reason, self-interest, and individual greed. The American dream of owning a car and a house, earning a fair wage, and enjoying freedom of privacy, expression, religion, and travel, while reasonable to our (American) sense of what ordinary life demands, is lamentably unexportable as a modern necessity from a global perspective. Indeed, it has now been widely acknowledged as no more than a dream for a significant segment of the American population as well.[21]

Ted Peters has also criticized the unrealistic optimism of transhumanists in regards to human nature. "And yet an item of looming significance is missing from this vision: a realistic appreciation for the depth and pervasiveness of what theologians call *sin*. As sinful creatures, we humans never lose our capacity to tarnish what is shiny, to undo what has been done, to corrupt what is pure."[22] To support his criticism of transhumanism, Peters made use of theologian Reinhold Niebuhr's analysis of personal sin. However, he missed a very important point in Niebuhr's analysis, namely, the complexities and ambiguities of structural sin (or "collective sin") beyond the realms of classical theology's psychological analysis of personal sin. As Niebuhr stated, "The group is more arrogant, hypocritical, self-centered and more ruthless in the pursuit of its ends than the individual."[23] Since structural sin is embedded in the sophisticated structure of collective power, Niebuhr argued, Christian theology and ethics need a more comprehensive and realistic strategy (a real Christian power politics) beyond a simple personal and psychological soteriology, namely, a Christian realism. This was a very important move for North American theological honesty within the global situation, motivating the rise of first world political theology and ethics. However, the Christian realism of Niebuhr has been criticized by liberation theologians in the third world,

---

21. Ibid., 4.
22. Ted Peters, "Progress and Provolution," in Cole-Turner, *Transhumanism and Transcendence*, 64.
23. Reinhold Niebuhr, *The Nature and Destiny of Man: A Christian Interpretation*, 2 vols., Gifford Lectures 1939 (New York: Scribner, 1964), 1:208-9.

because it later favored US foreign policy and national interests, a famous example of which was Niebuhr's unambiguous support for the US invasion of Vietnam. Although he was eager to examine the sinful natures of political, economic, societal, and cultural systems within the first world, Niebuhr failed to apply his method fairly in the global context but rather defended the hegemonic interest of the most powerful nation in the world.

At this point, I would like to raise five questions for transhumanist scholars (and transhumanism-friendly theologians), elaborating on some East Asian Christian perspectives on the related subjects:

1. Whose transhumanism?
2. What are the points of reference for transhumanism?
3. What type of humanism does transhumanism refer to?
4. What benevolence does it suggest?
5. Finally, what kind of transformation does it propose?

Although wrapped in the critical overtones of a hermeneutics of suspicion, these questions are not intended to denounce or condemn transhumanism but, on the contrary, to commence an honest search for the possibility of constructive dialogue with Asian theologies.

4. Transhumanism from an East Asian Christian Perspective

Whose Transhumanism?

The first question for transhumanism from an East Asian Christian perspective is whose perspective informs the understanding of transhumanism? Turning to the biblical source, the Sermon on the Plain describes "a preferential option for the poor," proclaiming, "Blessed are you poor, yours is the kingdom of God!" (Luke 6:24). The Christian Gospels are good news to the losers (or the unfit), the outcasts, the alienated, the disabled, the marginalized, and the minjung (simply, the oppressed), explicitly declaring "Woe to you that are full, for you shall hunger!" (Luke 6:25). In contrast, what is the techno-gospel of transhumanism? Transhumanism seems to declare a preferential option for the rich and the powerful, offering good news for the elite, the strong, the oppressors, and those winners in this ruthlessly competitive world for the evolutionary survival of the fittest. Peters has said, "Transhumanism is not a philosophy for the losers, for the poor who are slated to be left behind in the struggle for existence."[24] However, Jesus clearly declared, "How hard it is for those who have riches to enter the kingdom of God! For it is easier for a camel to go through the eye of the needle than for a rich man to enter the kingdom of God" (Luke 18:25; Matt. 19:25; Mark 10:25).

Even if transhuman projects are successfully achieved, they will be extremely expensive, and so only a limited number of people in the most advanced nations will be able to take advantage of their benefits, in a situation that will exponentially escalate economic and technological divides between the North and the South. Even if transhumanists somehow accomplish the building of a technological paradise on Earth or elsewhere in the universe, only the rich, the powerful, and the techno-elites who are financially and technologically capable will be able to enjoy the benefits. This will not be the kingdom of God Jesus talked about. Furthermore, transhumanist utterances in favor of the modification of human brains and bodies remind East Asian people of the nightmarish memory of human living-body tests for eugenics cruelly carried out by the special military units of Imperial Japan during World War II using the bodies and brains of other East Asians such as Koreans and the Chinese. Nevertheless, the current Japanese government is working hard to revise the Peace Constitution in order to remilitarize Japan using the excuse of military threats from North Korea and China, while persistently denying the historical fact of the criminal acts of the Japanese Imperial Army during World War II, on the issue of sexual slavery (so-called comfort women).

Which Points of Reference?

The second question I have for transhumanism concerns the goals of the movement. What are the points of reference to prove or

---

24. Ibid., 71.

evaluate the validity of these goals? I see listed in "the outline of transhumanism," mostly material goals in terms of modifying the brain and body by external means of science and technology.[25] But I do not see any convincing ideas for improving the global situation in terms of economic and ecological justice and morality. The goals of transhumanism along these lines are less impressive than even those that socialism offered. On the contrary, transhumanists seem to be more interested in pursuing superintelligence and controlling powers in order, even, to be able to play God: "We may be intended to evolve towards a posthuman apotheosis, or we may choose to become gods ourselves in order to challenge the Creator(s) for dominion."[26] However, the Christian God revealed in Jesus Christ is not an omnipotent God bent on domination but rather a self-emptying, kenotic God with the self-giving love of *agapē* (Phil. 2:6-8).

This may be the area in which transhumanism-friendly, first world theologians can play a leading role. The late Harvard theologian Gordon Kaufman provided helpful insight into the role of theology for a post-Christian, nuclear age. The significance of the notion of God, and so theology, from his North American perspective, is that it gave an ultimate point of reference "to which everything human was to be judged and assessed. Thus, the idea of God and of God's will functioned as a transcendent point of reference in terms of which everything human and finite could be evaluated."[27] This is a twentieth-century version of Anselm of Canterbury's definition of God as "that which nothing greater can be conceived." Kaufman set up the thesis: "Criticism and reconstruction of the image/concept of God will involve continuous reference to contemporary forms of experience and life—personal, social, moral, aesthetic, scientific—

---

25. http://en.wikipedia.org/wiki/Outline_of_transhumanism; also, http://en.wikipedia.org/wiki/Transhumanism.

26. James J. Hughes, *The Compatibility of Religious and Transhumanist Views of Metaphysics, Suffering, Virtue and Transcendence in an Enhance Future* (Hartford, CT: Institute for Ethics and Emerging Technologies, 2007), 30; http://ieet.org.

27. Gordon D. Kaufman, *The Theological Imagination: Constructing the Concept of God* (Philadelphia: Westminster, 1981), 85.

all of which must be related to, and thus relativized and humanized by, the concept of God, if God is indeed to function as 'ultimate point of reference' in contemporary life."[28]

In this age when humanity has the power to wipe out not only the whole human race but also entire ecosystems of our planet, I wonder how transhumanists can justify their goals, while explicitly declaring the end of *Homo sapiens* in order to advocate a collectively intentional alteration into the omnipotent *Homo cyberneticus*. Do they presuppose that genetic extinction is an inevitable gate through which the human race will pass in anticipation of the singularity that will result in the evolution of the posthuman? Transhumanists rationalize their cause by means of the Enlightenment values of reason and progress. As I already mentioned, the validity of these Enlightenment values has been considered questionable even in the Western context. Further, since the middle of the twentieth century, these values have been vehemently criticized as the primary causes of today's planetary ecological crisis.

Furthermore, from the vantage point of nonmonotheistic religions, the idea of salvation history moving in the course of linear time, which is the foundation for the Enlightenment optimism in progress and development, is an anthropocentrically reductionistic worldview that has brought about ecological disaster by neglecting the holistic relationship of humans with the cosmos and the Earth. Raimon Panikkar, an Indian Catholic-Hindu scholar, viewed this notion of history as a fallible belief in the myth of history.[29] According to him, the history of world religions presents three great religious visions: ancient cosmocentrism, medieval theocentrism, and modern historico-anthropocentrism. All of these are inaccurate, one-sided, reductionistic (monocentric) views of reality. In fact, God (or the Ultimate), humans, and the cosmos constitute three inseparable and concentric axes of the one reality. This triadic view is the theanthropocosmic (or cosmotheandric) vision that was presupposed not only in Asia but

---

28. Ibid., 274-75.
29. See Raimon Panikkar, *The Cosmotheandric Experience: Emerging Religion Consciousness* (Maryknoll, NY: Orbis Books, 1993).

also to some extent in the early and medieval eras of the West but which was lost in modern times through an excessive emphasis on historicism and anthropocentrism. In addition, new branches of science since Albert Einstein have demonstrated that the static notion of linear time flying like an arrow is false; rather, time is dynamic, holistic, and relational.

Which Humanism?

The third question from an East Asian perspective is, of what kind of humanism does transhumanism speak? An axiomatic pillar of Neo-Confucianism, which is a common religio-cultural background for East Asian people, is what has been termed the "anthropocosmic vision" inherent in the Confucian belief in the "mutual dependence and organic unity" of Heaven and humanity.[30] *The Doctrine of the Mean*, one of the Confucian Four Books, begins, "What Heaven imparts to man is called human nature. To follow our nature is called the Way [Dao]. Cultivating the Way is called education."[31] In this anthropocosmic vision, humanity (anthropology) not only is inseparable from Heaven (cosmology) but also is conceived of as its microcosm. This East Asian anthropocosmic approach to anthropology is quite different from the anthropocentric approach prevalent in the West.

This East Asian anthropology entails an "inclusive humanism," in contrast to the "exclusive humanism" dominant in the modern West since the dualistic rationalism of Descartes. Whereas exclusive humanism "exalts the human species, placing it in a position of mastery of and domination over the universe," inclusive humanism "stresses the coordinating powers of humanity as the very reason for its existence." Cheng Chung-ying, a Chinese-American Confucian scholar at the University of Hawaii, has criticized Western humanism:

---

30. Tu Wei-ming, *Centrality and Commonality: An Essay on Confucian Religiousness,* SUNY Series in Chinese Philosophy and Culture (Albany: State University of New York Press, 1989), 107.

31. Chan Wing-tsit, *A Source Book in Chinese Philosophy* (Princeton, NJ: Princeton University Press, 1963), 98.

In this sense, humanism in the modern West is nothing more than a secular will for power or a striving for domination, with rationalistic science at its disposal. In fact, the fascination with power leads to a Faustian trade-off of knowledge and power (pleasure and self-glorification) for value and truth, a trade-off which can lead to the final destruction of the meaning of the human self and human freedom. . . . Humanism in this exclusive sense is a disguise for the individualistic entrepreneurship of modern man armed with science and technology as tools of conquest and devastation.[32]

In contrast, he argues, the inclusive humanism that is rooted in Neo-Confucianism "focuses on the human person as an agency of both self-transformation and transformation of reality at large. As the self-transformation of a person is rooted in reality and the transformation of reality is rooted in the person, there is no dichotomy or bifurcation between the human and reality."[33] I would like to ask whether the humanism transhumanists have in mind is free from the exclusive humanism of the modern West and can welcome the inclusive humanism of East Asia.

Which Benevolence?

The fourth question is what kind of benevolence (or beneficence) does transhumanism suggest. Whereas the history of the religiously homogeneous West is filled with bloody religious wars and conflicts, such religious warfare is uncommon in the history of religiously plural East Asia. East Asian scholars assume that this is because the West is culturally based on a *conflict* model much influenced by Greek dialectical dualism, while the East is based on a *harmony* model exemplified by the *yin-yang* relationship.[34] In this

---

32. Cheng Chung-ying, "The Trinity of Cosmology, Ecology, and Ethics in the Confucian Personhood," in *Confucianism and Ecology: The Interrelation of Heaven, Earth, and Humans*, ed. Mary Evelyn Tucker and John Berthrong (Cambridge, MA: Harvard University Press, 1998), 213-14.

33. Ibid., 214.

34. See Shu-hsien Liu and Robert E. Allinson, eds., *Harmony and Strife:*

Neo-Confucian world, *rén* (benevolence), the primal virtue and the very definition of humanity, etymologically means the ontology of two people (or being-in-togetherness). Hence, Neo-Confucian wisdom commends the habit of the negative golden rule ("Do not do to others what you do not want them to do to you!"), for it is an attitude that entails "epistemological modesty" and "ethical *humility*," the crucial virtues needed in treating others as "guests" or "friends" and therefore in bringing harmony in the world. But the habit of the positive golden rule ("Love others *in your own ways!*"), though preferred in the Christian West, is carefully avoided. For it can cause the opposite attitudes of "epistemological immodesty" and "ethical *hubris*," which are prone to treating others as "strangers" or "enemies" in a conflict complex and can eventually foster the principles of domination and exploitation.[35] These attitudes served as a root cause for the modern failure of the arrogant Western Christian mission in Asia, not to mention Western imperialism. I wonder whether the benevolence transhumanism advocates (including "procreative beneficence") is free from these Western habits of epistemological immodesty and ethical *hubris*, the superimposing of one's own definition of benevolence (or love) on others (including future children) who may have different ideas in different contexts.

What Transformation? Cyborg, Sage, and Saint— Transhumanization, Self-cultivation, and Sanctification

Transhumanism basically refers to a transformation toward human perfection by means of science and technology. The fifth question refers to the nature of the transformation that transhumanism advocates. How does transhumanism define humanity and what is its *telos* of humanity?

First of all, the human person in the Neo-Confucian sense does not mean "a self-fulfilled, individual ego in the modern sense,

---

Contemporary Perspectives, East and West (Hong Kong: Chinese University Press, 1988).

35. Robert E. Allinson, "The Ethics of Confucianism & Christianity: The Delicate Balance," *Ching Feng* 33, no. 3 (1990): 158-75.

but a communal self or the togetherness of a self as 'a center of relationship.'"[36] The crucial Confucian notion of *rén* denotes the ontology of humanity as the being-in-relationship or the being-in-togetherness, which extends to an anthropocosmic vision (humanity and cosmos in harmonious relationship). In a famous passage of the *Western Inscription*, Zhang Zai wrote:

> Heaven is my father and Earth is my mother, and even such a small creature as I finds an intimate place in their midst. Therefore, that which fills the universe I regard as my body and that which directs the universe I consider as my nature. All people are my brothers and sisters, and all things are my companions.[37]

Further, Confucianism regards humanity as the heavenly endowment (*Tianming*), in a manner similar to the way in which Christian theology understands humanity as the image of God (*imago Dei*). A comparative study between John Calvin and Yi T'oegye, the most important scholar in the history of Korean Confucianism, describes this relationship: "The Christian doctrine of *Imago Dei* and the Neo-Confucian concept of *Tianming* [*T'ien–ming*] reveal saliently this characteristic of a relational and transcendental anthropology. Calvin and T'oegye both define humanity as a mirror or a microcosm to image and reflect the glory and the goodness of the transcendent ground of being."[38]

I have already asked about the *telos* of transhumanism, the goal of transhuman transformation or transhumanization by external means of science and technology. Confucianism and Christianity have carefully spoken on the issue of transformation. But their focus is on an inner transformation, a self-realization or a full humanization. In the Christian sense, the *telos* of self-transformation is to achieve sainthood, in and through the imitation of the eschatological personhood of Jesus Christ (*imago*

---

36. Tu, *Centrality and Commonality*, 53.
37. Chan, *Source Book*, 497-98.
38. See chapter 6 above.

Dei), and in the Confucian sense it is to attain sagehood in and through the cultivation of self toward a full humanization of what humanity originally ought to be (*Tianming*). This refers to the doctrine of sanctification in Christian theology and the teaching of self-cultivation in Neo-Confucianism, respectively. Both traditions endorse the dignity of humanity as the sanctity of life has been ontologically and eschatologically conferred in every stage; it is primarily given (relational) rather than innate (substantial). Yet, in existence, the human condition is ambivalent, because this transcendental potentiality has not been fully activated. So it requires a rigorous process of self-realization, that is, sanctification and self-cultivation.

From an East Asian Christian perspective, therefore, the sanctity of life implies the imperative for a life to realize to the fullest extent what it ought to be. This involves the diligent practice of sanctification and self-cultivation in reverence, including mindfulness, humility, and respect for others. Scientists and engineers should also engage in this rigorous practice of self-realization with an attitude of reverence. This attitude should be a prerequisite to exercising one's freedom to help others to accomplish their own imperatives for self–realization. It entails the attitude of humility in participating as a player rather than as a designer or a manager in the great transformative movement of the theanthropocosmic trajectory, that is, the Dao (the Way). The dignity of humanity from an East Asian perspective means a fulfillment and embodiment of the proleptic Dao, in its own freedom of life (*wu-wei*) and with a great openness for cosmic vitality, which is referred to as *ki* [*qi*] in East Asia and the Holy Spirit in Christianity. In an East Asian Christian perspective, therefore, freedom may refer not so much to "the freedom to alter," change, or modify nature or life systems but rather "the freedom not to alter" them unless such a change is ultimately helpful for ecological and cosmic sanctification.

I presume that transhumanist scholars would regard this Neo-Confucian mode of thinking as archaic (or "bio-conservative"), as they see the concept of the natural "as problematically nebulous at best, and an obstacle to progress at worst."[39] In East Asia, however, the way of thinking about nature is quite different from that of the West. The traditional Western understanding of "nature" carries a pejorative connotation inherited by the Greek and Christian hierarchical dualism between the supernatural and the natural. In contrast, Neo-Confucianism accommodates the profound Daoist insights pertaining to nature and *wú-wéi* ("actionless activity"), "a state of passivity, of 'non-action,' but a passivity that is totally active, in the sense of receptivity."[40] In Chinese characters, etymologically, nature means "*self-so*," "spontaneity," or "naturalness," that is to say, "the effective modality of the system that informs the actions of the agents that compose it."[41] In other words, *nature* in East Asian thought is the primary "self-so" (natural) manifestation of the Dao (the ultimate principle). The Bible also seems to endorse this affirmative sense of nature, because nature as God's creation is defined as "good" and the denial of its goodness as "self-so" would be regarded as the fallacy of Gnosticism.

Bede Griffiths, though a British Benedictine monk, after having studied world religions during a stay of many years in India, suggested a rather different insight from the views of tranhumanists, elucidating the relationship of the East and the West in terms of the *yin-yang* complementary opposite:

> This may sound very paradoxical and unreal, but for centuries now the western world has been following the path of *Yang* of the masculine, active, aggressive, rational, scien-

---

39. See http://en.wikipedia.org/wiki/Transhumanism, 6. See also Nick Bostrom and Anders Sandberg, "The wisdom of Nature: An Evolutionary Heuristic for Human Ehhancement," in *Human Enhancement*, ed. Julian Savulescu and Nick Bostrom (Oxford: Oxford University Press, 2008), 375-416.

40. Bede Griffiths, ed., *Universal Wisdom: A Journey through the Sacred Wisdom of the World* (San Francisco: HarperSanFrancisco, 1994), 27.

41. Michael C. Kalton, "Asian Religious Tradition and Natural Science: Potentials, Present and Future," unpublished paper, the CTNS Korea Religion & Science Workshop, Seoul, January 18-22, 2002.

tific mind and has brought the world near destruction. It is time now to recover the path of *Yin*, of the feminine, passive, patient, intuitive and poetic mind. This is the path which the *Tao Te Ching* sets before us.[42]

There still remains a very basic question about transhumanist anthropology. What kind of personhood is transhumanization looking for, after all? A posthuman cyborg, a machine-human being of the *Homo cyberneticus*, further self-evolved beyond the *Homo sapiens*? By choosing the path of transformation with the highest external use of science and technology, can transhumanism qualitatively liberate humanity from the ambiguous human condition of being a sinner (Christianity), a small person (Confucianism), or even a robot controlled by selfish genes (sociobiology)? How does transhumanism enable the transhuman "desire to control the body, to live longer, to be smarter and be happier," to be free from the habits which St. Augustine called concupiscence and which Neo-Confucianism called the existential human mind with selfish desires?[43] Brent Waters seems to have a similar concern: "To assert that humans should become posthuman requires the invocation of a higher and transcendent good that trumps the anthropocentric standard. What remains unclear in transhumanist literature is the source of this transcendent good that humans should pursue. . . . Or, posed as a question: what is the source of the 'trans' that justifies its affixation to 'humanist'?[44]"

This is the crucial point where both Confucianism and Christian theology begin their spiritual discourses on self-cultivation and sanctification. In a nutshell, the goals of both traditions are converging, as both lead one to seek freedom (of the sage and saint) from the habits of concupiscent and selfish desires, in and through a rigorous examination—an examination which aims to avoid such selfish desires in light of historically tested points of reference

---

42. Griffiths, *Universal Wisdom*, 27-28.

43. Hughes, *The Compatibility of Religious and Transhumanist Views*, 7.

44. Brent Waters, *From Human to Posthuman: Christian Theology and Technology in a Postmodern World* (Aldershot: Ashgate, 2006), 78.

(namely, "the innate knowledge of the good" endowed by the *Tien-ming* and "the humanity of Christ" embodied by the *imago Dei*).[45] Hence, from the vantage points of Confucian self-cultivation and Christian sanctification, the true meaning of freedom is not so much the choice to freely use science and technology for the sake of one's own material benefits, but, more importantly, it is a spiritual freedom from human propensities toward concupiscence and sin. In fact, Teilhard de Chardin, who has been regarded as a precursor to transhumanists, has also clearly articulated that, "it is upon its point (or superstructure) of spiritual concentration, and not on its basis (or infrastructure) of material arrangement [in other words, 'material paganism'], that the equilibrium of Mankind biologically depends."[46]

Finally, can the transhuman cyborg, so enhanced, modified, transformed, or created, be really better, wiser, and even holier than the Confucian sage and the Christian saint? Can she, he, or it become a real hope for the human race (and other life systems) in this divided, unjust, and possibly unsustainable world? In this regard, was not George Lucas a prophet who, through his film series *Star Wars*, presented a sort of prophecy about the true hope for humanity in a time far, far away? He seems to have foreseen that humanity's future hope will be neither in Darth Vader (a mightily enhanced trans-human-being) nor in the Empire equipped by the invincible power of science and technology, but in Jedi knights such as Luke Skywalker (a real human being) and Yoda (a sage), self-cultivated with the dignity of humanity and trained in communion with the natural Force of cosmic vitality which East Asians call *Ki* [*Qi*].

And so, "May the Force [*Ki*] be with You!"

---

45. For this discussion, see Heup Young Kim, *Wang Yang-ming and Karl Barth: A Confucian–Christian Dialogue* (Lanham, MD: University of America Press, 1996).

46. Pierre Teilhard de Chardin, *The Future of Man*, trans. Norman Denny (New York: Harper & Row, 1964, 1969), 317.

Glossary

Terms in Chinese Romanization

Pinyin	WG*	English	Chinese Characters
ài	*ai*	love	愛(爱)
chéng	*ch'eng*	sincerity	誠(诚)
chéng yì	*ch'eng-i*	the sincerity of the will	誠意(诚意)
dào	*tao*	the way	道
Dào xīn	*Tao-hsin*	the mind of dao	道心
dé	*te*	virtue	德
gé wù	*ko-wu*	the investigation of things	格物
jìng	*ching*	reverence, piety, mindfulness	敬
lǐ	*li*	principle	理
lǐ	*li*	propriety	禮(礼)
liáng zhī	*liang-chih*	the innate knowledge of the good	良知
liáng xīn	*liang-hsin*	good conscience	良心

* WG: *Wade-Giles Romanization System*

lì zhì	*li-chih*	the establishment of the will	立志
míng dé	*ming-te*	the clear character, the illustrious virtue	明德
qì	*ch'i*	material force, vital energy	氣(气)
qīn mín	*ch'in-min*	loving people	親民(亲民)
qíng	*ch'ing*	feeling	情
rén	*jen*	human being	人
rén	*jen*	benevolence, co-humanity	仁
rén xīn	*jen-hsin*	the human mind	人心
Shàng dì	*Shang-ti*	the Lord on the High	上帝
shēn	*shen*	body	身
shén	*shen*	Spirit, God	神
shén qì	*shen-ch'i*	vital energy, divine energy	神氣(神气)
shù	*shu*	reciprocity	恕
Tài jí	*T'ai-chi*	the Great Ultimate	太極(太极)
Tài xū	*T'ai-hsu*	the Great Vacuity	太虛
tǐ	*t'i*	substance	體(体)
Tiān lǐ	*T'ien-li*	Heavenly Principle, Principle of Nature	天理

Tiān mìng	*T'ien-ming*	Heavenly Endowment, the Mandate of Heaven	天命
Wàn wù yī tǐ	*Wan-wu i-t'i*	the Oneness of All Things	萬物一體 (万物一体)
Wú jí	*Wu-chi*	the Non-Ultimate	無極(无极)
wú wéi	*wu-wei*	non-action action	無爲(无为)
xīn	*hsin*	mind-and-heart	心
xìn	*hsin*	faithfulness	信
xīn jí lǐ	*hsin chih li*	the identity of mind-and-heart and principle	心卽理
xìng	*hsing*	Nature, human nature	性
xìng jí lǐ	*hsing chi li*	the identity of nature and principle	性卽理
yáng	*yang*	yang	陽(阳)
Yì	*I*	*The Change*	易
yì	*i*	righteousness	義(义)
yī qì	*i-ch'i*	primordial energy	一氣(一气)
yīn	*yin*	yin	陰(阴)
yòng	*yung*	function	用
yuán hēng lì zhēn	*yuan heng li chen*	origination, flourishing, benefitting, firmness	元亨利貞(元亨利贞)

zhèng xīn	*cheng-hsin*	the rectification of the mind-and-heart	正心
zhī	*chih*	knowledge	知
zhì	*chih*	wisdom	智
zhì liáng zhī	*chih liang-chih*	the extension of the innate knowledge of the good	致良知
zhōng	*chung*	equilibrium	中
zhōng yōng	*Chung-yung*	*The Doctrine of Means*	中庸

Terms in Korean Romanization

Korean	*Pinyin [WG*]*	*English*	*Chinese Character*
il-ki	yī qì [*i-ch'i*]	primordial energy	一氣[一气)
ki	qì [*ch'i*]	material force, vital energy	氣(气)
kyŏng	jìng [*ching*]	reverence, piety, mindfulness	敬
Mugŭk	Wú jí [*Wu-chi*]	the Non-Ultimate	無極(无极)
sin-ki	shén qì [*shen-ch'i*]	vital energy, divine energy	神氣(神气)
T'aegŭk	Tài jí [*T'ai-chi*]	the Great Ultimate	太極(太极)

* WG: *Wade-Giles Romanization System*

Index